JUST FOR THE RECORD

JUST FOR THE RECORD

THE AUTOBIOGRAPHY OF

FRANCIS ROSSI AND RICK PARFITT

BANTAM PRESS

LONDON · NEW YORK · TORONTO · SYDNEY · AUCKLAND

TRANSWORLD PUBLISHERS LTD
61–63 Uxbridge Road, London W5 5SA

TRANSWORLD PUBLISHERS (AUSTRALIA) PTY LTD
15–25 Helles Avenue, Moorebank, NSW 2170

TRANSWORLD PUBLISHERS (NZ) LTD
3 William Pickering Drive,
Albany, Auckland

Published 1993 by Bantam Press
a division of Transworld Publishers Ltd
Copyright © Acklode Limited 1993

A catalogue record for this book is available from the British Library

ISBN 0–593–035461

Typeset in 11/14pt Bembo by
Chippendale Type Ltd, Otley, West Yorkshire.
Printed in Great Britain by
Mackays of Chatham, PLC, Chatham, Kent.

ACKNOWLEDGEMENTS

Francis Rossi and Rick Parfitt would like to thank the following people who have helped make *Just For The Record* possible:

James and Jane Baker; Cindy Blake; George Bodnar; Audrey Carden; Celia Dearing; Broo Doherty; Catherine Hodkinson; Iain Jones; Roger Kasper; Julia Lloyd; Ursula Mackenzie; Christine Porter; Simon Porter; Claire Ward; David Walker and everyone at Handle; and Bob Young.

PROLOGUE

Two men in their early forties checked into a hotel in Minehead on a Friday night in October 1990. They were an unusual pair, one with a long dark ponytail, the other with shoulder-length blond hair. They certainly didn't appear to be businessmen on a weekend conference. They looked like rock stars. But what would a pair of rock stars be doing in Minehead in October?

After unpacking, the two left the hotel and went over to Butlin's Holiday Camp, strolling around the grounds on a trip down memory lane. They had met there as teenagers, one working in a rock band he'd formed at school, the other in a cabaret act with twin girls. That summer they had, in their different ways, entertained holiday-makers. At the same time they had entertained each other as only teenage friends can do. They'd slept out rough in deck-chairs, they'd sat smoking cigarettes and checking out girls, they'd laughed, joked and talked about anything and everything, developing a friendship which was to last them through the decades.

Now, revisiting their past, they were surprised that the buildings were much larger than they'd remembered. The rock ballroom was bigger, much more imposing than they'd seen it all those years ago. Butlin's had changed, obviously, but the atmosphere was the same. In those days, they used to look across at the hotel in Minehead and dream of staying there – since that time they'd stayed in thousands upon thousands of hotel rooms across the world, in ritzy suites, living a lifestyle most people can only dream about.

That night, when they went back to their hotel, they slept on their memories.

The next day a train set out from Paddington Station, destined for Taunton. It wasn't the usual British Rail train, it wasn't even late. At 1.40 p.m., one hundred and twenty people who boarded the first-class carriages – and all the carriages *were* first class – started on their journey, ready for fun. They were going on an outing, they were going to celebrate a twenty-fifth anniversary at Butlin's in Minehead.

This wasn't a normal twenty-fifth anniversary. It wasn't a silver wedding. This particular couple had been close for twenty-five years, but what brought them together and what kept them together over that time was one very special thing: music.

Music which, that Saturday night, would rock the Prince's Ballroom at Butlin's like it had never been rocked before.

Francis Rossi and Rick Parfitt were back where they'd first met. The band they'd made so famous – Status Quo – were going to play a gig at Butlin's. Rick and Francis had defied convention from the beginning of their career and they weren't about to stop twenty-five years later. Most successful rock groups of their standing would have held a posh party in a posh place to celebrate any milestone in the group's history. All the usual party people would have turned up and the usual press reports would appear the next day. Not Quo.

After the Quo Express train pulled into Taunton, the passengers were ferried by coach to Butlin's and checked into their holiday chalets, where a Quo goodie bag complete with albums, toilet rolls, soap, party poppers and condoms awaited them. At 6.30 they went to a reception. All sorts of faces from the past and present were there. The twins who had worked with Rick that summer of '65, Jean and Gloria Harrison, turned up to join the party, along with their landlady from those days. Disc jockeys Chris Tarrant, Alan Freeman and Annie Nightingale came for the bash, as well as television star Vicki Michelle from 'Allo 'Allo.

The ballroom was packed for the nine o'clock concert, and within minutes, as the *Daily Mail* reporter Spencer Bright put it: 'We were all rocking so hard the first floor of the Prince's Ballroom rocked too. The speakers threatened to topple. It felt at times like standing on a trampoline.'

Up on stage, Rick looked out and saw Chris Tarrant 'bouncing up and down like a punk'. Francis spotted him too: 'Mad, he is.' But Francis, after a few songs, wasn't watching Chris Tarrant's antics, he was concerned that something was wrong with the set.

'Suddenly I realized what was different about the gig,' he remembers. 'It hadn't been advertised. So, aside from our own guests, the others there – thousands of them – were all Butlin holiday-makers, regular campers who had never seen us before in their lives. They'd heard there was a famous band playing and they'd come to check it out.'

'They didn't know what they were letting themselves in for,' adds Rick. 'But they seemed to be enjoying themselves. The ballroom was shaking.'

There had been times in Francis's and Rick's twenty-five years together which had been as shaky as the ballroom that night. They had gone through bouts with drugs and drink, the break-up of the original band, and financial rip-offs. But they had survived. Throughout the bad times and the good, they'd kept a sense of humour and a commitment to the music.

And there they were, still up there, standing with their legs apart and their heads down, playing the music they loved. With more hit albums than any other band apart from the Rolling Stones and the Beach Boys, they showed no signs of stopping. Indeed, as they played, their twenty-fifth anniversary single 'Anniversary

Waltz' had become their forty-first hit single and stood at Number Two in the British Singles Chart. A landmark record, the single stringed together a stunning Quo medley of fifteen classic rock 'n' roll songs. In typical Quo humour, Francis and Rick hit back at critics who likened the single to electronic medleys released by Jive Bunny by featuring a squashed rabbit on the back of the sleeve, together with the words: 'It's live sonny!'.

Vicki Michelle remembers the Butlin's experience. 'It was a party from beginning to end. We started out at Paddington and carried on until the next morning. The concert was excellent and going to Butlin's was like going back to your childhood. Everyone was like a kid again. We were all leaping up and down, carried away by the music. Quo were brilliant – as usual.'

The party after the concert that Saturday was a blow-out; a summer holiday Butlin's extravaganza complete with raffles and karaoke competitions. Bottles of champagne were handed around like water. According to Rick: 'We're not generally big on parties, but this one was a laugh. Everybody was pissed. Everybody. We had a ventriloquist who performed and he was so bad, he was wonderful. We were giving him a bit of a roasting. Then I got up and called out the numbers for the raffle. It was really getting back into the spirit of Butlin's.'

All the guests were caught up in the Status Quo spirit, the kick-ass, hard-rocking fun their music brings out as soon as the first bar of the opening number is played.

As Chris Tarrant summed it up: 'When I first heard the idea of a concert at Butlin's, I thought they'd finally completely flipped. But I must admit, from the moment we boarded the especially chartered Quo Express train at Paddington and drank all the way to Minehead, none of us were feeling any pain. My memories of the concert are a little hazy, as are, I suspect, Rossi's and Parfitt's, but it did coincide with my birthday and I do remember at one point being dragged up on stage, presented with an enormous cake and forced to play "Caroline" on a rubber guitar.

'After that things got very, very silly. Suddenly it was three-thirty in the morning, I was smashed out of my brains somewhere in Somerset and I remembered I had to be on Capital Radio at six-thirty. Somehow I made it back, although I suspect *The Breakfast Show* the next morning was one of the quietest shows I've ever done.'

The next day, Francis and Rick boarded the Quo Express to go back to London. Francis remembers it well: 'All the people we invited had had a great winging the night before. So Chris Tarrant may have had the quietest breakfast show ever, and we possibly had the quietest train journey in the history of British Rail.'

1

Francis Dominic Nicholas Michael Rossi, born in Forest Hill on 29 May 1949, to an Irish mother and Italian father, grew up helping his Italian grandparents in their café, an all-day eating place which served typical English food: double egg, double sausage, chips, baked beans, two slices and a cup of tea in the morning; roast lamb, roast beef, Yorkshire pudding for lunch and dinner. Out the back, they made ice-cream and lollies which they sold at a window in front of the café and also from a fleet of vans.

FRANCIS: When I was really small, my head was much larger than my body. As a consequence, when I was at the top of the stairs looking down, the weight of my head would pull me and I'd fall down the stairs. When I hit the bottom, I'd start crying: 'Record, record'; someone would put a record on and I'd feel better.

When I watched one of the *Godfather* films a while ago, I suddenly understood why I like the 'shuffle' rhythm so much. There was a little guy singing a wedding song, an Italian song, and it was a shuffle. The song they used to play me when I fell down the stairs was 'Poppa Piccolino', which had a shuffle beat.

As I grew a little older, I was into Guy Mitchell, but one day I saw the Everly Brothers on television. Those voices really got to me and I thought: That's it. That's what I want to do.

Aged seven I was going to play the accordion, but after I saw the Everlys I convinced my younger brother Dominic that we should ask my parents for guitars for Christmas. My brother changed his mind and decided on a train set, but I got the guitar.

It was impossible to find someone to teach me how to play in those days. I went to a man for lessons and he said: 'What do you want? Foxtrots or waltzes?' Foxtrots or waltzes? I thought he was mad, and I asked: 'What about the Everly Brothers?' 'Oh no, not here, laddie,' he answered. No-one calls me laddie. I never went to him again. That taught me that if a child wants to learn, you shouldn't teach him what *you* think he should learn, you should find out what sparks him off and encourage him.

My grandparents had a café in Catford. They made ice-cream in the back and my mother and I would make lollies. We'd be up working at five, six in the morning and often I'd go out on the road with my father to sell ice-creams from one of our vans. The ice-cream business did well – we had between fifteen and twenty vans.

One day we were out on a trip – I must have been eleven or twelve – and I got my finger caught in the blades that scrape the sides of the machine. I started to bleed like crazy, but my father wasn't about to stop selling the ice-cream. We just told the punters it was strawberry flavoured.

The worst moment of my childhood was when I nicked some money from the wafer tin my parents used as a piggy bank. Nicking and spending it wasn't so bad, but getting caught was. The comeuppance was horrible. Not only did I get smacked, but my parents didn't give me a birthday present or a Christmas present that year. I was going to get a tape-recorder, which was really exciting, but of course I didn't get it – I didn't get anything. That really hit home.

I was used to punishment, though. I went to a Catholic primary school run primarily by nuns. We had one nun who would grab your hand, squeeze it and start to cry if you did something wrong. She was so genuinely upset, I couldn't bear it, and I'd say: 'Please, no, don't cry. I promise I won't do it again.' And I wouldn't because I didn't want to hurt her. The school authorities must have thought she was too soft because suddenly we had a different nun in charge, who was a short-assed, fat, little dumpy git – and that's being kind.

She used to slap me around, but I wasn't singled out. She used to knock us all about. One day she decided to set an essay for our homework entitled: How Teachers Behave at School. A kid named Costello, who had been the object of her fury all too often, wrote an incredible, very adult essay explaining why teachers shouldn't hit children. The rest of us in the class couldn't believe it – we were waiting for the earthquake to erupt. You could feel the tension in the classroom, but she didn't say a word. We were so relieved, and we thought, maybe he'll get away with it.

After prayers were finished at the end of the day, though, she said: 'Can I see Andrew Costello.' She then proceeded to knock seven kinds of shit out of him in the cloakroom. Costello was out of school recovering for a couple of days and we never saw her again.

A boy named Micky, who was a real trickster, came up to me one day and said: 'I've got a great joke for you. You go up to a girl and ask: "Are you a girl?" ' I said: 'Oh, that's a good one, Micky, very funny,' and he said: 'No, hold on. You ask: "Are you a girl?" and when she says: "Yes," you say: "Prove it!" ' So I went right up to Antoinette Miller, a girl I fancied – we were eight at the time – and I did this routine. As soon as I said: 'Prove it!' she ran straight off to the nuns.

Within minutes I was in the headmaster's office, being caned. Twenty-four times. I didn't rush home and tell my parents I'd been belted, I'd never do that. As far as I was concerned, I did something wrong, got caught and was punished and that was that. Today people might say: 'Oh, you poor thing, you must have suffered,' but I don't see it that way. It was part of my life.

In fact, I remember crying when I left my primary school. I was leaving all my friends and going to a big, strange school, out into the unknown. On the first day at secondary school, I saw this guy who looked as though he was three years older than me; he even had hairs down there. His name was Terry and he was my age. I thought, Dear me, I've got a lot of growing up to do. Terry took to me immediately, though. In the area he came from, he was the local tough guy, but he always seemed very pleasant and because I was a mate of his, I was OK from the start.

Terry was the first person who told me I talked with a 'poncey' accent. Alan Lancaster was the second. Alan was at my school as well, so we became friends, and I thought, I better find out what 'poncey' means. Whatever it meant, I didn't want to talk like that. I wanted to be like Alan and his family – I became very close to them. But I did find the way they spoke very rough and very intimidating. So I did my best to sound like them.

One day I was over at Alan's, watching television with him and his family. Some git was talking on the TV and Alan turned to his mother and said: 'That's the way Rossi talks.' They would never call me Francis – that wasn't a man's name. His mother said: 'Nah, he's one of us now,' and I was so happy, so pleased to be one of them, I couldn't believe it. I thought, Great, I've got that intimidating sound now. It has protected me ever since. If you can talk like that, people assume you're tough and confident.

I've never seen anybody beat Alan Lancaster, and he's only a short little bugger. Where he was brought up, though, you had to be tough. I felt a bit weedy and four-eyed when I was a kid, and I wanted to be liked. Sometimes I'd dream about being injured, so people would come to my hospital bed and be friendly. When Alan and I and the others formed the band in school, I got a taste for belonging to something, being a part of a group. People would say: 'Oh, that's the guy who's in the group – you know him, he's all right.'

At secondary school, I spent most of my time in classes saying:

'Yeah, right. Who needs this?' I was Jack the Lad, desperately trying to be tough and hard. I didn't have much respect for my teachers. There was one I quite liked, though, a woman who taught us French. She was impressed with me because I was the only kid who knew what the word 'chaos' meant.

One day she said, 'Rossi? You want to be a pop star?'

'Yes ma'am,' I replied.

'If you're a famous pop star, you'll have to travel all over the world, am I right?'

'Yes ma'am.'

'If you travel all over the world, you'll go to France at some time, so you should learn to speak French, shouldn't you?'

'No ma'am,' I answered. 'If I'm a famous pop star, somebody will speak French for me.' I was dead right about that, although now I have a fascination for languages, and I wish I'd been taught to speak Italian properly.

Just after I'd turned fifteen, I decided to leave school. There was a custom there I'd seen through the years. When you left, people would write all over your school blazer, on your shirt, everywhere. On the day I was leaving, of course, it happened to me, and I thought, Fine, that's the custom. But the headmaster called me into his office, caned me and expelled me for coming to class dressed so badly.

I remember standing outside on the pavement afterwards, staring at the school and thinking, This is really stupid. People have been doing this for years and he expels me on my last day. At that point I lost any respect I had.

We'd formed a band at school by then. Alan Lancaster was on bass, Alan Key and Jess Jaworski, also schoolmates, played guitar and keyboards and finally, John Coghlan on drums. I'd met Alan Key when I was playing the trumpet for the school orchestra. And we'd all met John when we were rehearsing in a garage at an Army Training Camp. He was in his blue Air Force gear and was full of it, showing off on the drums. Somehow we convinced him to leave the band he was in and come with us.

Most nights we rehearsed in Jess's place in Forest Hill. My father couldn't believe that I was actually rehearsing every night – he

London County Council

SEDGEHILL SCHOOL, S.E.6

PROGRESS REPORT   SUMMER TERM 1964

DOMINUS REGNAT

Name _Francis Rossi_   Form _4F17_ Age _15_ y. _3_ m.

	Grading	Effort		Grading	Effort			Grading	Effort
Art	D	D.	General Science			Mathematics		D	E
Commerce			Biology	D	D	Music			
Shorthand			Chemistry	D	E	Needlework			
Typewriting			Physics			Physical Education		D	D.
Divinity			Engineering Science			Technical Studies Woodwork		C	C
English Language	C	D	History	D	D	Metalwork			
English Literature			Housecraft			Engineering			
Geography			Languages French	D	E	Technical Drawing			
			German						
			Latin						
			Spanish						

Position of Responsibility

COMMENT. Due to frequent & prolonged absences, Francis' work has been well below the form standard. In no subject has he made any effort to work hard. His attitude is lackadaisical & the sooner he takes a serious look at the future, the more promising that future will become. At present he is living in a world of make-believe, waiting for a sudden & exhilarating success as a popular music idol. He has made no provision whatever for the possibility of failure in this direction. He must ask himself whether this is the action of a sensible & mature young man.

Form Master / Mistress _J macdonald_.

Parent's Signature _____

Head's Initials _JEB_

1000 (GB15624 6/60 (M0232

thought I must be up to no good. So he came to check me out. I didn't know at the time, but he'd be sitting outside, listening. He was worried about my chances of success as well. There were so many bands around, he didn't think I could make a real career out of it, although at the time the Beatles were just beginning to make it and he could see there was definitely money to be made. For a while we called ourselves The Scorpions, but then we changed and became The Spectres.

Our first gig was in October 1962, at a place called the Samuel Jones Sports Club. I'd turned thirteen five months earlier. Samuel Jones was a big engineering company reminiscent of one of those banks that has its own sports ground and sports club. We borrowed a van, and when we got there, Alan Lancaster went mad. His mum hadn't cleaned his shoes, and he said he wasn't going to go on. We could never start a gig without Alan's mum; for the first couple of years we had to wait to make sure she'd turned up before we began.

Our equipment then was less than basic. We didn't have any proper microphones, so God knows how they heard the voices. I used to have one which I got off a tape-recorder, but we didn't have a proper microphone stand either. So I ended up using a budgie-cage stand for my mike instead. The distortion from our pathetic equipment must have been horrendous.

It was that night that a man named Pat Barlow came up to us and said: 'Do you want a manager?' He was running gas central-heating showrooms, and he was a plumber, a very successful little businessman. As soon as he became our manager, he began to find us other gigs. He was a wonderful man, like a father to us all. No-one could say a bad word about us.

Wherever Pat worked, whichever showrooms he went to, he'd plug the band, talk us up. He arranged for us to play at the Café des Artistes in Fulham every Monday night from 10 p.m. to 2 a.m. That was pretty late for a thirteen-year-old kid, and we seemed to be gigging all the time, although we did have some weekends off. My parents knew that Pat was looking after us, so they weren't as worried as they might otherwise have been.

Any time one of us would look at a girl or make suggestive

comments, Pat would say: 'Don't do that. Remember, she'll be someone's mother some day.' He was strict about those things, very upright. However, one night at the Café des Artistes, he saw an absolutely stunning bird and said: 'I could fuck her till further orders' – an old Army expression – and we all said: 'Gotcha, Pat. She'll be someone's mother sometime, too.'

Alan Key left the band within a couple of months. His brother, who was in a band called the Didgeriedoos with Rolf Harris, used to encourage me to sing; he thought I was the only one in our band who could, so I went for it. Alan struck up a relationship with the girl next door, and that was it. He left us, ended up marrying her and they're still together as far as I know.

Jess Jaworski left after a while as well, because he wanted to stay in school and further his studies. While we were doing all this, I had a daytime job cutting lenses for an optician. Unfortunately, there was a big clock across the street and it never seemed to move. An hour seemed like a day, and I knew this wasn't the kind of life I could lead.

Pat had arranged for us to play a gig on the same bill as the Hollies, which doubled as an audition for Butlin's summer resident band. Clinching that job meant that we had a steady income for four months; it was also a huge break because a lot of big acts had come up through Butlin's. Cliff Richard had played there, so it was a great place to get a gig. Pat found an organ player, Roy Lynes, to replace Jess Jaworski, and at fifteen years old, I packed my bags for Minehead!

Richard Parfitt was sixteen years old when he met Francis Rossi at Butlin's that summer of 1965, and he was already an experienced entertainer. Born in Woking on 12 October 1948, an only child, he had led a happy childhood filled with sport and adventure. A sick baby at birth, Rick had his share of accidents and mishaps: his family's car was crashed into and overturned when he was two; he almost cut off the top of the fourth finger on his left hand when he caught it in a swinging iron gate aged three; he was run over by a taxi and survived with only a few scratches;

and once, playing naked in front of a fire, a cinder flew out and caught
him in the most sensitive parts, where he still bears the scar.

    Rick's father, Dick, a naval man who had served in the Second World
War, did odd jobs to earn his living, and his mother, Lily, helped out
by working in a café. They moved often, sometimes living with other
families, but ended up, in 1956, in a council house in Queen Elizabeth
Way, back in Woking – the first place Rick considered a proper home.
He had his own bedroom – a novel luxury – and he soon found a gang of
boys his age with whom he spent all his spare time playing, often acting
out scenes he'd seen in Zorro *or* The Lone Ranger.

    At that point Rick's real interest in life began: music. Buddy Holly,
Cliff Richard and Lonnie Donnegan inspired him. He watched them on
television, listened to their songs, and decided that he wanted to be like
them. When his parents gave him a guitar for his tenth Christmas, he
took the first step in his rock 'n' roll life.

RICK: I never had any guitar lessons. Instead, as a teenager, I'd
go to the local Co-op in Woking and watch other bands – beat
groups – play. I'd put on my mohair sweater, winkle-pickers and
skintight jeans – jeans so tight I had to rip the leg from the bottom
to get them on, then sew them up so I could wear them. The tighter
the jeans, the more cool you were. I'd put on as much Brylcream as
I could get my hands on and go over to the Co-op and study the
band. I'd concentrate on one chord a guy was playing, remember
it, then go back home and practise. The next week, I'd go again,
focus on another chord and learn that.

    After a while, I'd built up a series of chords. I had a natural ear
for tuning, anyway, which came from my mother who played the
piano. From a very young age I was introduced to really old songs
which my mum would sing and play. Ever since then, if I hear a
song to which I know the melody line, I can chord it immediately
without even thinking about it. It's a great asset now, if I hear an
old song, to be able to pick up the guitar and play along with it
straight off. Back then, the first song I ever played on my guitar
was Harry Belafonte's 'Mary's Boy Child'.

My father had no show business in him at all, but he could see I had a talent and he wanted to see me get on, so he began to steer me in the right direction. He began to take me with him to his working men's club in Woking. He'd say: 'Put your box in the car,' and I'd say: 'No, I don't want to.' I was embarrassed about getting up and singing at this club, but he always convinced me.

The club had a great atmosphere. Throughout the evening people would get up to sing on a foot-high stage. Eventually my father would coax me to get my guitar out of the car and perform, then I'd be off. I sang 'Baby Face' and a country track called 'Down The Trail of Aching Hearts'. The chorus went: *Nobody's hiding their tears/You led me to where sadness starts/Down the trail of aching hearts.*

I was only in short trousers at the time, and I was shy about performing. To play in front of an audience of sixty was daunting for an eleven year old, but once I was up there and doing it, I loved it.

Dad entered me in a talent contest and I won a fiver singing 'Baby Face'. At that point I was dubbed 'Woking's Budding Tommy Steele'. The problem was, I didn't want to be Tommy Steele, I wanted to be Buddy Holly or Cliff Richard.

Then I won another talent contest which Dad entered me in – I tend to think he put my name up for things like that when he'd had a few. The top prize was a week's holiday at Butlin's in Cliftonville, Kent. Once I was there, of course, there was yet another talent contest which I lost in the final. I was broken-hearted, distraught. Afterwards my mother found me under a hedge, crying my eyes out.

By the time I was thirteen, I'd built up an act. I'd play working men's clubs all over London; I'd gone down well as a novelty act, because I was so young. My voice hadn't even broken. Thinking back, I must have been hilarious. Sometimes I wonder whether I should have been a comedy act.

Someone who heard me at one of the clubs in London suggested that I go for a recording test at Decca Records. Out I came with the old favourites – 'Baby Face' and 'Living Doll'. Frankly, I was so nervous, I was crap. The studio frightened the life out of me. At that point, I thought an 'echo chamber' was an actual room you went into, I didn't know a thing about recording.

The man in charge, Marcel Stellman, told my father that I should come back when I'd learned to breathe properly, a phrase I've always seen as a gracious way of saying: 'He's no bloody good.' Marcel suggested I sing in a church choir because that helps with breathing, apparently. Somehow I never quite saw that as an option.

Soon after that fiasco, I got another break. There was a TV music quiz for kids called *Midwinter Music*, hosted by Steve Race. Every week a guest soloist appeared, and one week I was chosen. The show was in black and white, so I wore shorts and a white shirt. Before I went on, though, they made me change into a blue shirt because white dazzles the screen.

I'd been nervous before, but never as nervous as I was then. The programme was live on Associated Rediffusion, and after it had finished my father asked Steve Race if he saw any future for me. Race said: 'No,' because, as he explained, there weren't many children's television shows at the time, and there was nowhere else for me to perform.

Naturally, this was a blow for me and my parents. My father, still determined that I'd make it in the entertainment business, decided I should have acting lessons and sent me to Cambridge Manor in Addlestone, near Weybridge. I was supposed to learn how to speak properly and was given sentences like 'Come round to my house and bring a pound of round raspberries'. I felt like Eliza Doolittle trying to pronounce: 'The rain in Spain' and I thought, What the bleedin' hell have I let myself in for here?

My mother is from Bethnal Green in the East End, my father from Newmarket in Suffolk, so my own accent was somewhere between the two. It wasn't too easy to pull off a posh speaking voice. Added to that, I found myself being told one day to act as though I was a fried egg in a frying pan. That did it for me. Besides, I couldn't act to save my life. At the time I went to an audition for *Oliver* in Drury Lane. I took my guitar along and sang 'Baby Face' – of course. It didn't come as a huge surprise to me when I wasn't given the part.

My father walked in to the acting school one day and saw me teaching the other kids how to play the guitar. He wasn't best pleased as he was paying people to teach me to act and there I was giving guitar lessons for free. So he hooked me out of there and I concentrated on my music from then on.

From the time I'd learned to play the guitar, my academic studies went completely out of the window. I knew from the age of eleven what I wanted to do, and I was totally committed to it. At school I was one of the lads, naughty as hell. I wasn't bothered about English, Maths or Geography, and I didn't take my education seriously. All I was interested in was games. I'd captained the football and cricket teams and I loved sport, but academics weren't my strong point.

Luckily my big break came soon enough, when I went to do a 'shop window'. The venue was a small room above a pub called The Feathers in Euston. There was no stage, no microphone and various acts would go out and do their bit. It was called a shop window because booking agents from all over the country would come and watch to see if they liked any of the acts.

I got up, played and was hired for the summer season by the Mayor of Hayling Island, an entertainments manager, at the Sunshine Holiday Camp. Dad and I were leaping up and down. There I was, aged fourteen, with a real job which was going to pay me ten pounds a week. Believe it or not, my father told Gordon Mitchell, the mayor, that ten pounds was too much; he didn't want me to get spoiled or big-headed. Five pounds would be fine. The silly sod.

Still, that meant I could say two fingers to school. I couldn't get out of there quickly enough, and within a couple of weeks of leaving school, I was down at Hayling Island, rehearsing for my summer season.

All of a sudden I was alone, without my parents, in a new, different world. I had to grow up quickly and join in with the group.

The first people I met at the camp were seventeen-year-old twin girls – Jean and Gloria Harrison. They were identical in every way: they wore the same clothes, the same jewellery, their hair was done the same. I'd never met twins in my life and I was fascinated; in fact I fancied them both immediately. All sorts of thoughts sprang into my head.

They were dancers, a speciality act. That first night when we met, they said: 'Coming down to the pub, then?' I said: 'Yeah, all right.' I was wearing a pork-pie hat. I had on my red socks and hush puppies. I was a little Mod.

Within minutes of getting to the pub, I'd started smoking because Gloria smoked and I'd fallen for her right away. Two days later, I fell for Jean. I didn't know then that this was an indication of how the next thirty odd years were going to be as far as women were concerned.

The three of us began to sit around in the late evenings singing harmonies, old Springfield hits, and one of the senior guys at the camp heard us. He suggested that we team up and do a show in the bar. We called ourselves The Highlights and put an act together. The audience liked us, so we continued, although we were still doing our solo spots as well.

After the season was finished, Jean and Gloria asked me what I was going to do next and I said nothing. They suggested that I went with them to London where we could rehearse some more and see if we could get some work. I had no better options at the time, so that's what I did.

We got our act together quite well. By that time my father had dropped out a bit and the twins' dad had found us an agent, so we started to do shows up and down the country. The clubs required us to do two fifteen-minute spots and we had learned at least twenty songs, so we could vary the set. We played two clubs a night, seven nights a week. I'd end up with twenty-five pounds a week in my pocket. Then we were hired without even auditioning for the summer season at Butlin's.

So off we went . . . to Minehead!

In 1965, the year in which Winston Churchill died, the Beatles were awarded MBEs. The music explosion which they'd set off in 1963 was still shaking the world, and the phenomenon of pop had been recognized

by everyone from screaming, hysterical fans to the Queen herself.

That May 'Ticket To Ride' was Number One in the charts in the UK and another British band, Herman's Hermits had the Number One single in America with the unlikely title of 'Mrs Brown, You've Got a Lovely Daughter'.

While the Beatles went off to tour America and Cliff Richard released his twenty-eighth single, 'The Minute You're Gone', the Rolling Stones were in the public spotlight: Mick Jagger, Bill Wyman and the boys were in court for indecent behaviour following an innocent pee up against the side of a petrol station. Meanwhile, Elton John was struggling along in an unknown rhythm and blues band called Bluesology.

At Butlin's in Minehead, musical entertainment was part of the holiday scene for the campers. Catering to different tastes and styles, the Butlin's management hired a variety of acts, from cabaret to rock. Rick Parfitt was singing 'Baby Face' with The Highlights while Francis Rossi was belting out 'Bye Bye Johnny' with The Spectres. On the surface, their meeting and friendship may have seemed unlikely, but they soon found that they had the same drive, the same passion for music and the same sense of humour.

FRANCIS: When The Spectres first got to Butlin's, we were put into a bar we called the Wig and Pisshole – it was actually the Pig and Whistle, a glorified barn that held about one thousand people. We complained to the camp, saying: 'We're a rock 'n' roll band, we can't play here,' so they put us in a rock 'n' roll ballroom.

We were delighted to win our first battle. The camp had the last laugh, though, because the punters flocked to the bloody Pig and Whistle to drink all night. Then they'd come to the Prince's Ballroom for the last half-hour of our set – from eleven-thirty to midnight. They'd go back to their chalets pissed and happy, but we were frustrated playing to a half-empty ballroom night after night.

The dressing-room was pretty ropey. We shared it with a

wrestling team who always argued about the arrangement of their fights. We played in the afternoons as well, usually to about a dozen people. We'd play songs like 'The Wanderer' and 'Runaround Sue' and the best reaction always came when Roy Lynes, the keyboard player, sang 'I Can't Help Falling In Love With You'. That was the only applause we got. Quite honestly, we were awful.

RICK: One evening the twins and I had just finished rehearsing our cabaret act and I heard this rock 'n' roll blasting from some-where. I thought, Jesus Christ, that's out of our limit. Where's it coming from? I wandered over towards the noise and I saw the ballroom. When I went in, I took one look at the band and thought, Fantastic, magic. That's for me. They were really steaming, playing 'Bye Bye Johnny'. 'Jesus Christ,' I said to myself. 'Do I want to do that!'

FRANCIS: I was playing when I saw this bloke wander in with twin girls on either side of him. He walked up to the stage and nosed around, looking like any musician does when he sees another one play – that OK, show-me-what-you-can-do look. At first we thought he was a poof – anyone who was that slim and good looking had to be, but Alan Lancaster got talking to him and then I did. We became friends within days. He was a little embarrassed about singing songs like 'Baby Face' and 'The Sheik of Araby' in his cabaret act, but we were quite impressed by the show business aspect of it all – he was far more show business than I ever was.

The first day I walked into Butlin's with John Coghlan, I went through the gate, to the right, to get my pass and the first person I saw was Jean, the woman who later became my first wife. She was working there as well, and she told me I had to put on my pass. I turned to John and said: 'That's going to be the one for me.'

After a while I started to sneak her into my digs. Our landlady used to come in every morning and wake me up by putting her hand on my bum. One morning she felt two bums in the bed and that was that. We got thrown out.

RICK: Jean and Gloria, the twins, had moved out from our digs to a caravan site, which was fine by me, because I had total independence and freedom. Consequently, when Francis was thrown out and his girlfriend Jean had nowhere to go, I suggested to my landlady that Jean came to stay in the twins' old room. She agreed, which solved Jean's problem. But Francis still had nowhere to stay.

I thought, I can't have him out on the road on his own with no place to sleep, so I left my digs and went out on the tiles with him. We slept anywhere and everywhere: in phone boxes, little sheds on the front, in between deck-chairs.

FRANCIS: We had to avoid the security guards because we were supposed to be off the camp by midnight. We weren't residents. We'd dodge around the back of buildings, and some nights we'd sleep in a bath tub down the chalet lines. That meant that we had to wake up at five or six o'clock so the guards wouldn't catch us.

RICK: The worst night I remember was once when it was cold and wet and we'd been sleeping in a bath. We got up at five and realized that if we became pals with the kitchen staff, who had to start work then, we could ask them to let us sleep in their beds for a few hours. That worked out fine, except those beds smelt of grease and fat – it felt like sleeping in a vat of chips.

FRANCIS: This went on for a couple of weeks, until my landlady accepted me back. Jean had left me and run off somewhere, so Alan Lancaster went to her room at Rick's place and Rick moved back as well.

RICK: Those times out on the tiles were great fun, though. We were so young that we didn't give a fuck. It was all one big adventure. Francis and I were inseparable. During the day, we'd sit in the coffee bars smoking Kensitas and ogling all the girls. At night, I'd do my show and then go over to the ballroom to watch the band play.

FRANCIS: There was a similarity, a kinship between Rick and me. He was the only person I'd met who laughed at the same things as I did – whether they were stupid, infantile things or whatever. The others never laughed. I'd say things to John Coghlan and – nothing. I'd get no response.

RICK: In the early days we established a mental relationship, we talked about so much, about anything and everything. We didn't know then how much those first weeks together would stand us in such good stead in the years to come.

After the Butlin's summer season ended, Rick promised to keep in touch with Francis and Alan Lancaster, but he wasn't sure what to do with his own career. He knew, after seeing The Spectres, that he wanted to be in a rock group, but he was earning a decent living with the twins as The Highlights, and he had no other offers at the time. He continued with his cabaret act.

RICK: The twins and I kept working around the clubs, although I felt the act was starting to get a little tired. At that point I was calling myself Ricky Harrison, because we figured we'd get more bookings if people thought we were a brother and sister act. The Parsnips were around in those days – the Partridge Family – so it seemed the thing to do. I didn't like my name anyway when I was young.

The Highlights did get some bookings abroad, at American bases in Europe. During any show, we'd start off as the three of us, The Highlights, and at a certain point in the act, Jean and Gloria would go off to change into their dance costumes.

I remember being left on stage on my own at this naval base in Naples, dressed in a cummerbund and bow-tie, singing my best tune – 'Baby Face' – to four hundred pissed sailors. Needless to say, it wasn't going down too well. They were waiting for the girls to come back on. This was excruciatingly embarrassing. I knew the act wasn't working for me any more and something had to give, but I had nothing else to do, no other options.

From time to time, I would see Francis and Alan. We'd get together when neither of our bands were playing. Once I watched them playing a gig at Eltham Baths, supporting the Yardbirds, Eric Clapton's former band. I thought The Spectres were magic that night. Francis wore red strides with an S belt and a black-and-white checked shirt. He had a Mod haircut and looked great. I went backstage and was thrilled to be involved in it all, rubbing shoulders with the Yardbirds. I wasn't happy with what I was doing professionally, and I was even less happy about my lack of success with girls. This was a major worry back then.

I'd had no real sexual experience when I was at school – apart from going into the scout hut at the back of the playground. Various other boys and I knew ways of breaking into it, and we'd take girls in there and get them to get their tits out. Feeling and looking was as far as I'd gone, though.

When I left school, I was getting pretty concerned about this because a lot of the other lads were saying: 'Oh, I had a fantastic time last night with so-and-so.' It started to make me think, Christ, I haven't done this yet. I couldn't even lie and try to brag about it.

As soon as I met the twins at Hayling Island, I was sexually attracted to them, but nothing ever came of it. On Saturday mornings at the camp, other male members of the staff and I would watch the busloads of people arriving and we'd eye up what was getting off those buses, peruse the coachload. The Canaries, which is what they called the staff there, weren't allowed to be seen with the campers socially, however. So I saw plenty of very nice girls, but I didn't approach them.

However, one day, it just happened. I was talking to a girl, doing my normal Canary duties, and I said: 'Well, I'll see you around.' She responded by giving me her chalet number and telling me to come down later. I knew exactly what that meant and I must confess I was a little frightened. In those days I was a skinny little thing and she was a big girl – a lot taller and larger than me. She was older as well.

I finished my duties at eleven o'clock and I thought, What have I taken on here? But here I go. This is it – I'm going to get it on tonight. I got a packet of johnnies and off I went for my first adventure.

My nerves were jangling, because in my mind she was experienced. I figured that she knew what she was doing, she'd done it before. I didn't and I hadn't. Still, I knocked on her door in a hell-for-leather mood, ready to get in there and have a go. We snuggled up and started messing about and as these things happen, the moment came when she was ready and I was too.

I turned away from her and said: 'Hold on, I've got to get one of these things.' I was shaking like a leaf, desperately trying to rip it out of the packet and put it on and everything was going wrong. It seemed to take an eternity to get this thing on. I turned back over to her and I realized the whole episode was turning into a nightmare. I tried, but it didn't really work. It was all over.

She threw me out then. I think she must have been very frustrated because I was getting nowhere. In those days it was bang or bust. This disaster stayed in my mind for quite a while. My attempts were marred after that during the summer season, because I'd had this bad first experience, and something like that can hit you pretty hard. I had needed it to work.

So there I was, a couple of years later, at seventeen, and I still hadn't screwed a bird. The twins and I were doing a summer season at Skegness at that point and things were going very wrong. I had an obsessive crush on Jean then; she was going out with other blokes and I was staying awake half the night until she got back. We had rented a little cottage, and I had even wrecked my bedroom once because she was off with someone else.

All three of us were pissed off with each other. One night in the theatre, before the show, the mood between us was just terrible. I was in their dressing-room and I said something. A verbal fight escalated, and I ended up announcing that I'd had it. Enough was enough and I was off.

They both turned on me and told me I couldn't walk out just before a show. I said I certainly could. That's when the physical fight began. Gloria and Jean both came at me, attacking me with their stiletto heels, smashing me over the head. I was getting a heavy battering. There were a thousand or so people out in the theatre waiting for the show to start; meanwhile backstage the real fireworks were going on.

I was down on the floor, cowering under the dressing-table, bleeding and crippled, my head split open by a well-aimed stiletto. The whole cast were backstage before this show, watching me receive this beating. When I managed to get up, I said: 'I'm off,' and I walked out of the door. The twins had to go on on their own that night. My parents came down, I dumped all my stuff in the back of their car, and that was the end of The Highlights.

Rick's future looked bleak at this point. With nothing to do, nowhere to go, and very little money, he moved back in with his parents. His father had lost the will to push him in the show business world, and Rick knew he had to get a nine-to-five job. He was employed first as a baker's roundsman, delivering bread and cakes, but was sacked after a couple of months. He then became a petrol pump attendant, but was sacked from that as well. Finally he became a clerk. He was, he admits, 'absolutely useless' at this job, but he believed his music career was finished.

RICK: One night a call came through from London. Pat Barlow was on the telephone asking me if I wanted to join The Spectres. I'd been in touch with Francis and Alan all along, but I couldn't really believe I was being asked to join them. Did I want to join *the* group? I couldn't even try to sound nonchalant and cool. I jumped at it. They figured they needed another voice in the band. I couldn't believe my luck.

In 1966, the year after the summer season at Butlin's, Pat Barlow sent a demo tape The Spectres had done of a Shirley Bassey cover, 'I (Who Have Nothing)' to songwriter Ronnie Scott. Record producer John Schroeder, a friend of Scott's, was so impressed that in July he signed up the group for

a five-year deal with Piccadilly Records, a company licensed to Pye.

The Spectres released 'I (Who Have Nothing)', written by Lieber and Stoller, in September, but it failed to make any impact on the charts. During that month the Beatles were topping the charts in the UK with 'Yellow Submarine/Eleanor Rigby' while the Supremes reigned in the US with 'You Can't Hurry Love'.

A second single, the Alan Lancaster composition 'Hurdy Gurdy Man' also flopped, and the last single released by The Spectres as such was 'We Ain't Got Nothing Yet', in February 1967.

That March, The Spectres changed their name to Traffic, a move which caused problems when Stevie Winwood, who had split from the Spencer Davis Group, formed his own new group, also called Traffic, on the Island label. Winwood's Traffic had a hit single 'Paper Sun' which prompted Pye's Traffic to change their name again, this time to Traffic Jam. Under that new heading, the group put out a Francis Rossi single, 'Almost But Not Quite There'.

FRANCIS: 'Almost But Not Quite There' was banned. It's about leaving a woman in a slightly frustrated position. At the time I thought, Hey, they've banned my song, that's pretty cool.

Around that time, Pat Barlow brought in a bloke named Joe Bunce, who was going to put some money behind the band. He was a waste-paper merchant and we always thought it was funny that his name was 'Bunce' because that was a slang word for money.

I remember he once gave Rick and me a fiver when we were broke and it lasted for a long time – it was wonderful. One morning Joe found Rick asleep in a car outside his house, which wouldn't have been so bad, but Joe's daughter was in the car with Rick. That didn't go down so well.

Three months after 'Almost But Not Quite There' was banned, in June 1967, Francis married Jean, the woman he had met when he first went *to Butlin's. He had said, as soon as he saw her, that she was the woman for him, and they were married in a Register Office less than two years later.*

FRANCIS: I had just turned eighteen, and I wanted to be accepted, grown up. The day of the wedding there was a lot of acrimony between our families. My parents didn't want me to get married – I suppose they thought I was too young. We went to a Register Office, and afterwards we had a little celebration in a pre-fab place where my mother-in-law lived. I was wearing a blazer with green and yellow stripes, a pink shirt and white trousers. Rick used to wear my wedding gear on stage after that.

My parents and my brother Dominic were there and we had some dodgy ham sandwiches. A few photographs were taken, then my parents said: 'Well, we better be going.' I got up to leave with them, and it took me a few minutes as I was walking away with them before I suddenly realized that I wasn't supposed to be going anywhere. I'd just got married and I was supposed to live with my wife, not go back to my parents' house.

At that precise moment, I remember thinking, Uh-oh, this is not what I want. I'd been married two or three hours and I knew I'd made a mistake. However, there was a huge part of me that was keen for it to work. I liked the idea of being in love – I wanted to have a wonderful marriage and a happy domestic life.

On 20 August 1968 my son Simon was born, and I was immediately labelled a 'family man'. I found it strange to think that one baby constituted a family, and that I'd moved from being a married man to a family man so quickly and at such a young age.

I had been fifteen when I had my first sexual experience. We were playing a gig in Peckham and singing that Rolling Stones song, 'Tell Me You're Coming Back To Me'. A girl was standing right in front of me crying while I was singing, so naturally I figured that I must have got to her. Afterwards we began to talk and then we started to go out together.

We took a train ride to the country – a place called Shoreham down in Kent – and we found some open space where we couldn't be seen, and we did it. I remember being well pleased with myself at the time. I'd had bits and pieces when I was at school. A girl named Stella, who had huge tits, took a shine to me, and she taught me how to kiss, along with some other stuff. But I also had lots of girlfriends at school, I mean *friends* who I used to hang out with.

The trouble with men is that we're blind when it comes to women. We have only one eye and that's in our private parts. Women aren't the same, they approach sex differently. This eye of ours sees a woman and says: 'Oh, I'll have some of that.' We're controlled by it. And we're conditioned to think like that at school; we're supposed to be macho to the point where we see a woman and think, She needs me. We see two lesbians and say: 'They need me.' It's emotional baggage which I've grown out of now, but was a big part of my past.

Three weeks after I'd first met her at Butlin's, Jean ran out on me, saying she couldn't take it any more. Often, during the twelve-year course of our marriage, she'd threaten to take off; sometimes I'd come back from a gig and she would have gone to a hotel with the kids. Finally, in 1979, she said she was going to leave and I told her there was no turning back if she left.

In the early days, Jean criticized everything about my career; she thought I didn't have a chance. Before we got married, she said it's either me or the band, and I thought, You're on a sticky wicket there. That's like asking someone to cut off his arm for you.

The November following my marriage, Pat Barlow telephoned Rick and asked him to join the band, saying we needed another 'voice'. At that point, we were calling ourselves Traffic Jam – it was just before we became The Status Quo. We rehearsed with Rick for a while and then did our first gig at The Welcome Inn, supporting a group called Episode Six, some of whom went on to become Deep Purple. Rick wasn't playing well at all that night and he forgot a lot of the set.

I thought, This isn't going to work, and was a bit pissed off, because he was my mate, and you always think your mate is going to be all right. There was no way I wanted him to leave the band, though. I wasn't about to try to get rid of him because I could relate to him so well, our humour was so similar. By the second or third gig, Rick was absolutely fine and we were on our way.

Still dissatisfied with their name, the band played with the idea of calling themselves The Queers, thinking that at least might get people talking about them, or The Muhammad Alis. They even considered writing to Ali to tell him about themselves and perhaps get some publicity, but then Pat Barlow suggested Quo Vadis. He'd seen it written in a shoe and liked the sound of it. Not entirely happy with Quo Vadis, they then decided on The Status Quo and went on that night in 1967 officially announcing the birth of The Status Quo.

2

The Status Quo broke through into the charts in 1968 with 'Pictures of Matchstick Men'. It reached Number Seven, while Love Affair cornered Number One with 'Everlasting Love'. The success of 'Matchstick Men' secured Quo a performance on Top of the Pops *and the group appeared in the national newspapers for the first time: the* London Evening News *reported the rumour that 'Pictures of Matchstick Men' had replaced the usual jingles playing on Rossi's grandfather's ice-cream vans.*

FRANCIS: I wrote 'Matchstick Men' in the toilet to get away from the wife and the mother-in-law. I used to go into this narrow frigging toilet and sit there for hours, until they went out. Finally, I finished it in the lounge.

'Gentleman Joe's Sidewalk Café', a Kenny Young song, was going to be the A side and 'Matchstick Men' the B side.

Pat Barlow was the one who pushed and pushed to turn it over and release 'Matchstick Men' on the A side. I've always been worried about promoting my own songs. You think people think you're pushing it only because it's yours.

When it first came out, we thought it was marvellous. With a hit single and a spot on *Top of the Pops*, we believed everything was going to change and life was going to be wonderful from there on. It takes a few weeks before you realize that you still wake up every morning being just you and that one hit record doesn't constitute a career. We were on half a per cent retail with the record company so we didn't earn that much compared to what we'd get now for a hit like that.

RICK: At the time of the release of 'Matchstick Men' we were Madeleine Bell's backing band, and I was still clerking during the day. I remember going into work and saying to my boss: 'Look, I may not be able to work here very much longer because I'm in a group and we might have a hit record.' He said: 'Yeh, yeh, sure, just get in there and do your job.' As soon as 'Matchstick Men' went high into the charts, Pat Barlow announced: 'You can all give up your jobs now. You're professionals.' We leapt around like young boys do, thinking, Fantastic!

Francis got fourteen hundred pounds for 'Matchstick Men' even though millions of copies were sold. We were rehearsing in Brixton when I heard that he'd got this money. I looked over at him and thought, Fuck me! He's got over a grand! That was really something then, it was outrageous.

FRANCIS: I was told at the time that I shouldn't be called Francis, that Mike Rossi was the name I should use and it stayed that way through the mid-Seventies.

After 'Matchstick Men' we released 'Black Veils of Melancholy' which died a death. It was almost a carbon copy of 'Matchstick Men'; some reviewer for *Disc*, a big selling pop paper, said: 'The Status Quo have rewritten the words to their last hit.' It didn't feel that way to us at the time.

Even though we'd had a hit and we'd been on television, we

weren't worried when the second one flopped. We thought, This one hasn't worked, so what? You just carry on.

RICK: That September our début LP, 'Picturesque Matchstickable Messages' was released, but failed to reach the charts as well. In addition to the singles, it included covers of the Bee Gees' 'Spicks and Specks', 'The Lemon Pipers', 'Green Tambourine', and Tommy Roe's 'Sheila'. We didn't have a hit until October, with 'Ice in the Sun', which Marti Wilde and Ronnie Scott wrote.

FRANCIS: I've always thought the lyrics of 'Ice in the Sun' were strange – *'I'm not a little boy/ I've lived alone and loved so many more'*. I've lived alone and loved so many more? I keep wondering what the fuck they're talking about.

RICK: We didn't exactly go from strength to strength after 'Ice in the Sun'. The next single failed again, so it was an up and down period for us.

FRANCIS: We weren't *that* big, and there were so many bands at the time who might be up for a month and then gone. We were lucky to survive at all; even some huge bands like Amen Corner and Love Affair disappeared in a short time. We hung on to the fact that we were The Status Quo and that we were going to keep playing, whatever happened. It was a good job we did, really, because if we hadn't been so committed, we might have gone our separate ways in the late Sixties.

In April 1969, three months before Neil Armstrong set foot on the moon, and four months before the famous Woodstock Festival in America, The Status Quo supported Gene Pitney on a UK tour. Marvin Gaye was topping the charts with 'I Heard it Through The Grapevine'.

FRANCIS: There were some strange bills in those days. Englebert Humperdink might be on with The Who – it was weird.

We went on the Pitney tour, all of us in the same bus. We would meet at a little bus station near Baker Street and wait in a canteen for everyone to show up; we weren't the only other band on that tour – there were others like Amen Corner, Don Partridge and Simon Dupree and the Big Sound, acts who were selling a serious amount of records, but none of us could sell out a tour on our own.

We'd meet up, stow the gear underneath the bus and set off. There wasn't much gear anyway – we were plugged into little speakers around the hall. Nobody had the power to be loud.

Gene Pitney always sat in the back of the bus, but when we arrived at our destination, he'd stay in a different hotel from the rest of us, a posh one. And every show, he would read out the same bloody letters from fans.

RICK: He still does that, to this day.

FRANCIS: The next morning we'd be dropped off back at Baker Street and we'd have to make our own way home. We'd been in the charts then, but we certainly weren't treated like stars.

RICK: That tour was the epitome of being bullied into doing what you didn't want to do. We had to dress in absurd clothes. I actually used to go on stage dressed in a red and gold lamé coat, yellow trousers, pink shirt and white shoes – playing my red guitar. All I needed was a splash of blue and I would have looked like a walking rainbow.

FRANCIS: One night I had a peek through the curtains before we were going on stage and Ron King, the tour manager, rushed up. He said: 'If you ever, ever do that again, you'll never work in this country. You can't do things like that.' So there I was, standing in my frilly shirt, having to say: 'Sorry, sir.' That wasn't what we thought rock 'n' roll was all about.

We first met Bob Young, who has written a lot of songs with us, on the Pitney tour. Bob was working with Amen Corner at the time. Alan Lancaster used to take an eternity to tune up and I heard Bob, who was sitting on the side in the wings, say something about fucking bass players. A couple of weeks later, Pat Barlow said: 'Here's your new roadie.' After some time spent being a roadie, Bob became our tour manager. He took care of us and pretty soon he and I were writing songs together.

RICK: Pat said at the time: 'You think you're pop stars – you wait till you see this guy.' Bob was a very handsome young bloke. He played the harp, he wrote songs and he was a great guy to be around. Bob and Francis and I became fantastic pals – we were like the Three Musketeers. We never stopped laughing.

'Ice in the Sun', an out-and-out 'pop' record, saw us through a year of being 'famous', but we found we didn't really like it. After the Pitney tour, we were working the circuit, the Mecca Ballrooms around the country, big venues with revolving stages and mirror balls. We found that we weren't so much appreciated as screamed at.

FRANCIS: Lots of girls went to the Mecca Ballrooms to see pop groups who had been on television and the guys went to try and pull the girls. At first the audience would be knocked out to see us, but after a few songs, they'd get bored – the girls would stand in the audience practically filing their nails. Nobody was there for the music.

RICK: There were a phenomenal number of hit bands on the billing every night at the Meccas in those days. Amen Corner, Love Affair, Marmalade, The Status Quo – three or four nights a week every week, they'd have these big acts in. It makes you wonder now where the kids – you couldn't really call them fans – got the money from to go to all these shows.

The four big 'faces' on the pop scene then were Steve Ellis, of Love Affair – he was a huge teen idol; Andy Fairweather-Lowe of Amen Corner; Peter Frampton of The Herd and Francis. Funnily enough, Dean Ford of Marmalade didn't quite make it into that league. The *New Musical Express* had a 'Face of the Year' every year and Francis was put forward to be the 'Face of '69'. I remember Peter Frampton won it that year.

FRANCIS: The problem with things like that is you may be Face of the Year one year, but what happens the next? If you're hot one year, be careful because you can't always maintain it. Pop stardom like that can disappear almost overnight.

Around that time, I saw a college band called 'Suck' playing a gig. They were dressed in jeans and T-shirts, playing what they wanted to play and I thought, That's what we should be doing. We'd been taken to Carnaby Street, told what to wear and how to look in order to make it as 'pop stars', but it wasn't for us.

RICK: When we played the Mecca Ballrooms, we were booked at a set fee. Most nights we'd play for £125, which was not bad money, but when you think about it, you've got a couple of crew members to pay; somebody to set up the gear and somebody to drive the band. Then you've got travelling expenses, and of course you have to split it five ways anyway. In the end, you probably come out of it with a tenner in your pocket. So we weren't exactly raking in the money.

We began to get really hacked off with it all, because we did have aspirations and we wanted to be creative. The move from pop to blues-based rock was everyone in the band's idea. We were sick of playing for screaming groupies. We thought we were a better band than that, that we weren't just after hit records. Even though it might have jeopardized our career, we knew we had to move on – we didn't want to keep playing to soppy audiences.

FRANCIS: Before, when we used to go to gigs, we'd do a sound check in the afternoon and we'd be playing the kind of stuff we do now, and we thought, Wouldn't it be great if we could get the stuff we're playing in the sound check into the set? That was what we really wanted to do. So we came off the road and began to rehearse.

RICK: Of course we were happy to have had the hits, but it didn't change our outlook. We were still just 'the band' and the feeling between us hadn't changed. Our feet hadn't left the ground at all – they never have. When we first started rehearsing the new set, we were up above this pub in Brixton and we were going apeshit. Guitar necks were swinging all over the place, we were really enjoying ourselves.

FRANCIS: Our second LP, 'Spare Parts' hadn't gone anywhere, and we were ready for a change of direction and a change of image. We began to wear ripped scruffy jeans and dirty trainers. Also, we'd shave at night, so the next day we'd have what's now called 'designer stubble'. At the time we didn't think of it as trendy – we were just fed up with looking clean-cut. I had pierced my ear and begun to wear an earring as well. People thought I was a gypsy.

No-one could tell us what to do once we decided to follow our own instincts. We looked weird for that time, and we had an angry young man kind of attitude.

Having played all those Mecca Ballrooms, we changed gear completely and after we'd rehearsed the new set, we went into sweaty little back rooms of pubs. We weren't an overnight success; there were times when we first started in the underground clubs when people sat there listening as if they couldn't be bothered, stoned out of their minds. At that point you have to ask yourself what you're in the music business for – screaming teenyboppers, adoration, Number One hits, or the chance to play the music you want to and the hope that someday someone will appreciate it.

RICK: I remember one night at The Castle at Tooting. It was an underground gig and our name was out front. People who came along thought they'd come to the wrong place. They thought The Status Quo was a pretty little pop band, not a serious group.

We were supporting Mott the Hoople with Ian Hunter of All the Young Dudes fame. The atmosphere was new to us. Everyone was sitting down on the floor in trenchcoats with pints and we thought, Blimey, what's going to happen here? But we went on and strutted our stuff because we were confident. We were pretty heavily armed with some good material and we liked what we were doing.

FRANCIS: Once we started playing, we got really into it. Rick and I were enjoying it so much that our heads started to nod, it was just a natural movement. Then we noticed the people in the audience putting their heads down and nodding too. We thought, Great, finally we're moving, we're not standing on stage like a couple of gits. This is the way it should be. And that's how the whole heads-down approach came about. We were really into it, the audience was really into it, and that developed into the legs apart stance and the heads-down playing.

RICK: After that, we didn't look at the audience, but by the end of the set they were up on their feet, going bananas. For the first time we felt like we'd achieved something. They *liked* what we were doing. There was no stopping us then.

Making the switch from pop to a harder sound may have been rewarding musically for Status Quo, but financially, it was less than easy. The fees and royalties were getting less, the gigs in clubs weren't on the Mecca Ballroom scale, and money was tight. They managed to scrape along, but the change of direction invariably meant a change of management as well.

Pat Barlow, who had been such an enormous influence and respected father figure, was, as of 1970, no longer in a position to run their career. He had been a part-time manager, continuing with his job in central heating, and a parting of the ways was almost inevitable. He'd had great success as an amateur in such a competitive field, but the time had come to move on. For a brief period Nigel Thomas, who also managed Leon Russell from the Grease Band, took over.

FRANCIS: Nigel Thomas managed us for about a weekend. He put us on at the Albert Hall and those were the days when everyone in the audience would sit down and be very cool. We were singing: 'Is it really me? Have I got to go home?' There was an instrumental bit in the middle when Alan Lancaster and I exchanged pieces of music. It was all very quiet when suddenly some bloke stood up in the audience and shouted: 'Load of fucking rubbish!' Then he sat down. We struck a few more chords, said: 'Thank you, good night,' and got out of there as quickly as we could.

We'd played the Albert Hall before in the late Sixties with a load of other bands including The Move. That time, we were on stage playing when Alan just flaked out, keeled over. The audience was laughing and Rick and I said: 'This isn't funny.' We managed to get him off stage only to find out that he'd done it for a bet. Somebody had bet him he wouldn't and he went ahead and did it, the bastard. We were all concerned and he'd just been messing about.

After their short-lived link-up with Nigel Thomas, Status Quo approached Colin Johnson of Exclusive Artists. Johnson, who thought they were the most exciting band he'd seen, decided to take up the challenge of managing a group who had turned their back on easy commercial success and were trying to make it the hard way.

Pat Barlow was not the only person close to the band to depart that year. Roy Lynes, the keyboard player, also left about that time. On a train trip to Glasgow for a gig, he announced that he was getting off at Stoke. He never came back.

FRANCIS: Roy had told us he was leaving the week before, but we didn't believe him.

RICK: There was no explanation at all, he just said: 'I've had enough of this,' and walked off the train. He wasn't really cut out to be gallivanting around the country. He was a bit laid back, the Open University type who liked tinkering and finding out about things. He loved cars – he had an Aston Martin and then an E-type Jag.

One day he was filling up his E-type at a petrol station and he met a girl and fell hopelessly in love with her. It got a bit much. At one point we were playing a gig in Bexley on a stage about six inches high; the place was packed, absolutely jammed – you couldn't move. Roy was playing the keyboards and holding hands with this girl at the same time. If he came to an awkward bit on the keyboard, he'd play it with two hands and then go straight back to holding her hand again. I think she largely affected his decision to leave.

FRANCIS: Years later, ten or twelve years later, he showed up at a gig we were playing in New Zealand. He'd married her and was living over there, so he just came up and said hallo. We hadn't seen him since he got off the train. He seemed a much happier bloke.

RICK: Roy wasn't really one of the lads. In those days we were sussing out each other's personalities. Francis and I had pretty much worked one another out, but with the others, especially John Coghlan, it was trickier. I never really wanted to be close to John. And though Roy and I had a love for cars in common, I never really wanted to be close to him either. Alan Lancaster was definitely one of the chaps though.

FRANCIS: Alan used to be very funny when he smoked dope, he used to cry with laughter. At first Rick and I thought we had to hide the fact that we were smoking from him, but then he joined in. John Coghlan never did, and it must have been hard for him, because we'd all be laughing at silly things and John wouldn't be on that level. He'd say something and the rest of us would laugh and he couldn't see what was funny, of course.

RICK: Because of course it *wasn't funny* if you hadn't smoked. This was the time when some of the rhyming slang and daft sense of humour started. When you're spending that much time together and you're smoking dope as well, you begin to do some things that just don't make any fucking sense.

Alan and I started to roast one another verbally, giving each other a hard time about any defects or weaknesses. Alan was a little hard to roast because in his own mind he was pretty perfect – he was attractive, well-built, you didn't argue with him. The only thing you could get him on was the fact that he was short. But if you started getting at him for that, you could end up with no teeth. Things began to get a little bit mangled. What had initially been just a laugh got a little less funny and some of the tensions that eventually surfaced in the band go back to those days.

In the spring of 1970, down to a four-man line-up: Alan Lancaster, John Coghlan, Francis and Rick, Status Quo set to work on their third album for Pye, eventually titled 'Ma Kelly's Greasy Spoon'. It included Junior's 'Wailing', a cover of a song by blues band Steamhammer. When the boogie-tinged single 'Down the Dustpipe' was released in July, Tony Blackburn dismissed it on Radio One with the comment: 'Down the dustbin for this one.' It climbed to Number Twelve in the UK charts.

FRANCIS: We came up with 'Dustpipe' – Carl Grossman from Australia wrote it, Ronnie Scott suggested we do it – and it took about six months to break. A guy called Peter Prince had this poster made up to promote it which he thought was really wild. It was a shot of someone's bum with air coming out of it. We also did a programme called *The Golden Shot*, hosted by Bob Monkhouse. We had to shoot it the day before the audience came in, and they had us playing on a huge JCB digger.

RICK: Why on earth were we on a digger?

FRANCIS: Ah, down the dustpipe, mate – see? No, neither do I. It made no sense at all.

I remember seeing Elton John – or Reggie as we call him – at a restaurant across from Pye, and he told me he'd just been recording our 'Down the Dust Cart'. In those days they had compilation albums of hits, like the 'Now' albums these days, but the hits were all done by unknown artists. It was cheaper that way. Reggie was pissed off because he couldn't get arrested at the time, but about six months later Rick and I saw him driving up Oxford Street in a lilac-coloured Aston Martin. When I first heard 'Tumbleweed Connection', I thought it was wonderful.

Rick and I have always called Elton 'Reggie', but we were all at a do once and someone came up to him and said: 'Reggie,' and he turned on him. He said: 'Don't you call me Reggie. These two can, but you can't. Nor can Stewart or that other one, Jagger.' He wasn't being nasty, he was just teasing.

RICK: Reggie suggested an album title for us once: 'As The Quo Flies'. We haven't used it yet.

FRANCIS: We had another single after 'Down the Dustpipe' which didn't go anywhere, then we had 'In My Chair' which had a total of seven plays on the radio, but still, incredibly enough, reached Number Twenty-One on the charts. We had an appearance on *Top of the Pops* for that as well. The lyrics which Bob Young and I wrote for 'In My Chair' sound outrageously psychedelic. We may have been smoking dope, but we certainly weren't on acid.

At the time we couldn't get any airplay because we were considered too noisy and too brash. We did occasionally do live radio shows and once Marc Bolan was there with us – he'd released 'Ride a White Swan' at the time and we had 'In My Chair'. I remember him saying to me that he thought we'd broken the mould.

Few people in the music media were willing to take Status Quo's change of direction seriously. At the time Pink Floyd and Chicken Shack were the obviously cool bands, and Quo, because of their first pop hits, were still struggling for the recognition they deserved.

One breakthrough came when Radio One DJ John Peel saw them perform at a heavy rock festival in Leicester in 1970. 'I couldn't get over how cocky they were,' he commented later. 'They bounded on – in front of about four hundred hippies sitting gently on the floor – and shouted out: "Right, you're not going to like us, so get ready."

'Despite myself I have to confess that I found myself liking them. They were loud and abrasive and very exciting. And although I didn't play their first single that year, precisely because of who they were, I did play "In My Chair". By the following year we brought them in for a session on Night Ride.*'*

RICK: We worked the clubs all through London and throughout England playing to scruffy people, people who really appreciated the music. We began to get a following – people would come distances to see us. We hit the college circuit; we'd be playing at a college gig along with Manfred Mann, Marsha Hunt, Julie Driscoll. They'd get the best spots, the ones which started at 1 a.m. and we'd go on at 5 a.m. and play until six. Even if the audience was pissed out of its brains or half asleep, we'd play. If not for their pleasure, for ours.

FRANCIS: During that transition period, at the time when we had the single 'Make Me Stay A Bit Longer', we were in Margate for two nights getting two hundred quid a night which was quite big money in those days. On one of the nights a total of three girls turned up. That was our entire audience. We played for them, about forty-five minutes. As I recall, we were never paid for that one.

In those days we would do doubles – lots of bands did. We'd play one show and then go somewhere else and play another the same night. Once we turned up at a farm for a gig and we realized that if we did our set there, we weren't going to make it to the next gig in time. So we asked Bob Young to talk the farmer's wife into letting us go on early.

RICK: He managed to convince her and we were finishing our set as the majority of the punters were arriving. They couldn't believe it. There they were, streaming in to see us and the next minute, we were off. We'd finished.

We'd play anywhere – sometimes we'd be playing on the back of a hay lorry. You'd see a tractor going round a field with a load of hay – they'd just take the hay off and we'd play on the trailer.

FRANCIS: Small stages never suited us, though. With our set, we need lots of room on stage. Back then Slade, us and maybe Mott the Hoople were the only bands around that moved at all on stage and spoke to the audience, encouraging them. We'd get the crowd going by moving around the stage. I remember my brother came to see us once and afterwards he said: 'My mates think you look like a fucking formation dance team.'

RICK: We weren't capable of just standing there strumming. The music was too pumping for that.

FRANCIS: There are some memorable moments from those days. There was a girl who used to follow Rick around. She wouldn't leave him alone. At every concert, she was always in the front, always standing as close to him as she could possibly get. We used to swing the necks of our guitars around on the intro and I suddenly saw Rick's guitar head swing through the air with a mop of blond hair hanging from the end. She was wearing a wig, and the thing just came flying off.

RICK: We were standing well low in our characteristic Status Quo stance and I was swinging the neck of my guitar. My head was down, so I didn't notice anything at first. Then I saw this mop of hair. Bloody hell, I thought, where's this come from?

FRANCIS: She ran off holding her head. She never came back.

RICK: One night we were on stage, we'd just started, I was in the usual heads-down position and I heard this almighty clatter. I looked around and Francis had gone. He'd just walked off the edge of the stage, like Freddie Starr or someone. There he was in a complete heap, and we were only a few bars into the first song.

FRANCIS: There was a gap in the stage, and when we went on, I thought, Here we go, we're opening. Turn right, turn left, turn right again – you have the pattern in your head of the movements you're supposed to make – and suddenly bang, I'd fallen in the gap. Rick went up to the mike and said to the audience: 'It's not funny,' and of course he was cracking up. They were all pissing themselves. I picked myself up and kept going.

RICK: Another of the great cock-ups happened when we were playing at the Imperial Ballroom in Nelson, which had a revolving stage. It was one of those places where an orchestra would come on first playing hits of the day, and then a group would follow them. By this time we'd amassed a whole lot of equipment because it looked fabulous. We had eight-foot-high stacks with amplifiers on top. The only people who had stacks taller than us were Slade.

After the orchestra faded, the stage would revolve and we were supposed to fire up immediately. So there we were, all set to come round and do the whole moody face, rock 'n' roll thing, and of course we hadn't allowed for the aerial draft of the stage. As we were revolving, the top of the stage just started wiping all the amps off the top of the speakers. We were getting quieter and quieter and eventually there was nothing. We were yelling: 'Turn the stage back, turn the bloody stage back.' It was like a scene from *Spinal Tap*.

After 'In My Chair' and the follow-up, 'Tune to the Music', Status Quo released their final LP on the Pye label, 'Dog of Two Head'. DJ David 'Kid' Jensen, then hosting his own progressive music programme, Dimensions, on Radio Luxemburg, was one of the first DJs to pick up on the album.

'I thought it was a great rock album. I'd loved "Down the Dustpipe" of course, but unbelievably they were still put in that whole Marmalade/ Casuals bag, despite what they were doing live. I just went ahead and played the album and ignored what was meant to be fashionable. They were a great, go-ahead, steaming rock band.

'After that we brought them over to Luxemburg to record them live at the Blow Up Club, which was a huge success. It was such a good night that I ended up on stage singing "Bye Bye Johnny" with them!'

RICK: 'Dog of Two Head' was an album much more in keeping with what we wanted to do – heavier stuff. The feeling was good and relaxed and we thought, Hey, this is where we want to be. The pumping rhythm turned me on; it made your hips sway and you felt sort of horny playing it. We were growing our hair at that point too, and we began to write more hard-rocking songs – it came naturally to us.

By that time Colin Johnson realized Pye wasn't behind us to the extent that he thought they should have been. John Schroeder, the producer at Pye, was a lovely guy, but he wasn't into hard rock. He was Medallion Man: the barnet was permed, he was beautifully pressed, he had high-heeled Beatle boots and a chain around his neck – everything was perfect. So he wasn't going to be right for us when we got into our jeans and T-shirts.

FRANCIS: In early 1972, we left Pye and signed with Phonogram's rock subsidiary company, Vertigo. Brian Shepherd was in charge of Vertigo. He'd been a roadie with a band called Magna Carta, but he'd moved up in the world. He came to see us play a couple of times, before he signed us, but I remember the night that clinched it was a gig we did in New Cross. He was desperate to get us on his label after that.

Brian was never one of those people who'd put in his two penneth for the sake of it. He wouldn't say: 'Oh, this needs a remix,' just to flex his muscles. He'd say straight off whether he thought it was crap or great. He was good to us all the way through.

That July we made a big impact when we played the Great Western Rock Festival in Lincoln. They put us on the bill at the last minute and we played on the afternoon of the third day. The conditions were horrible – the rain was pissing down, the place was like a mud bath and there we were, playing in the daylight in the midst of all this mayhem. The punters loved it. They see you out there going on when you're drenched and they think it's great. We broke out of the pack then.

RICK: We always get a good reception when it rains. There's no glamour about this band. When we did Wembley Stadium a couple of years ago, it was pouring, all the audience had their umbrellas up and we went out deliberately from under the tarpaulin cover to the front of the stage. We figured if the audience was going to get wet, we'd get wet with them. We were getting drenched, and there's always the chance that you're going to get a charge. Even though you have a skilled crew with you, you're out there playing an electric guitar in the rain.

After the Great Western Festival at Lincoln, we went to the Reading Festival, which was, again, a great gig. If you could tear the place up at Lincoln and Reading you were going somewhere. We managed to do that. Reading was a big breaking moment. Any band who was going to move on to bigger and better things would do that festival.

In those days there were two gigs that really tested you – one down south and one up north. The one up north was in Glasgow – a place called Greens Playhouse, better known as The Apollo – that was a real cauldron, a real tester gig. The Scottish were a hard-nosed audience – if they didn't like you, they'd let you know, but if they did, they'd let you know that, too – and they did like us. Reading was the same. There were a million bands on and you knew it could either kill you stone dead or it would make you. It made us. By that time we'd left Marmalade, Amen Corner and all those bands behind. We were the only ones who survived through that period.

FRANCIS: Recently, I saw Andy Fairweather from Amen Corner on *The Eric Clapton Unplugged Video*. He was playing acoustic guitar.

RICK: He was an amazing guitarist. We couldn't believe at the time that he was the lead singer because he was such a good guitar player.

The Sixties music sound was moving on. Hair, the tribal-rock musical had just closed on Broadway, Alice Cooper's hit 'School's Out' was Number One in Britain and David Bowie was playing to sell-out crowds at the London Rainbow.
'Paper Plane', Quo's début single on the Vertigo label, was the song which began a virtually uninterrupted string of hits.

FRANCIS: 'Paper Plane' was a title I figured I'd ripped off from 'Virginia Plane' by Roxy Music. I like the word 'plane'. We were watching somebody play at the Marquee around that

Deep within the earth
There lives a man
Who holds the key
to where I am.

I have seen him there
I ~~took~~ a trip
~~they to~~ Into the mazes
I did slip

Riding on a big white butterfly
We turned our backs toward ~~the~~ sky
We closed our eyes to find the way
I saw myself in yesterday
And there we came upon ~~this~~ land
I saw a friend hold out his hand
Though what he said I never heard
I understood his every word.

Days that never turn
Into a night
And singing birds
~~I~~ all feathers white

Crystal waters running
Clear and deep
There are no tears
For one to weep.

Riding on my big white butterfly
We turned ~~our~~ faces to ~~the sky~~
We closed our eyes to find the way
I found ~~myself~~ back in today
I turned to look but all was gone
I knew we had to carry on.
But in my mind at last I've been
Into a place I've never seen.

Original poem adapted to become 'Paper Plane'.

time and we ran into one of the guys in Sweet. He was doing this 'I'm a big time rock 'n' roll star and you're just a little band' routine and he said: 'Good Luck with that Paper Planes,' which I thought was very funny.

A couple of weeks later we met up with him again and we were doing better in the charts than he was. It made me think of that old saying: Be nice to people on your way up the ladder, because you might meet them again on your way down.

Even though 'Paper Plane' had little radio airplay, it reached Number Eight in the charts in February 1973. John Peel said that it was the best single he had heard in years and it had set a lot of people talking. Charles Webster in Record Mirror *wrote that 'Status Quo has been through a lot and now they have the image of being a hard-working road band who only need a hit like "Paper Plane" to make it big again. If they do make it, it will be purely on merit – not on gimmicks like glam rock.'*

RICK: 'Paper Plane' was on the 'Piledriver' album, the first LP we produced ourselves. It was as rough and raw as the title suggests, as close as we could get to a live sound, and we had a great time recording it.

FRANCIS: For the first time we were on our own. We had no excuses. Up until then if mistakes had been made – and they had – we could have blamed them on other things – the producer, the record company, whatever. With 'Piledriver', everything was on our heads.

The 'Piledriver' album cover, a classic of the time, shows Francis, Rick and Alan, heads down, legs apart, long hair completely covering their faces. By 1973 Status Quo had set the style and pose for a myriad of UK heavy metal groups.

3

*After the success of 'Paper Plane' and 'Piledriver', Status Quo's popu-
larity began to spread further afield. 'Pictures of Matchstick Men' had
reached Number Twelve in the American charts in 1968, and there had
been plans to make a US tour then, but those had never materialized.
By 1973, Status Quo were more than ready to embark on international
tours. Their first stop, in January, was Australia.*

RICK: Australia was wild. On one internal flight, a few groups
were all together – us, Lindisfarne and Slade. It was a small airline
and the hostesses were all pretty game.

We'd all had a few on this aeroplane and pretty soon there
were paper bags on our heads and banana skins being thrown –
it was developing into a real party. Unfortunately, for us, there
were a few civilized people on the plane, passengers who were

poor unsuspecting innocents. A banana skin landed smack on this Japanese guy's face. It was all happening.

We'd gone through one of Dave Hill's cases – he was in Slade – and in those days he used to do the glitter bit. We got the glitter out and started lobbing it about the plane. Dave had tinsel in his bag as well, so we're hanging it up from the clothes racks, anywhere – the plane looked like a fucking Christmas tree.

After a while, the hostesses were starting to get a little hung up. And they didn't even know we had mirrors on our shoes so we could see up their frocks.

FRANCIS: We were sitting in lines of three, with an aisle in between us and the guy across the aisle would say: 'Excuse me' to the hostess and ask her something, so she had to bend over. When she did that, another guy could position his shoe with the mirror stuck on it so we could check her out. We nearly got arrested for that trick once.

RICK: I was sitting beside the tour manager and he was reading a newspaper, and I set his paper alight – like you do, you know, just like that. He was reading away happily and suddenly he noticed the paper was alight and he panicked. In a broad Australian accent, he said: 'A joke's a joke but that's not funny.' On that plane though, anything was fair game – Francis even dropped his trousers. We got a severe ticking off and were fined at the end.

It was harmless fun until I lit the paper – that was getting a bit dangerous in a pressurized plane. On flights after that, the airline hired two armed guards to sit at the back and watch us. I think they were supposed to make sure we behaved.

FRANCIS: Six months after our tour of Australia, we went to America for the first time. We were the opening act for Savoy Brown. When we arrived in Los Angeles, Rick and I were staying in a Travel Lodge, a real piss hole. It was the bottom end of the hotel chain, you couldn't get any lower. But we thought it was fabulous. We had twenty-four-hour TV, an excellent shower, two double beds each. Compared to the hotels in England, it was bang on.

We'd been in the room five minutes and the phone rang. Rick and I went, 'Yeah!' because it was just like on the television – we'd only ever heard that sound on telly. Los Angeles was like cloud-cuckoo-land, it wasn't real. Afterwards we went to various other areas, Detroit and places like that – that was almost too real. We thought, Shit, this is depressing.

In Los Angeles, we played at the Whiskey a Go Go. We'd heard about it before and thought it was going to be a great venue. When we got there, it turned out to be a poxy club. The stage was in the corner, up in the air – you came down this funny tunnel to work on it. We weren't used to that kind of club – people sitting there with a little lamp on the table and waitresses walking around serving them. They were bored shitless and so were we. It was one of the gigs over there that just didn't work – most gigs there did.

RICK: Everyone in the Whiskey was out of it. You were playing to an audience that was totally out of its tree, because the Whiskey was known to be the place to go to get out of it. We played one night to a group of record company executives and the whole thing about our set was the fact that we were active, we used to run around the set – we were alive on stage. The stage at the Whiskey was about six foot across. You just couldn't move.

We had a conversation before about it and said that we'd just have to go up there and do it, stand our ground. The audience were the type that wouldn't clap anything unless it was in the charts with a bullet. One English journalist who saw us there said that we looked like four guys who were trying to swim in blancmange. We had a week there and it was crap.

FRANCIS: We tried to break in in the States the way we had everywhere else – we'd work a small town, go back and work a larger one, and – except for at the Whiskey – we always went down extremely well with the audiences. But we couldn't get any radio airplay. They said we were too noisy, too crass. Or they'd say: 'You need more drums on this song,' so we'd put in more drums and it still didn't work.

In the end we thought, What are we doing this for? The way it was put to us at the time wasn't helping either: I'd been told that to make the break there we had to have an American manager. I didn't want some Yank coming in and telling me what to do, taking over. If we'd given away a percentage of our management, had an American representative who would have got a slice of the action once he delivered for us, that would have been different. That's probably what someone should have suggested to us.

But as it was, we were in trouble because if you start doing too well, you get pushed down the bill. The top act gets worried about the competition. On one of the US tours we played the Longbeach Arena with Aerosmith and it was one of the best shows we've ever done in terms of audience reaction. They went fucking crazy. The day after that we'd been moved down the bill.

I remember our second American tour in 1974. We were supposed to do gigs with Nazareth and Fleetwood Mac. We got there and Fleetwood Mac weren't Fleetwood Mac at all, they were somebody else. The original group had split up and gone home. This other lot came out and took their place. Imagine an audience, especially an American audience, realizing that the band, when they came on, weren't really Fleetwood Mac.

We were supposed to be with them for five weeks, but it was ridiculous. It was our second trip to the States, and we were second billing in some places and headlining in others. We did only four out of the eight gigs and then we came home.

As time went by, it got to the point where we were making money everywhere else, then going to the States for a tour which cost us an arm and a leg and coming home broke. I thought, If this is all over in a few years' time and we're all broke, people will think we're complete dickheads. So I felt it was cut-and-run time.

RICK: I thought we'd totally blown it when a punter came up to me at the end of one of the best shows we'd ever done in America. He said: 'Man, you were really bad!' I said: 'That's fucking nice – we've been rehearsing for weeks for this gig and all I do is come out here and get insulted.' It was only weeks later that someone told me that bad meant good and he'd been paying us a huge compliment.

The situation in America was put to me like this: if you want to have a US hit, you have to pay for it. The idea was that certain influential people in the recording industry there get Ferraris or their mortgages paid, something to sweeten the pot and you get a hit in return. I said no way – if we do it, we do it on our own merit. I saw paying for it, hyping it, as immoral. Sometimes I think that we should have gone to do a tour there in 1968, when 'Matchstick Men' came out. It had a big success in America and we might have capitalized on that. Then we would have been in the same position as we were in England – we would have changed our style and gone into the heavier stuff anyway – but at least we would have had one big tour there when we had a hit record. We were supposed to have gone then – we were going to be sponsored by Coca-Cola – but it never came off. I don't know if that was our management's fault or what exactly happened to stop that tour.

FRANCIS: But looking back on it, I think early success there would have destroyed us. It would have meant more drugs, more drink, more outrageous and starry behaviour.

RICK: I'd probably be dead.

FRANCIS: Yeah, but think how rich you'd be. We've always had this joke – I can't wait to die, then I'll sell some fucking records!

When we came back from our first trip to the States, everything we'd been doing was suddenly being done by bands all over the charts, contemporary acts – Suzi Quatro, Mud, Sweet – all with loads of guitars. Up until 'Paper Plane' we'd been given the impression that there was no way what we were doing was ever going to make it to the charts and become successful. Pye, our ex-label, recognized that we were now popular and brought out the single 'Mean Girl' from 'Ma Kelly's Greasy Spoon'. They also released a compilation album of the songs we'd done with them called 'The Best of Status Quo'.

After 'Paper Plane', everything we did hit. Our second Vertigo LP was another self-produced album, 'Hello!'. It came out in late 1973, and actually *entered* the charts at Number One. At the same time we brought out 'Caroline', a song Bob Young and I had written years before. I remember writing it with Bob on holiday in 1969. At the time we were writing '*Take my hand, together we can rock 'n' roll*', I thought, You can't say that – 'rock 'n' roll' wasn't cool then.

Later, when we did 'Rockin' All Over the World', I was surprised when it was received as quite a 'cool' song. I would have thought that '*And I like it, I like it, I like it, I like it, I la-la-la like it*' was dreadfully unhip. But we did it and then the Stones did 'It's only Rock 'n' Roll but I like it' and I thought, Oh, I see. Rock is cool again.

On 23 August 1973, seven months after the release of 'Piledriver', Rick married a German woman, Marietta Böker.

RICK: I met Marietta after we played a gig in a university town in Germany. After it was over we went out to rave at a party. Francis and I walked into a pub with half a dozen Dutch clog dancers – I have no idea where we picked them up from. They were dressed in their native costumes and were a real sight. The dance floor was directly in front of us when we walked in and I saw this girl dancing away. I turned to Francis and said: 'Wow – I'm going to marry her.' It was as simple as that.

She stopped dancing, walked past me and I stopped her to say hallo. She said hallo back, I invited her for a drink and that was that. We all went back to her place for a party and I realized that I had totally fallen for her. Back then I was a true romantic.

The band seemed to be on a continual tour at that point, but Marietta and I kept in touch. On the odd occasion when I went home, I'd write her a letter. I'd never written letters before in my life, but these came naturally to me so I must have been hopelessly in love.

Three months after we first met I invited her to come stay with me in England. We had a terrific time together, but there was trouble back in Germany. Her dad was a hard-nosed German businessman and he didn't exactly approve of me. I went over to Germany to meet him because we both knew it was getting serious.

When I arrived at Hanover, Marietta and her dad were there at the airport to meet me. Imagine what her father saw when I walked through customs. My hair was nearly down to my waist, I was wearing platform shoes, jeans with leather patches all over them – a walking advert of a complete scruffy git.

His jaw literally dropped. I don't think he could believe what he was seeing. In fact, after that, he told Marietta he'd give her twenty-five-thousand pounds to give to me to sod off. In those days that was a hell of a lot of money, and he wanted her to give me the money and get rid of me. If not, he said, he'd disinherit her, cut her off completely.

Marietta and I knew it would never work if her father had his way, we knew we could never get married with his approval. So she came to England and after a little bit of deliberation, we decided to go round the corner to the Register Office and get married on our own.

The next day I borrowed three quid off my dad for the fee and we did it, went to the Register Office and got married. Then we had to phone her parents. When we told her father, it was as if a bomb had exploded. The telephone was practically glowing from the heat. He was completely gutted, but there was nothing at all he could do about it.

She went back to Germany to pick up her stuff, and she gave up her university studies. Her father, now that he was faced with the inevitable, said that he wanted to see her married properly, in a church. So I actually bought a suit for about thirteen quid – it was horrible black velvet – and I flew to Germany, where we had a church wedding.

They lived in a tiny village and whenever there was a wedding, everyone came out for it. The bride and groom walk to the church arm in arm and the entire village follows them. We did all this, so we'd been married twice. When we came back to England, we lived with my mum for a year and then bought a bungalow right on the London to Portsmouth railway line. The track was twenty feet behind our bedroom, raised above us.

At five o'clock every morning the milk train went past and the whole house would rumble, but we didn't care. It must have been difficult for her, though, because I was off touring so much. From 1968 with 'Matchstick Men' right through the Seventies, we never stopped. We were touring every day, every week, every month of every year.

I'm sure it wasn't the best recipe for domestic bliss, but we were having a ball, really enjoying ourselves. Gigging, being up there playing, was great. Now it has become much more of a business, but in the early days we weren't thinking about how much money we were earning – it was just a charge to get up on stage and play.

FRANCIS: Before gigs, we'd play a five-a-side football match, forty-five minutes each way, then come in, shower, and get on stage. After the show, we'd climb into the Bentley we'd finally bought after going through a series of highly unreliable cars, and we'd get absolutely wongaed – stoned – and off we'd go, with Bob Young driving. It was a lovely, immensely comfortable car, an S2 with power steering. We had a music system put into the glove compartment and extra speakers on the back window.

Alan, Rick and I would sit in the back and we'd make sure that we were giggling sufficiently and then, wherever we were, we'd yell: 'Bob, stop!' and he'd come to a screeching halt. The angle of the window was just so that we could put our heads back and look up at the stars. We'd be looking at the stars, wongaed, and we'd line up this tape – there was a Byrds' song, 'Aldridge, Armstrong and Collins', about the moon landing – and it was a marvellous bit of a recording with a space rocket blasting off. It sounded so real, it was fantastic. We'd wait till the countdown on the song, and we'd say: 'Go, Bob, go!' and he'd accelerate like mad.

RICK: We would love it. We did this every night. Then we'd put Chicken Shack on after that and it was like that film,

Wayne's World. We were well happy. Imagine other cars on the motorway seeing this Bentley roaring past with sounds coming out and smoke pouring out of the window.

FRANCIS: Later on we were given a driver named Jim McAndrews. The first time Jim drove us we were going to Bristol in a Daimler limo. The heat was stuck on and I felt sick. We encouraged him to go faster, egging him on to see how fast the Daimler would go and all the time we knew there was a police car right at the back of us. He couldn't see him. He could barely see the road in front. So he was stopped and booked of course, and after that first day, we said we didn't want him to drive us. He was as blind as a bat. We were told he had to stay on for three days, and then a replacement would be found. We had him as our driver for six years.

RICK: How we're still here, I don't know, the way he drove. But we kept him and we loved him in the end. He was a great character, he just couldn't drive. The car we were in had a partition between us and him, one of those ones you can put up and down. We'd put the partition down, ask him a question, then put it back up and just watch the back of his head bobbing up and down as he was talking away.

   One night we were crossing one of the bridges over the Thames and Alan Lancaster leant out of the back window and tapped on Jim's window. He shit himself and nearly smashed the car. Once he actually backed right into my house, and rumour had it that on one occasion he'd backed into a boat.

FRANCIS: I heard he backed into a plane. It was like, 'Yeah, go on Jim, go on, Jim' . . . *Smash!*

RICK: There was a do in Blackpool – Rod Stewart and The Faces were there and they were having a party at their hotel. We went over with Jim in an old Daimler and after a while the party got out of hand. Jim had parked the car as best he knew how and was waiting outside. Inside it was getting totally out of order. People were getting thrown in the pool – I'd been thrown in, Ronnie Wood had been thrown in – everyone was getting chucked in. Somehow, at the end, we'd more or less smashed the place up and had to do a runner.

We went screaming out of the hotel, dived into the back of the car and yelled: 'Go, go, go!' to Jim. He said: 'But I can't.' He was partially blocked in by two other cars. We yelled: 'Step on it!' and he put his foot down. He took both sides off the limo – everything was dented. You've never seen such a mess.

FRANCIS: Sometimes we'd stop somewhere and send Jim in to buy some Wimpys and some cigarettes. Then we'd move the car forward sixty feet or so and he'd come out, look around, totally confused and lost. He never had the presence of mind to realize what we'd done.

RICK: One day we unscrewed the dashboard and rewired the whole thing. We switched all the wires from one thing to another, linked everything up and then switched on every switch in the car. As soon as he got in and turned the ignition on, the hooter went off, the wipers started, the hazard warning started to blink – everything was going all over the place.

FRANCIS: He was a bit part player in films. In *The Guns of Navarone* he was one of the German officers who got blown up.

RICK: We'd ask him something about a film and he'd turn around to answer us and the wheel would turn with him, so we'd be careering across the motorway. We'd be screaming: 'JIM!'

FRANCIS: Or, other times, we'd be shouting: 'Jim, Jim – there's a roundabout in front of you!' and he'd go straight over it. He was a wonderful man but not a born driver. A lot of the time one of us would end up driving and he'd be in the back.

By 1974, the year that Patty Hearst was videotaped robbing a bank with her former abductors, and Harold Wilson became Prime Minister, Status Quo kept their string of hits going strong with 'Break the Rules', a song written by all the band, with a title which especially appealed to all the fans. The LP 'Quo' reached Number Two in the album charts.

In January 1975, 'Down, Down' became Status Quo's first Number One single.

FRANCIS: I remember Bob Young came in to tell me that 'Down, Down' was Number One when I was taking a bath. I splashed the water everywhere. We had trouble with *Top of the Pops* with that one – they refused to have us on, even when it was at Number Three, because they thought it was going to go down in the charts. When it went to Number One, they were after us to do it, but we weren't in the country at the time.

When I was writing 'Down, Down' I'd done the whole thing except the lyrics. It was all in place and I was desperately trying to come up with something for the chorus. From 'Dum, dum' to something I'd heard in a T. Rex song and then I came up with *'down, down'* and thought, That'll do. It means sod all really – but everyone thinks it's sexy, they think, 'I know what you mean.'

I know a lot of bands and artists who think that you have to have a Number One or nothing, but I've never understood that. Number Two is great as far as I'm concerned. Three of our songs which could have been Number Ones were up against serious, hardcore competition. Abba stopped us on 'Rocking All Over the World', Barbra Streisand on 'What You're Proposing', and at the height of the *Neighbours* craze, one of those *Neighbours* people beat 'In the Army Now' to Number One. You don't mind losing out to someone like Streisand.

There are times when you think that one song will make all the difference, it will change everything, work a kind of magic – sort out any personal problems, stop the arguments between me and the wife, whatever – but it never happens. What does happen is that you immediately start thinking about the next song, what you're going to do next.

RICK: That's why we've never felt like stars, really. We've had this success and we're pleased, but we're always thinking of the next one and that's how it still is today.

get ~~Drive~~ ~~DOWN~~ ~~GET DOWN~~ DOWN   Rossi/Young

~~Keep~~ down deeper and down
"   "   "   "

~~You mean all~~
I want all the world to see
To see you're laughing
And you're laughing at me
I can take it all from you
Again again again -- - - - - -
Get down deeper and down
"   "   "   "   "

I have all the ways you see
To keep you guessing
~~Stop~~ you're messing with me
Keep you guessing about me) ???
You'll be back to find your way
Again again - - - - - - -
Get down deeper and down
"   "   "   "   "

I have found you out you see
Know what you're doing
What you're doing to me   why?
I'll keep on and say to you
Again again - - - -
Get deeper and down

Original lyrics for 'Down Down'.

FRANCIS: Each song is important. Once we were being interviewed by a journalist who didn't like us. She didn't like our reputation and she had already judged us before the interview started.

In the middle of the interview, I asked her to hold on for a minute while I went to find out how a song of ours was doing on the charts. When we heard that it had gone from something like Fifteen to Number Five, we went nuts. She was gobsmacked – she couldn't believe we cared, that it meant so much and for a while I think she thought we were putting it on. But we weren't. We're still excited by it all.

RICK: When a record is climbing in the charts, it's fabulous. Once it has peaked, then it's over. We think, That's gone, what are we going to do next? I can clearly remember going weak at the knees when 'Matchstick Men' went into the charts. Now, if one of our songs went to Number One, I'd probably go out and get pissed.

FRANCIS: Some people think 'I've had a hit!' and go crazy and never move on. It's nice to know that we've had more hit singles than any other band in this country, but you still need to say, 'Well, what have we got going today?' If you stop doing that, you're finished.

RICK: 'Down, Down' was from the LP 'On the Level', and that was Number One in the album charts as well. Another batch of our old material from the Pye days came out on an album called 'Down the Dustpipe', so we had the charts well covered in the spring of '75. We did another one of our American tours, and then we released a three-track live EP with Junior's 'Wailing', 'Gerdundula' and 'Roll Over, Lay Down'.

FRANCIS: At the time when I was writing 'Roll Over, Lay Down', with Bob Young, my wife had the hump. She had a go at me for something, and she'd deliberately stay on my side of the bed. When I'd come into the bedroom, I'd say: 'Roll over, lay down and let me in'; in other words, 'Fucking move over and let me get in,' but you can't put that in a song, so I had to keep it to 'Roll Over'.

I remember a girl coming up to me in Australia – she was only about thirteen and she had tattoos on her arms, and she said: 'Roll, over, lay down . . . ah, wooo . . . ' I couldn't figure out what she was talking about, but then I realized she thought it was all about sex. It had nothing to do with sex whatsoever. I've never written a song about sex except when I was trying to be sexy in 'Almost But Not Quite There'.

At the end of 1975, as Middle America was trying to recover from the fact that John Denver had confessed to smoking marijuana, and Keith Moon, dressed in a policeman's uniform, was frisking Who audiences for illegal substances, the record buying public was listening to Queen's new song, 'Bohemian Rhapsody'. Status Quo, in the midst of an incredibly prolific period, had acquired the reputation of being a 'people's' band. They not only wrote song after song, they also performed at concert after concert.

RICK: On New Year's Eve, in 1975, we played the Great British Music Festival at Olympia, along with Procul Harum, Barclay James Harvest, Bad Company, Nazareth, Thin Lizzy – lots of big names. We just kept churning songs and albums out – the next one was 'Blue For You' and the single from that – 'Rain' – was different for me because it was the first time after we'd become pretty famous that I sang lead vocal on a record. Francis usually sang the lead, so it was a huge change.

FRANCIS: When we were doing the 'Blue For You' album, we had some sulphate – speed – and I used to put a little bit into Rick's tea. One day I put too much in.

RICK: You put a whole teaspoon of the stuff in – as if it were sugar.

FRANCIS: Anyway, we worked through the day. When we'd finished I was going to give Alan Lancaster a ride home.

RICK: I was as high as a 747.

FRANCIS: Around midnight Alan and I left Rick in the studio strumming the intro to 'Mystery Song'. We came back the next day, around noon and there he was, still on the same stool, still playing the same song. He'd been there all frigging night.

RICK: But I finished the song.

FRANCIS: 'Rain' was from that same album – 'Blue For You' – that's why it sounds a little speedy too.

In an unusual move for those days, Levi Jeans decided to get on the Status Quo bandwagon. Levi sponsored a Quo tour in what was one of the first tie-ups between the commercial and rock worlds in Britain. Quo members were paid to have pictures taken of them in Levis; since they wore jeans all the time anyway, this was hardly a sell-out. Levi was allowed to advertise at the Quo gigs, and 'Blue For You' was, in turn, advertised in some six thousand clothes stores.

FRANCIS: You couldn't go anywhere without seeing a picture of us on a Levi poster. It was embarrassing to go into a shop to buy some jeans and see myself hanging up on a wall. But we didn't see a penny from it. You do a Levis deal today and you get serious bucks, but we didn't. It wasn't like Michael Jackson and his Pepsi deal.

In the late Sixties and the early Seventies you couldn't go just anywhere in a pair of jeans – if you went into a restaurant with jeans on, you'd usually get turned away. You couldn't go to work in jeans. Parents never wore denims. I wonder sometimes whether we were instrumental in changing all that. Everyone used to come and see us in their denims and it got on your tits at the end – looking out and seeing this sea of blue.

How can I see what Im heaving for,
How can I give what I gave before.
How can you tell me that you want me to stay
How can I stay when off Im trying to say,

That I cant live without the rain.
so yes.   "   "   "   "   "

Where can I go when Im feeling so here

How can I feel what Im trying to feel.
How can I move when Im steel to steel.
Your always shouting about the doubt in my eye.
But I cant answer when my eyes are so dry.

And Now I can live whithout the rain
yea I can live without the rain.

"SOLO"

I can live without the rain thats falling on my Head,
Rain thats falling on my Head
   "   "   "   "
   "   "   "   "

Rain's thats falling
Rain thats fallen on my Head.

I started thinking back to you know when
Id like to write but
Id like to send a line but then again.
How can I write ya when there aint no light
I feeling tight tonite & thats allright.

Now I can

Parfitt's handwritten lyrics for 'Rain'.

By the mid-Seventies, the band had managed to accomplish what they had set out to do in 1970. They'd moved from pop to rock, they'd escaped from the image-conscious industry, and in the process, created an entirely new image which the public loved. They didn't see it as an image, however, they were just being themselves. Without actually trying to be, they'd become trend-setters – simply by doing what came naturally.

The addition of Andrew Bown, in 1976, as a session keyboard player was another inspired move. Bown, an ex-Herd member, had met John, Alan, Rick and Francis before: Herd and Status Quo often stopped at the same motorway café. He added to the sound and also fitted in with all the different personalities of the group.

4

In March 1976, after an incident at Vienna airport, Francis, Rick and Alan Lancaster were arrested. Long-haired rock musicians were frowned upon by certain authority figures, and although Rick and Francis had actually been trying to break up a fight, not instigate one, they were taken off to jail. It was an experience which stayed with them and still produces the occasional nightmare.

FRANCIS: The band was having a day off. Rick, Alan and I left the Hilton in Vienna to go to Stuttgart. John Coghlan went off somewhere else, which pleased us because he was having one of his bad times and wasn't too wonderful to be around. When we got to the airport, we saw Rick Wakeman and his band so we had a little chat with them, then wandered off towards the gate. We went down some stairs and at the bottom there was this young guy standing with a gun and a hat on. I said to Rick: 'Look, there's Benny Hill.' We both laughed and carried on.

Because we didn't have any hand baggage, we thought we could show our tickets and go straight past the line of people waiting and through the security barrier. But as we waved our tickets in the air and tried to get through, a guy said: 'Whoa – stop. Go back to the back of the queue.'

Of course we did, although there didn't seem to be much sense in it, and an English fellow who was back there with us turned and said: 'Looks like they've got it in for you.' We waited and waited until finally the queue had cleared through and I said to Rick: 'You go first.'

There was a small booth with a curtain around it. They took him in there and I could tell they were frisking him behind the curtain. Then I saw his trousers drop on to the floor and I heard him say to me: 'Hang on, it's getting funny in here.'

RICK: They asked me to take my shirt off and I thought, This has never happened to me in my life. When he told me to take my trousers off, I was embarrassed and I found it insulting. This man was stripping me down in a little booth and there were loads of people about. Then he pushed me against the sides.

FRANCIS: I knew Rick was playing it as cool as you can play it, and finally I saw that they'd let him through – he was out the other side. Then the man motioned to Alan Lancaster. As Alan went up to him, the guy grabbed him by the lapels. I cried out: 'Nooooo,' because I knew right then you don't do that kind of thing to Alan and get away with it. Lancaster hit him – bam. When Alan fights, he's quick. The two guys who tried to hit Alan couldn't – he was too fast. They didn't stand a chance. Compared to what Alan could have done, they got off lightly.

RICK: I'd gone through, but I heard this commotion behind me. I didn't know what was happening, all I could see was pandemonium. I ran back, realized that it was Alan and rushed into the booth to try to separate him from the guards. Francis was trying to do the same – break them up – and suddenly we were surrounded by men with machine-guns and big black dogs.

FRANCIS: And the Benny Hill lookalike rushed up, the one we'd been laughing at before. He was a young kid and he was standing pointing his gun at us. You could sense how nervous he was and I could see the gun wobbling. I thought, Hell, if he gets *too* nervous, we're gone, we're dead. So we froze.

RICK: We were read our rights, arrested and then taken to a room in the airport to be interrogated, one by one. I got off fairly lightly, with just a heavy talking to.

FRANCIS: So did I, but Alan got a bit of a beating. Rick and I were sitting in a room outside the interrogation office when Alan went in for his turn. He never said a word, never even murmured, but they were beating him underneath his arms. He was all black and blue, but he wouldn't give them the satisfaction of showing any pain. He just took it.

RICK: They kept us there for three or four hours, under armed guard. We couldn't even go to the toilet without the guards, and when we did go, they wouldn't let us close the door. We had to stand there in front of them.

FRANCIS: Luckily, Bob Young hadn't been arrested, because he'd been a few minutes behind us, but he was in the interrogation room with us. He went to get a cigarette out of his pocket, and he found a little bit of dope in there, too. Obviously he had to get rid of it somehow, which was hard considering we were surrounded by guards with machine-guns. So he snuck it into the ashtray, lit his cigarette, put the match in the ashtray and the dope accidentally lit as well and started to smell. We were terrified, but luckily no-one noticed.

RICK: Finally we were told that we'd be taken back to Vienna and spend the night in a police station, behind bars. It didn't matter that Francis and I hadn't hit anyone – the airport police guy who had grabbed Alan by the lapels had it in for us and the rest were backing him up. We were at the point of accepting this

– one night in a police station cell, the three of us together. And because Bob hadn't been arrested, we knew that he could get on the phone and call London. Thank Christ.

It was late in the afternoon by then and they put us in one of those Volkswagen vans with bars at the back, some right heavies on either side of us. They stopped at a police station halfway back to Vienna and took us in to make statements.

FRANCIS: The guys there were quite light about it. They seemed to think it was funny that this airport man had been hit. We thought that they'd ease off us for a bit.

RICK: We kept asking them what was going to happen to us, and they said, in low voices: 'Oh, you don't have to be too worried.' They took all our statements, exactly what had happened, then trundled us back into the Volkswagen.

We headed for Vienna, not sure exactly where we were going and then suddenly we saw it. We saw the prison doors.

FRANCIS: Those doors that go on for ever, massive, twenty-foot-high gates. This wasn't some little police station. This looked like Colditz. We watched as the gates slid back and in we went.

RICK: That was where it really started to get nasty and we thought, Uh-oh.

FRANCIS: They took everything off us.

RICK: Even the gold cross my grandmother had given me. They ripped that right off me. They separated us, put us in rooms with no windows, no nothing, and then two guys with guns came and marched me away down the hall. I remember about eight doors being locked behind me as I walked. I was being taken into one of the prison wings. The guards stopped then, threw a blanket at me and pushed me into this cell.

There were two bunks hanging on chains; I looked around and saw two guys in there already. I asked if they were sleeping in the bunks and they said: 'Yes,' so I just lay down on the floor and slept there.

FRANCIS: Meanwhile, the same had happened to me. The guards marched me away, prodding me in the small of my back with a stick. If you lose your balance and fall, they can say it's just an accident. Finally they pushed me into a cell and I tried to figure out where to sleep. There were three people in there, no available bunks, so I ended up lying on the floor too, and I put my head on the base of the pan.

I woke up in the middle of the night and I had no idea where I was. I was completely disoriented. Then I saw a leg, and I thought, What's this? What's a leg doing there? It dawned on me then, Oh no, fuck me. There was a guy up above me having a shit. I had no place to go, nowhere else to move, so I closed my eyes and went back to sleep.

At half-five in the morning, they woke everyone up for something I guess was coffee.

They poured out the coffee from these big beakers, then they took me into what looked like an office. There were people typing away at desks, but there were other prisoners as well, standing there. Fifteen or twenty of us. I was stripped down stark naked – which was very belittling and then they brought Rick in too. As he walked past me, he tried to put his hand on my shoulder, but the guard belted him off. Neither of us looked at each other after that.

RICK: The three of us were locked in a cage in the corner of this office. They brought in all our possessions and made us identify them and sign for them. As soon as I'd signed, they put all my possessions in a box, took a piece of lead and sealed it up.

FRANCIS: That's when you think, We're going to be in here for a while.

RICK: After that, we were marched off and given a shower.

FRANCIS: I had some big brute watching me in the shower. I thought, If he takes a shot at me, I've had it.

RICK: And of course I've got no ciggies, have I? Apart from the fact that I've been banged up, I don't have any smokes. There was a lifer in the shower with me. Since I could speak a little German, I asked him for a cigarette. He told me he didn't have any, but he could get me one. I thought, Uh-oh, that's a bit hairy. What's he going to want in return?

He came back with a roll up and half a loaf of bread. Then I was taken away to another cell and locked up with a bloke named Franz who was an armed robber. He was in for thirteen years. Before he was an armed robber, he'd been a croupier. So we sat down – I had my own bunk in there – and he started to teach me how to play poker.

FRANCIS: After I got out of the shower I was taken to a prison wing. I could have sworn the guy in charge of that wing was Ernest Borgnine playing one of his nasty roles. He went nuts when he saw me and screamed that there was no way he'd have me in his wing, not with my long hair and everything.

No-one seemed to want to cross this nutter, so they took me down another corridor to another wing and another cell. I thought it was a bit funny because the door of this cell was open. I noticed a kid in there a little younger than me and he had long hair too. I thought, Fantastic, a kindred spirit.

Along with him, there was an old boy who had been in about thirty years, and a huge, fat, beer-bellied German who didn't like the look of me at all. I thought, What have I done? Also there was a bloke who looked like Chuck Berry – I liked him, but I was thinking, Christ, I'm not turning my back on the man with the beer belly, so I sat myself up against the wall.

It was a strange kind of cell – the door kept opening and they seemed to walk in and out to suit themselves. So I reckoned, perhaps this won't be so bad. Chuck Berry looks nice, and the blond kid with long hair kept smiling at me. I smiled back. Then he went and sat next to the other bloke and started jiggling his balls. Oh no, I thought, oh no.

RICK: During the day I'd been let out for a fifteen-minute walk. There were some very nasty people out there. This was the one time I wished that I didn't have blond hair down to my waist. I didn't dare to look around. I heard all these remarks I couldn't understand. But I got the tone.

FRANCIS: I fell asleep and Chuck Berry woke me up, saying: 'You be free, you be free.' There'd been something on the radio about us, which the others had understood. I wasn't sure whether I could believe him or not. We got some food which looked like dogshit, a funny kind of sausage and bread which they banged on the floor. Why were they pounding this bread against the floor? I wondered, until I saw the bugs falling out of it. I knew then I couldn't eat anything.

RICK: They gave me a gristly piece of pig in greasy soup. I was playing cards with Franz when he said: 'You'll be going.' He'd heard it on the radio too. My heart leapt. I couldn't believe he was serious.

Our record company had paid our bail money that afternoon. When Alan, Francis and I got out and walked across the courtyard, we heard this deafening noise. All the prisoners were banging their tins against the bars – they'd heard about us and a lot of them were Quo fans. The whole prison was clapping.

FRANCIS: It was strange – as soon as we got out we went straight to an ice-cream parlour. All we wanted to do was have some ice-cream.

RICK: We went back to the airport, got on a plane to get out. One minute we were sitting in jail, not knowing when we'd be set free, the next we were sitting in First Class. It was wonderful. Unbelievable.

Although they'd been let out on bail and were allowed to leave Austria, Rick, Francis and Alan still faced the prospect of a trial in three months' time. They debated whether or not to go back and face the court, knowing that, if convicted, the penalty for assaulting a policeman was a three-year prison sentence. After a twenty-four-hour stint, they were all too familiar with prison life.

However, if they didn't return for the trial, they pictured the authorities coming to get them, dragging them, handcuffed, back to Vienna. The case for the defence rested on the fact that none of the Status Quo members were aware that the men Alan hit were airport policemen, not civilian security monitors. At the time, they hadn't seen any badge identifying them as members of the police. Hitting a civilian might be bad, but hitting a policeman was a much greater charge. The fact that Rick and Francis hadn't hit anyone, but were trying to break up the fight, was one which the police refused to admit. Francis, Alan and Rick decided, in the end, to go back for their trial.

FRANCIS: We had no suits at the time. I had a borrowed tie, Rick did as well. We were advised to cut our hair for the court appearance, but there was no way we were going to do that. Two women sitting on either side of the judge were making jokes about the way we were dressed.

RICK: I brought along my wife Marietta because she was German and could understand what was going on. We all gave our individual statements. Apparently the guy who Alan walloped was claiming that he had a fractured skull and suffered from severe headaches, but we had a doctor examine him and this doctor said there was absolutely nothing wrong.

FRANCIS: Alan was asked if he could have hit these two more than a couple of times, and he said: 'No.' So of course the judge believed that Rick and I must have hit them too. Alan wasn't trying to be funny or save his own skin; as far as he was concerned he hit them a few times only and that wasn't what he would have called a fight. For Alan, that was nothing.

One of the policemen stood up in court and said: 'The blond was kicking me.' Up until that point, and this shows how naïve I can be, I believed that people went into court and told the truth. As soon as he said: 'The blond was kicking me,' I thought, Wait a minute, Rick never touched him, he never kicked him. You think when people swear to tell the truth by Almighty God, they will. But there we were in court and he was lying. I thought, Oh, that's the game, is it? I see.

RICK: We were lined up in front of the judge and he was prattling on in German. I kept looking over at Marietta to try to figure out what was going on, and then suddenly the judge got a black hat out and put it on. I saw Marietta's head snap back and I thought, Blimey! We're going to be shot. We're going to be fucking shot.

Well, we weren't down for the chop, but we were given three months in prison. He couldn't find us guilty of assaulting a policeman because the guy's police badge was on his belt, covered by his shirt and his jacket, so it was impossible to know who he was. But we were guilty of causing a *fracas* at the airport. All I could think was three months – in that place. I was devastated.

FRANCIS: I couldn't hear a word he was saying after that. I kept trying to work out what I could do in that time. Could I get my guitar in there? How could I possibly spend three months back in that hole?

RICK: Suddenly the judge pulled a calculator out of his robes and we realized that he had converted the jail sentences into fines. Francis and I were going – absolutely, good idea. That's just the thing to do. We paid the money and we came away.

FRANCIS: Since then, we've heard various stories from other bands and roadies about trouble in Vienna. I still dream about it occasionally. It was probably the most frightening experience in my life.

RICK: The next time we went back there we took in a private jet and the same guy was there, the one Alan had hit. He'd been promoted and he was in an office. He saw us pull up at the private aviation terminal. We got off, looked at each other and didn't say another word.

5

Any rock musicians, especially successful, famous ones, have access to a lifestyle most people can only fantasize about. In the famous line 'sex, drugs and rock 'n' roll', sex comes first. From the early days, Status Quo members found that girls screamed at them and didn't stop there. Living in an era before AIDS began to change everyone's attitude to sex, Quo scored high in charts which had nothing to do with music.

RICK: I got off to a bad start with that girl at Hayling Island, but I made up for it later. Even though nothing happened between me and the Harrison twins – Jean and Gloria – I soon met another set of twins. These next two were tall, slim and blonde, which was right up my street. Francis and I met them on *Top of the Pops* – they were dancers – and I fell for Yvonne and Francis fell for Sue. We had a thoroughly good time. I was eighteen at that point and

I made up for what I had missed out on. The same year, I met a married woman who was twenty-eight and I spent five years with her, off and on. I had a fantastic time.

FRANCIS: We were all envious of that at the time.

RICK: She was a wealthy woman, and I'd go over to her house to visit. Her husband knew I used to go around there, but he didn't know what was going on – at least I think he didn't. One afternoon we were in bed, and suddenly I heard a car coming up the gravel drive. I got up and peered out of the window and saw it was her husband.

I did the most amazing 'get dressed, get downstairs, get into the kitchen, pick up and read a newspaper, try to look casual, stop breathing heavily' routine imaginable. I think I did it all in under ten seconds. It was one of those situations you see in a film and hope to God will never happen to you. He came in and said: 'Where is she?' And I said: 'Oh, she's upstairs having a rest.'

FRANCIS: When we were seeing the twins, Yvonne and Sue, we used to go around and stay the night at their house. There were three or four beds in one room, so you could hear what was going on. One night I heard Rick say that he was going to leave, he was going home – and this bird lost her rag.

These twins both had incredibly low voices and they talked in a very tough way. She said to Rick: 'Listen – you have a choice. You can stay here or you can go home. Right? Either you stay here with me or you go home.' So Rick says: 'Fine, see you then, I'm off.' Then she goes: ' 'Ere where ya goin'?' She'd told him he had to go home and then she couldn't figure out where the fuck he was going.

RICK: Most nights it was gut-bustingly funny. We used to have such a laugh with them, and we couldn't help laughing at the way they talked.

After we'd had 'Matchstick Men' and we'd been on *Top of the Pops*, there were groupies everywhere. They came in all shapes and sizes. All these birds were throwing themselves at our feet, but I had to fancy a girl to do anything. I wasn't one of those blokes who would bang anything – I've never been like that – I had to look at the woman and like something about her or I wouldn't do it. But they were definitely up for it. You'd see a woman you fancied and you only had to smile or wink at her and she was yours. It was that easy. Pull them into the van or the car and away you'd go.

FRANCIS: We had nicknames for some of the groupies – there was a lot we used to call the Manchester Heavies. Certain ones always took the guitarist, certain ones the drummer and so on. We'd drop them off and they'd go to another group and then come back again.

RICK: The first ones we called The Elephant Mob, because they came from the Elephant and Castle. There were nine or ten of them who always used to come to rehearsals and would be outside *Top of the Pops*. When everyone else was shouting for whomever, they'd be going: 'State-us! State-us!'

Even though we had the groupies, some people used to think that Francis and I were queer. We were such good pals that if we were on an aeroplane and it got scary, we'd hold hands, thinking, Well, if this fucking plane goes down, we'll go down holding hands. In the early days, we'd get identical clothes made up and we'd phone each other and ask what the other was going to wear to a gig so we could wear the same things.

After a gig in Germany one winter we went back to our room and jumped into bed together because it was freezing cold. We were sitting in the same bed having a natter and a cigarette when this photographer burst in from nowhere and snapped our picture. We were saying: 'Wait a minute, hold on,' but he'd gone, vanished. We were expecting to see ourselves all over the papers with that photograph, but nothing ever came of it.

We didn't think anything of it ourselves, because we were pals and we just wanted to get warm and have a chat.

FRANCIS: After Sue and Yvonne, we got involved with another set of twins – Scottish ones. I was with one of them in one room, Rick was with the other in another room when mine got hung up about something and said: 'I'm going off to Rick.' I said: 'OK, fine,

I don't care – go off with him.' I did care, but I wasn't going to let her know that. I said I didn't give a shit.

RICK: That really turned me on, because she was nice and I was in bed with her sister when she came in. I should have stuck with both of them, but I sent my one over to Francis. In those days, the Seventies, Francis and I would be in the same room with different girls and I would see his little white bum going up and down and I'd be thinking, Hey, he's doing all right. We'd swap them around – anything went back then. It was real rock 'n' roll.

I figure we must have screwed as many as eight or nine girls each in our time.

FRANCIS: Maybe eleven or twelve.

RICK: I had a really weird experience with a girl in America. We were playing in a club in Atlanta, Georgia. It was a hip place and we were with Little Feat. After the show, this bird came into the dressing-room. I'd had a smoke and I was feeling pretty good; she'd had one, too. Everybody had. We were all wongaed. That night I was particularly wrecked.

This bird and I had some eye-to-eye contact and we'd had a good laugh together, when suddenly she started getting a bit heavy and asking me some strange questions. I began to talk to her about my wife and she asked: 'Does your wife get on your wick?' I don't know why, probably because I was so wongaed, but I just couldn't handle that question. I thought it was an incredibly weird thing for her to say.

The smile left my face and I immediately felt frightened. She'd given me a ring and told me she was a witch, and I'd been saying: 'Oh, of course you are,' and having a laugh, and all of a sudden she'd just bowled me over. She told me that if I ever took the ring off, life was going to be a real problem for me. I totally freaked out. I motioned to Bob Young to get her out of there, and I went straight back to the hotel, shaking. I was feeling really spooked.

When I got to my room I thought I'd take a shower, that then I'd feel better, so I was standing in the shower, trying to wash off these witchy feelings when I dropped this sliver of soap. It stood bang upright on the shower floor, which is an impossible thing for a sliver of soap to do, and I looked at it and I couldn't believe it.

Then the phone rang – and I thought, It will either be one of the chaps or it will be her – if it's her: help! The phone carried on ringing and I couldn't decide whether to answer it or not – but eventually I figured I'd get it. At the same time, I thought, If it stops just when I get to it, I'll freak. And that's exactly what happened.

I had to lie down on my bed, but as soon as I did, my body started contorting. I suddenly thought, Yes, of course, she *is* a witch and she's made a little dummy of me and she's poking it and that's why I'm twitching. Any minute and she'll skewer it with a knitting needle and I'll be dead.

I managed to survive, but since that night, at least fifteen years ago, I've never been able to smoke a joint. I can't handle it. Every time I've tried to take a puff since then, my mind goes straight back to that night and I start thinking about the devil. That was one bird I could have done without.

FRANCIS: Speaking of showers, one night we met these two girls who had some amazing stuff on them – it was a 'stud spray' – you spray it on and it makes you stay harder longer. So I sprayed some on and I thought, This is pretty good. I was merrily working away on this girl and she must have thought I was wonderful. We started at about one in the morning and I was still going strong at half-past four.

I was going at it, no problem at all, when suddenly the other bird came in and said that Rick was having a problem.

RICK: I'd OD'd on this spray.

FRANCIS: I came out of the room and I'm still up, so I'm walking around as proud as you like, and there's Rick, standing in the shower, screaming with pain.

RICK: I was standing there with my knob under the shower. It would not go down and the harder it got the more it hurt. It was stinging beyond belief. One of the girls said: 'It's all right, I can help. I'm a nurse.' I yelled: 'Don't touch it! Don't touch it!' God knows how long I stayed there in the shower. It was the only relief I could find. I was desperately trying to get it down, trying to think about anything but women. I think I was in there all night.

FRANCIS: The sight of him bent half-back in the shower, moaning, was something.

Foreign trips were always wild when it came to girls. For instance, in Australia the women outnumbered the men something like seven-to-one and a lot of the men were gay anyway, so we were quids in.

RICK: We were in Sydney once, in the Sebell Townhouse, a beautiful hotel. We had a couple of days free and there was nothing to do. I remember going into Francis's room and he was knee-deep in women. There were about fifteen birds all over the place – on the chairs, on the bed, probably even in the closets, and I'll never forget his face. I was gobsmacked when I walked in and saw this scene and he was just laying back on the bed saying: 'Not a bad life, is it?'

FRANCIS: But after a while, the groupie thing can get a little much. If the band were all sitting in a club and a bird walked in, I used to think, OK, I'm going to get that one, and maybe the other guys might be making eyes at her too, so if I cracked it, I'd think, Great. Then we'd get up to my room, and suddenly something would change. I'd see all my personal belongings there, and I'd start to think, I can't take a piss with the door open because this bird is here. And I could have just gone to bed and read a book, but now I have to perform. So I'd come back in the room from the toilet and there she'd be, lying on the bed, totally undressed. There I was, presented with a stark-naked woman, and I would think, No, don't get undressed. I like women with their clothes on, like wrapping on a Christmas present.

That situation is similar to a gig: when I imagine a gig, I see it as a full auditorium, with the lights on and everything, not an empty stage. These naked groupies were like an empty stage. And some of them used to do the rounds – they'd be with us and then we'd drop them off with The Move, and then The Move would pass them back to us and it was all a little sticky and messy – you knew they'd been on the road for weeks.

RICK: There were times, when I was at my wildest, going out on the town for three days on the trot, when I'd wake up with a bird beside me and think, Who the fuck are you? and for all I know, they felt the same. That's when it's no fun at all.

FRANCIS: People put so much emphasis on sex now. I know men who say: 'Unless I come four times, she's no good.' Really? I'm not saying that I didn't go through it myself. I used to think, Yeah, this is the way to be. I've done it four times in a night, I'm great, but that's part of the pressure put on by society. Everybody's under pressure with sex. Married couples are supposed to do it three or four times a week, but are they doing it because they want to or because they think they have to keep up the national average?

And this whole business with women and their orgasms really got to me for a while. I used to think, Why don't you just do it for yourselves then? Get on with it and buy a machine.

I wonder sometimes what Madonna is going to do next. What's she going to suck next? I don't see how she can make a record like 'Like A Prayer' and then go smack into porno. When I see that she's got bondage in her videos, I think, Come on, this is a bit much. People might snigger and say: 'Oh we're being prudish, are we?' and I say: 'If that's what it means to be prudish, then yes, I am.' I can't see that it's good for society or the world for young children to see that kind of thing.

When you're a teenager, fine, you have to rebel and push the edges out, but now I think we have to take some responsibility. I didn't used to think that we had responsibilities, but we do. When 'Down, Down' came out, people would say to me: 'Oh, my little three year old loves that,' and I'd think in a dismissive way, Sure, fine, great, but now I realize that what I sing is listened to by kids and I have to be aware of that.

6

In October 1976, seven months after the incident at Vienna and two months after 'Mystery Song' hit Number Seven in the charts, Andy Bown, who had worked on recording sessions with Quo before, joined the live line-up. The Rolling Stones' mobile studio was brought to Glasgow's Apollo Theatre to record three live concerts – tickets for the shows had been sold out within hours.

At the same time as George Harrison was found guilty of 'subconsciously' plagiarizing The Chiffons' 'He's So Fine' for his song 'My Sweet Lord', and Patti Smith was announcing that 'every man I've ever screwed has thrown up on me at least once', the Sex Pistols were signed by EMI Records. A spokesperson for EMI commented: 'Here at last is a group with a bit of guts for younger people to identify with.' Punk was well on its way.

FRANCIS: The punk people used to say that they didn't want fame, they didn't want major record company deals, they didn't want limos, they didn't want this and they didn't want that. They claimed to be completely outside the 'Establishment'. And I always wanted to ask them: 'Right, if that's the case, why do you play at the Marquee? Why do you play at Hammersmith? Why don't you just stay at home and play in your front room and then you won't have to have any of those things you don't want?'

Once we were recording at the Marquee in the studio at the back, and somebody said there was a punk band playing next door, so we decided to go in and see what was happening. We hadn't been in there for two minutes when we heard someone yell: 'Fuck off, you boring old farts.' We were twenty-six, twenty-seven years old at the time.

RICK: We just wanted to check it out; it was the start of punk and we thought, Hallo – we'll take a look. They used to do this pogoing thing, jumping up and down – other people had been doing it for years and suddenly it was called the 'punk movement'. When we went in, it was awful. There was spit flying around, everything.

FRANCIS: Before punk, we were described as rebels, but after punk I think we must have been seen as quite pleasant.

RICK: I think we must have looked positively smart. I always got off on the fact that we were loud, but then when I saw them, loud didn't come into it. It was a complete mess – it looked like a plate of sausage, beans and chips all mashed up together. It sounded like that, too.

FRANCIS: They were the hip thing and we weren't, so we figured we'd best leave the room.

RICK: The one band I took particular umbrage to was Sigue Sigue Sputnik.

FRANCIS: That did it for us. Rick said something not so kind about Sigue Sigue Sputnik and we got into trouble. The next hit we had was anything but punk. We were Tommy Quickly's backing band for a while in the old days – he was a Brian Epstein protégé – and 'Wild Side of Life' had been his only single. When we did our version of it and released it, some reporters said they thought that we were going 'country'.

The first time I went to the States, I thought all the people I was into were pop stars. Instead I found out that they were country people – Guy Mitchell, the Everly Brothers, Connie Francis – everyone except Johnny and the Hurricanes, who were rock. Country, blues and rock are similar, they intermarry.

We used to love the lyrics of country songs, lines like: *'I'm going to build me a bar at the back of my car and drive myself to drink.'* Or: *'I bought a pair of shoes that just walked out on me,'* and *'I've got tears on my ears from lying on my back and crying over you.'* They're funny, but they're brilliant. I like *'I never knew there were honky-tonk angels'* from 'Wild Side of Life'.

We recorded 'Wild Side of Life' at a studio in Stanhope Place and they brought in a producer, Roger Glover, the Deep Purple bass player. He recorded Rick and I first, then a really basic drum pattern, then the crashes and cymbals and all sorts of stuff.

RICK: It was a great record, that.

FRANCIS: We went to Australia with it thinking it was going to be blinding, but someone in the record company didn't think it was quick enough, so Roger Glover dubbed in the bass part while we were away, which I always thought was a mistake. So when we got back to England, it was a slightly different single than we had made, and that's the only time that ever happened to us. It was a hit, though, so who cared?

Before we got to Australia on that tour, we went to Japan. On the way over, we were joking about the things they might say, how they talk. We got to the airport and got masses of flowers and when we got to the hotel, our Japanese promoter said: 'You not go to sreep till you velly, velly sreepy.' That did it for us, we just couldn't stop laughing.

RICK: We had no preconceived idea about how big we were there, and we were met by all these kids giving us all these presents, wonderful wooden toys which I still have. I have a memory of the audience over there and it's in black and white – a mass of men wearing white shirts and black ties in the crowd.

FRANCIS: They kept to the schedule absolutely exactly. If they say the show is going to start at four, it starts at four. If it's supposed to be over at eleven-thirty, it's over – the doors are closed, the trucks are going. It's all precise. And the audience is a register above any other audience. If you listen to an audience anywhere else at a large show and the band is walking on, getting applause, it's usually a deep roar. In Japan, it's a shrill screech.

RICK: They took us to a bath house – it was a fantastic experience.

FRANCIS: I missed out on that – the others all came back saying: 'Marvellous, that is.' I couldn't think what they were on about.

RICK: They had no inhibitions at all about giving us a good rub down.

FRANCIS: One afternoon, on a day off, I was sitting around with the crew, there were about ten or twelve of us, and we were smoking joints. The room started to shake, and I said: 'Did you feel that? It must be outrageously strong dope.' We all said: 'Wow, amazing stuff!' The next day we found out we'd sat through an earthquake tremor.

RICK: The fans were everywhere. They followed us when we went on the bullet train. It was very flattering. I liked Tokyo because I love gadgets. We were buying cameras and camera equipment – we had Nikons coming out of our ears, casefuls of gear. We were cameraed up in a big way.

FRANCIS: That was the phase when we decided that we were great photographers. I remember setting up a shot – taking hours to set it up – and it was a picture of a load of cameras on a windowsill. Very arty.

RICK: When we came back from Japan and Australia, 'Rockin' All Over the World' was released. It was a massive European hit, but bombed in Japan, Canada and the US. We had been huge in

Australia, we were really kicking some butt over there and then all of a sudden, 'Rockin' All Over the World', possibly one of the strongest singles we'd ever had, wasn't even released there. In fact, we haven't had a release there since 'Wild Side of Life'. And 'Rockin' ' didn't get a single radio play in America, even though it was written by John Fogerty of Creedence Clearwater Revival fame. That's never made sense to me.

FRANCIS: Alan Lancaster thought that 'Rockin' All Over the World' should not have been released. He felt the same about 'Marguerita Time', too. He used to say that he could never face his family if we released a song like that because it wasn't 'man's music'. Alan was very into that, 'man's music', although he liked 'Wild Side of Life' which surprised me. I remember being in a limo with Alan and his second wife. They were both laughing about what a mistake we'd be making if we released 'Rockin' '.

By this time, 1977, Alan was spending a lot of time in Australia and he wasn't doing as much with the band. He was there when we were doing the video for 'Rockin' ' and he told us he couldn't come back over to be in it. We decided to go ahead with the video anyway, but we knew people would notice Alan's absence, so we had a lifesize puppet of him made up.

Colin Johnson was up in a gantry working the wires, and it looked incredibly realistic. There were a couple of times during breaks in the shooting when they'd take the puppet down, and it would be sitting in a chair with its jeans and jacket on and I'd go up to it and start talking before I realized: 'Oh shit – it's a puppet.'

In 1978, for tax purposes, all Status Quo members lived abroad. Alan Lancaster stayed in Australia, John Coghlan went to the Isle of Man, Rick lived in Jersey and Francis moved to Ireland.

FRANCIS: I went to Ireland to do the tax year and I was down in the country, in County Clare, living in this castle owned by an American. Bernard Frost and I had started to write songs together at that stage. We first met Bernard in 1969 or 1970 – he used to turn up in a truck and he came into the dressing-room a couple of times. He'd pick up the guitar, sing a few songs, and then he and I started writing together in the early Seventies – the first song we wrote was called 'Naughty Girl'. Bernie came over to Ireland and we did a lot of writing. We were spending eighty pounds a day for rooms – and that's without food – so we thought, Hang on a minute, we can get one room and spend the extra we've saved on studio time to make some demos.

We looked around for cheaper rooms for a bit, and then someone suggested we go to Dublin and get in touch with Liz Gernon, a woman who had worked with us on a tour the year before as a promoter's assistant. She was in Ireland and she could find a place for us. She did. We ended up in adjoining rooms in Dublin which cost us forty-five pounds, and Liz then booked studio time for us. I slowly got to know her. It was a long process. I admired her because she was so good at her work and I liked her very much.

My marriage had broken up before Liz came on the scene. Jean, who was continually threatening to divorce me, decided that she was going to go off yet again, and this time was the final straw. Although Keiran, our third son, was born in 1979, we had come to the end of the road. Eventually, Liz and I started up together.

RICK: When I was in Jersey I was going through my mad phase – taking foreign substances and drinking far too much. The only good thing that came out of it was a couple of songs I wrote – particularly 'Living On An Island', which I co-wrote with Bob Young, who used to come out and visit me there.

I smashed up a couple of cars during that time in Jersey and I was nearly killed one night when Marietta and I went out to a Chinese restaurant. I had a mane of blond hair then, very long, and I was sitting, eating peacefully. There were three Scotsmen at the table opposite and they didn't like the way I looked. I was facing them and I could see they were building up to something, but I was trying to stay cool, when one of them got up and came across at me with a knife. I got Marietta out of the way, but I didn't know what I was going to do next – he was going to stab me for no reason at all. I hadn't provoked him. His mates got hold of him and there was a struggle and they managed to get him out, even though they were all drunk.

The police came down and the owner of the restaurant explained what had happened – they'd smashed a couple of chairs and tables up in the fracas. I ended up paying their bill. I knew they hadn't paid and it didn't seem fair on the proprietor, so I paid for them.

During that year, I spent some time in Germany as well. I was pissed off, bored and I wanted some action. I decided to go see Francis in Ireland. My mother, Marietta, and our two children, Richard and Heidi, set out in my car for Amsterdam. I was going to drop them off there and then fly on my own to Ireland. The boot was piled high with the kids' stuff, while my mother was in the back with all the gear and the nappies – she'd never liked sitting in the back of a car. I was hammering down the autobahn, doing about one hundred and forty miles an hour, because I wanted to get there as quickly as possible.

My mum was feeling sick in the back, and she was trying to say something, but she couldn't quite manage. I was steaming along and I heard the back window go down, and my mum being sick out of the back. She got her head back in, I slowed down and she tried to say: 'That's better,' – but she couldn't. She'd lost her teeth – they'd flown out of the window. The cars behind us must have seen her teeth winging by. You can't exactly stop and go and search the autobahn for a set of flying teeth, so the only thing I could do was buy her a new set later. I eventually made it over to see Francis, but whenever I'm driving in Germany, I wonder if I'll run into my mum's teeth.

7

1978 was an important year in Status Quo's history, a year when the cracks, both within the group itself and the individuals, began to show. The wear and tear of a decade of constant touring, constant performing and constant recording started to take its toll, and the second item in the sex, drugs and rock 'n' roll litany crept on to the scene. Until that time, although they had smoked their fair share of dope and done some speed, Francis and Rick had managed to avoid the more dangerous drugs.

RICK: I didn't feel any pressure to do drugs – I just wanted the experience, and I suppose I fell into it – everything was there for you in our position. It was very easy to get. We were in Toronto when we were offered our first line of coke. Francis and I did it at the same time at a party. It didn't really do anything for either of us at the time. It wasn't until about six or seven

Francis Rossi: Pictures of Matchstick Boy.

Rick Parfitt:
Woking's answer to Tommy Steele.

Francis and The Spectres breaking the rules.

Rick and The Highlights in their full glory.

The Status Quo kitted out in their Carnaby Street frills. (© *London Features International*)
The band after the switch from pop to hard rock. (© *Mike Putland/Retna*)

Francis and Rick in action. (© *Ara Ashjian*/©*Adrian Boot*)

Relaxing after a gig.

Alan, John Coghlan, Rick and Francis after the ball was over. (© *Robert Ellis*)

Francis and Alan Lancaster matching mugs. (© *Robert Ellis*)

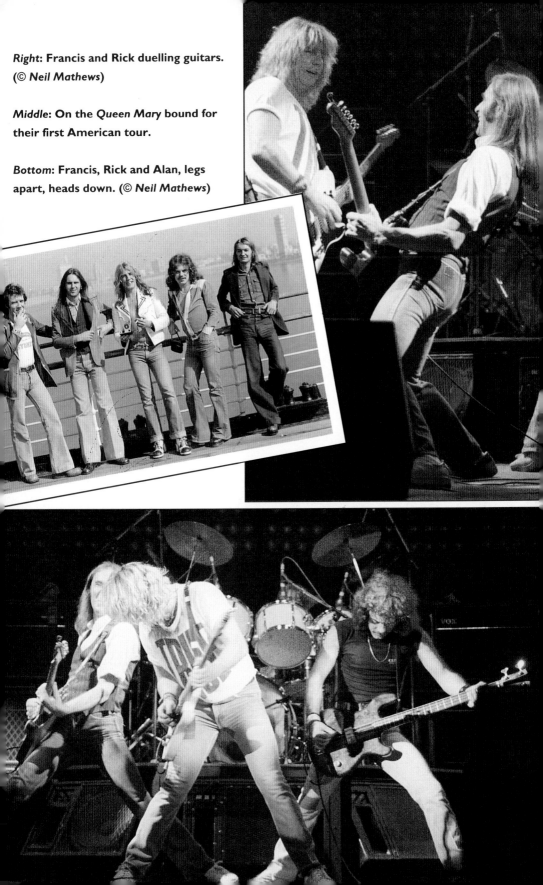

Right: **Francis and Rick duelling guitars.** (© *Neil Mathews*)

Middle: **On the *Queen Mary* bound for their first American tour.**

Bottom: **Francis, Rick and Alan, legs apart, heads down.** (© *Neil Mathews*)

Left: **Francis: this year's model? (© *Fin Costello/Redferns*)**

Below: **Rick putting himself in the driving seat.**

Francis and Rick in the studio. (Above: © *Bob Young*, below: © *London Features International*)

Quo Live. (© Robert Ellis)

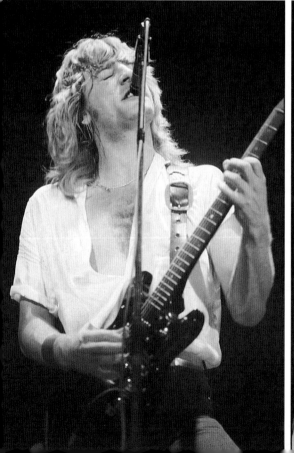

Marguerita Time? (© George Bodnar)

months later, when we were in Ireland, that we both thought, There must be *something* in this, let's give it another go. And *that* time we realized how out of it you can get and away we went from there – on a coke binge.

FRANCIS: There are lots of things I used to say I'd never do. I said I'd never marry a redhead – I married one. I said I'd never marry an American – I married one. I said I'd never have any more children after my first marriage – I had them. I said I'd never shag a friend's wife – I've done that, too. And I used to see people doing cocaine and think, What a gross habit, I'll never do that. I did it.

I slowly started to get into it and then I began snorting sulphate as well, but it's cheap and nasty. Once I'd started, down the slope I went.

Rick and I did most things together. If it was two o'clock in the morning, Rick would finish up the coke that was around, whereas I'd be panicking, thinking, No, I need some for tomorrow morning. That was the difference between us: he would do it all and get in a state the next day trying to find some more, whereas I would always hang on to some.

When we were doing coke, we got into this crazy routine. First we had to find the score – where we could buy an ounce, and an ounce of coke at the time cost about a thousand pounds – and a thousand pounds in cash in the late Seventies was a problem to find.

The logistics were incredible. We had to arrange to get the cash, so we needed two cash cards to get it out of the cash point because one card only covered five hundred pounds, and then we'd sit back and wait for the delivery. It was always 'coming at nine', always about to arrive. We'd sit and wait and wait and then finally it would get there. Then we'd have a cup of tea and a line. It took over our lives.

RICK: Years before, when I was in The Highlights, I'd seen a guy who was dealing Purple Hearts – the Ecstasy of the Sixties. He looked so awful, so ill, that I remember thinking, If Purple

Hearts do this to him, then I'm not going to touch them. He looked strung out, drawn, with black under his eyes. It scared me off the hard stuff until many years later. But when I did get into it, I lost a lot of friends.

At the time, I felt it was fun. I didn't think, Oh, Christ, I'm living a rock 'n' roll lifestyle. I just enjoyed doing it and it was totally crazy. I smashed two cars to pieces, got banned from driving, my marriage went haywire, life began to collapse, but I wasn't in any shape at the time to do anything about it.

FRANCIS: It took us a while to straighten out.

The band was devastated in February, 1978, during a difficult tour in Germany, when one of their fans was killed in the middle of a gig. As Harry Doherty reported in Melody Maker:

A six thousand-capacity bowling alley had been converted in Wolfsburg for the concert and halfway through the set, the promoter asked fans not to stand on the window-ledges upstairs. He mentioned casually – in German – that one person had fallen through the window. What he didn't say was that there was a fifty-foot drop to the pavement and the poor kid who mysteriously smashed through the glass was a mangled mess when found.

RICK: I didn't know it had happened until afterwards. I couldn't believe it – someone had died at our gig. Someone had paid to come and see us and it had killed him. I hope to God that will never happen again – it was horrible. We were all gutted and sent flowers to his family. I still find it hard to believe.

In August 1978, after an Australian tour and a stint in Holland to record the LP 'If You Can't Stand The Heat', the band made its

only UK appearance of the year, headlining the Reading Rock Festival. The following month, the single 'Again and Again' made it
to Number Thirteen in the charts.

RICK: I wrote 'Again and Again' with Jack Lynton and Andy
Bown. Lynton, who we had met on our first tour in America
when he was with Savoy Brown, was a complete nutcase. He
used to have us in stitches. We met him when we were touring
in the US and we were laughing all over America because he was
such fun. It's the most basic of all our songs, dead simple. The
chorus is very difficult to learn: *'Again, again, again, again, again,
again, again, again, why don't you do it, why don't you do it again?'*

FRANCIS: I thought it was the usual story – someone can't get to
me so they get to Rick. Jack was painting Rick's house at the time,
and I'd gone over there to do some work with Rick. I was sitting
in the kitchen with him and suddenly there was Jack. So we sat
somewhere else, and again, there was Jack at another window. So
we moved again and we thought to ourselves, How can he paint
so many windows at the same fucking time?

When 'Again and Again' came out, I heard rumours that Jack
was going around saying: 'I've fucking done it. Have you heard
that single? I wrote that.' I thought he was taking the piss, so I
was very much against that track going out. I think I can see
when someone's taking advantage of Rick before he can, but I'm
sure it works the other way around too. These days I don't find
'Again and Again' half so bad.

RICK: We put it together in about three and a half minutes.

FRANCIS: Actually, I thought the verses were excellent.

RICK: Well, I don't know about excellent.

FRANCIS: I like *'Once upon a time not so very long ago there wasn't
such a thing as a rock 'n' roll show.'*

RICK: Funnily enough – it's remained a firm favourite for years in the set. It's a good turn-on kick-ass number. When we did 'Accident Prone', the album which came out in December 1978, I think we were starting to get a bit too clever. We'd smoothed out – the rawness was gone. It could have been a great record, but the drums were awful.

FRANCIS: That was because for one of the first times we were following a trend instead of doing our own thing. The fashion at that time was for drums to produce what we called a 'pea-soup' sound, so John Coghlan did this 'pea-soup' thing; it was a perfect example of why you shouldn't follow the fucking trend.

RICK: We weren't good at 'pea-souping'.

FRANCIS: We definitely weren't. We were doing this 'pea-soup' and Honda sound as we called it. I thought the track 'Accident Prone' was wonderful at first and I pushed like mad for it – I thought it was going to be the biggest hit we ever had. It wasn't. In fact, it was our first big accident.

RICK: I loved it, though. I thought the actual groove was great and it was the most enjoyable video I'd ever done. We did it in the middle of the night in a scrap yard and we were out of our trees – or I was, anyway. I decided to wear Wellingtons for the filming – fuck knows why. There were cars being dropped from immense heights, others being crushed, there was smoke and dust everywhere – it was outrageous.

My favourite of the songs I've written is 'Whatever You Want', which came out in October 1979 and went to Number Three in the charts. The intro to that is a classic – it's been written about as one of the all-time great rock 'n' roll intros. I wrote it with Andrew Bown on the guitar and piano and it just worked immediately. And if you start with a line like 'Whatever You Want', you can write about whatever you like.

FRANCIS: I've always seen that one as operatic. A couple of years later Hale and Pace did a bunch of Quo songs all dressed up in black tie, and they did 'Whatever You Want' as if it were an aria from an opera.

RICK: They were great. I've always found anybody's impressions of us highly amusing. When the two Ronnies did us I thought it was immensely flattering.

FRANCIS: How somebody so short could be Rick and someone so heavy be me, I couldn't believe, but they pulled it off brilliantly. They did 'The Wanderer' and sang *'Because I'm fond of her, I'm very fond of her . . . '* They had Rick and me in hysterics.

RICK: Little Ronnie was portraying me as a bit of a poof and was doing it rather too well for my liking!

FRANCIS: We couldn't believe how they could do us so well.

RICK: People tend to think that we'd be insulted by someone taking us off, but we love it.

Rick's ballad about his year in Jersey, 'Living On An Island', finished the Seventies with Quo high in the charts. They'd barely been out of the charts since they had found the music that suited them, and the decade had been one of tremendous success brought about by incredibly hard work and creative drive.

Bob Young left the band at the end of the decade and Iain Jones, who had started as a roadie in 1978, working on keyboards and guitars, then took Bob's place as tour manager and became an integral member of the Status Quo team.

But the tensions in the band and in their personal lives which had been fermenting in the late Seventies blew in like a vicious hurricane as the Eighties dawned.

RICK: Through the Seventies, we were making a lot of money and I was spending a lot. I've always been of the belief that if I've got the dough, I'll spend it because I've worked hard for it. I had no idea of how to manage it, I wasn't thinking how much I could put in the bank. If I want something, I'm impetuous – I have to have it. Nobody was telling me I had to save it, so I didn't.

By 1980, Marietta and I had moved to a fantastic pad in Surrey called Hydon Ridge. It was 560 feet above sea level, on top of a beautiful hill. There were uninterrupted views for twenty-five miles, and I had it lit up like something out of *Close Encounters*. If you were driving along the A3, you could see the glow of my house from five miles away. Whenever I drove home, I'd see it from a distance and think, That's my pad.

At that time, I was living the rock-star life with a vengeance. I had a Mercedes, a Porsche, a Range Rover, a little jeep for my son Richard, a Studebaker Hawk, a Corvette Stingray, and in the house itself I had a twenty-four-track recording studio, jukeboxes, pin-ball machines, a billiard room; all the things that people imagine rock stars have. I had them. And I had a beautiful wife and two beautiful children. Everything could have been perfect, but I began to get bored with the country, and that was when I started to go to London for three-day binges.

I was into drugs in a big way and blowing a fortune on coke. Until coke came into my life, I'd been all right, but once I had started that, I began to fuck myself up completely. Marietta tried a few moves to get me off drugs because I wasn't responding to her and she could see what a wreck I was becoming. She could also see that the children were suffering because they would always see their dad in bad shape. I don't remember ever changing a nappy – I was a terrible bloke.

Without telling me, Marietta learned to fly a plane. She knew that once I'd found out, I would think, If you're going to fly a plane, so will I. Anything that went that fast was a challenge. And she thought that if I began to fly, I wouldn't take drugs. I did take flying lessons, and we even bought our own plane. But it didn't make any difference, I couldn't kick the habit.

On 10 August 1980, my daughter Heidi died.

It was a Sunday afternoon. My wife Marietta was cooking lunch and I was watching television with my four-year-old son, Richard. I got up to go to the kitchen to check on lunch, and Marietta asked me: 'Where's Heidi? Is she with you?' I said: 'No, I thought she was with you.'

We didn't panic at that stage. We went all around the house calling her name, but got no response. Then we went outside and started shouting for her. That was when the fear began to set in. Suddenly it hit me – I felt a lightning bolt go through me – 'Oh, my god. The pool.'

The pool was about thirty metres away from the house and there were steps down to it. I saw her from a distance, floating on top of the pool, face down. I ignored the steps and leapt down the terrace nearly breaking both my legs, dived into the pool and dragged her out. I began to pound her, pump her out, give her the kiss of life. I was using life-saving techniques I didn't know I knew, but they came naturally in a crisis situation like that.

She showed no sign of life at all, and I could hear Marietta, who had followed me to the pool, screaming. I didn't know what to do any more. I'd picked her up and she was hanging, completely drenched, on my shoulder. We called the ambulance, and the time spent waiting for it seemed like for ever. I was walking around with Heidi, dazed. I kept trying to bring her back to life, but she was blue. There was absolutely no response.

Finally the ambulance arrived and I put her in the back. The medics wouldn't allow Marietta and I to get in with her because they had to do some very hefty treatment on her during the ride to the hospital. Marietta, Richard and I followed in the car – I think we must have been going about seventy miles an hour, and when we got there we sat down to wait, hoping against hope that they'd managed to shock her back to life.

A nurse came in to see us and said: 'There's nothing we can do. Would you like to see a priest?' We just sat there sobbing. Then I had to do the hardest thing I've ever done in my life. I had to go and identify her body. When they pulled the sheet down and I saw her, it really hit home. I was devastated.

We saw the priest. He said whatever he said. I couldn't take it in.

Then Richard, Marietta and I drove back home. When we arrived back it was unreal. All her dolls, all her toys were there lying on the floor. The lunch was still sitting in the kitchen, half-prepared. Within such a short space of time, our whole lives had been changed. Heidi had been taken from us and we were supposed to go back to what we were doing before. It was impossible.

Someone must have leaked the story at the hospital because the Press were at the house, hounding us. I forget what I said to them, most probably: 'Fuck off.' The police were there as well, some detectives walking down by the pool. We found out later that she must have been in the pool for about five minutes before I got to her.

The children were never allowed down by the pool. They knew that, so it didn't make sense for Heidi to be there. Later on we tried to piece it together, and we figured out that our little dog, Friday, had gone down there to bark at the electronic pool-sweep which fascinated him. His barking must have enticed Heidi to follow him, and then she fell in.

I remember calling Francis when it happened and he said: 'Are you sure? Go check.' He couldn't believe it. He'd been playing with her a few days before.

Like any parent who has lost a child, I said: 'Why her? Why me?' When Eric Clapton's son died, I knew what he must have felt, I really did. After Heidi's death I cried for ages. Sometimes I would even hold myself under water in the bath to try and feel what it had been like for her, what she had gone through, until I thought, What am I trying to prove to myself? Am I trying to drown myself? What good will that do?

For nights afterwards I would run into the garden and literally rip my shirt open and yell: 'God, if you're there help me now.' I waited and waited for a sign, but it was like waiting for a train that was never going to come.

Marietta called Cliff Richard and asked him to see me. She believed he might be able to help, and I thought it would be a good idea, too. It was fantastic of him to make the effort, and I liked him for what he was trying to do. I even went up to a couple of Bible studies in London when Cliff was addressing them, hoping they would help me come to terms with what happened, but nothing he said then made sense to me. Nothing anyone said made sense to me.

She was buried in a churchyard about a mile down the road from our house. I could see her grave from the house with a telescope. I went to visit it and I sat down under a tree beside her and I heard her name in the breeze. Also, a few weeks after her death, I had the water changed in the pool and I dived in. I swore I heard her underwater. Maybe it was the condition of shock I was in, but I choose to believe otherwise.

A child's death can cripple you for the rest of your life. I know parents who have been destroyed by it. The sooner you accept that someone has gone, the quicker you learn to live with it. And you have to learn to live with it because that person is not coming back, at least not as themselves, the person you knew. You must accept that. Then you can start to rebuild your life. If you think it's all been a bad dream, and they're going to come back, you're not going to go much further.

I know Heidi's death shattered my marriage, it shattered me for a long time, but now I try to get something positive out of the negative. I've tried to salvage something from her death, and I have. Life does have to go on. It had to go on for Richard's sake. I felt like ending it all, but it's not the way. It took a long while to come to grips with it, but when I'd accepted it, I started to rebuild my life.

I draw strength from Heidi now. She's like a tonic to me. Sometimes when I need a boost, when I need confidence, I think of her and I can get it. Every night on stage when we go into a certain part of 'Rockin' All Over the World', I think of her. She's with me all the time. I wear her necklace as a bracelet and I've never taken it off. I never will.

8

In 1980, Status Quo released two albums, the first, '12 Gold Bars', was Number Three in the LP charts, and seven months later 'Just Supposin' ' went to Number Four, while the single from that album, 'What You're Proposin' ', reached Number Two. The next year was also full of releases, with the LP 'Never Too Late', the single 'Something 'Bout You Baby I Like', and the ballad 'Rock 'n' Roll' all doing well in the UK charts. As 1981 ended, however, a major upheaval in Status Quo took place at a recording studio in Montreux, Switzerland.

FRANCIS: Some people say that friction between guys in a band works, and I can see why they say that, but I don't reckon it's the way to be myself. John Coghlan used to have major tantrums. Once, at a dinner in Germany with some record company executives, he decided he didn't like it, got up and just walked right over the top of the table and out the door. Another time, in France, he stormed out of another dinner and just as he got to the door, he threw a pear straight at my head. It missed.

He had been a very nice bloke when he was younger, but at that time I think he was trying to annoy people, take them on. Once he had an argument with Rick about the relative merits of tequila sunrises and Porsches – a weird argument to have in the first place – and he got very annoyed and went off to sit with Snafu, who were supporting us that night. We saw him pointing to us and apparently he said: 'You see those bastards over there – they're all horrible fuckers, every one of them in that band,' which we thought was funny considering that he was one of the band himself.

We were always a very visual, energetic act and we used to give each other a sign, a signal which meant we'd go off and bop together stage right. But John would start to get softer and softer on the drums and one of us would have to move around to the side of the drum kit to get him going again, because otherwise he'd slow down and all the sound signals to the mixing desk would get screwed up.

Sometimes I think – with all due respect to drummers – that they can be difficult if they don't play another instrument or sing. When the Eagles were doing 'Hotel California', the drummer was singing, so he was aware that there was a song going on, he wasn't just sitting there bashing away. Drummers can get into their own world and lose track of the song.

John's favourite saying used to be that he had three dislikes in life: gigging, rehearsing and recording. Well, there's not much else you do in a band. In Montreux, he just went and kicked his drum kit in – a kit we'd spent two days setting up – and said: 'I'm leaving.' He'd kicked his drum kit in before – on stage, at the beginning of a gig, which wasn't a very good move. At Montreux, we said: 'Right, if you leave, you're not coming back,' and off he went.

That night we made a phone call and got another drummer – Pete Kircher from the Original Mirrors. Pete is a very nice bloke, very quiet. His passion in life is bird-watching which might seem like a strange hobby for a drummer in a rock group. He fitted in well with us, though, and he was a pleasure to work with.

After John Coghlan left, the LP which they'd been recording in Montreux, '1982', became Quo's fourth UK chart-topper, and the single from it 'Dear John' went to Number Ten. That spring they received a very unusual invitation.

RICK: We were asked to do the first Prince's Trust gig in May 1982. We started the whole thing off. When we were approached to launch the Prince's Trust with a show at Birmingham, we thought that Prince Charles would eventually hit the throne at some stage—

FRANCIS: That's one way of putting it. Hit the throne.

RICK: And we figured he was looking for a way to get through to people of his own age, that he needed a new generation to accept him. Also, he genuinely wanted to set up something to help people who were struggling. We thought, Great, we'll do it for nothing because it's a good cause, we'll kick the whole thing off.

FRANCIS: We used to think about inviting Prince Charles to play the 'cello on one of our songs. I remember watching some film clip of him when he was playing the 'cello and one of the strings broke and whacked Edward in the face. I figured it would be funny if we could get him to play for us.

RICK: He helicoptered in to the NEC at Birmingham and we were all lined up – it was the first time we'd met any royalty. He was very gracious to the fans outside; he did a walkabout and met them, and we found that quite touching. We thought, He's all right, this bloke.

I was quite nervous about meeting him. We had a brief chat – I remember he said that he should have been wearing his jeans. We laughed and then left to get ready for the show. Prior to the gig, we recorded a version of 'God Save the Queen'.

FRANCIS: It's tricky. Each member of the royal family gets a specific amount of 'God Save the Queen' played when they come in somewhere. The Queen gets the whole lot, but the rest get only so many bars. Prince Charles is allowed the first bit.

RICK: We played our recorded version of it – an instrumental, but in Status Quo style. The lights dropped, the spotlight came on, and he came into the auditorium. You've never seen or heard anything like it. The place went completely berserk, all eleven thousand of them. We reckoned we'd torn it up at Glasgow, but this was outrageous! I wondered if he'd ever had a reception like that before.

FRANCIS: We thought, Blimey, how are we going to follow this? He had all these dignitaries with him and we heard later from someone we know who was in his group, that he knew that if he stood up, everyone else with him felt obliged to follow suit; if he sat down, they'd have to as well. They must have felt like yo-yos.

We gave Prince Charles earplugs before the show – very large earplugs.

RICK: After about an hour he left and we carried on playing. A few weeks later we got a letter from him saying: 'Thank you very much.' It was flattering to have been the first band he'd asked to play a concert for the Trust.

A while after that, I received a telephone call from one of the Prince's aides asking if I had some spare studio time available which I could give to a struggling young band who they believed were very good. I had the twenty-four-track studio at my house in Surrey and I said that of course I did. That's what the Prince's Trust is all about: giving people breaks. I said: 'Yes, by all means,' and I arranged for a time when they could come in.

The band turned up on that day, they got out of a van and I couldn't believe it. They had orange hair, tattooed heads, spikes on their elbows. They were out-and-out punks, Gothic-looking punks. I thought, 'Oh fuck – wrong!' Despite this I went into the studio with them. However, if I had known what was coming, I would have helped them out long before they arrived.

As soon as they'd plugged in, they started making the most awful noise. I said: 'You better tune up, you're dreadfully out of tune. What key is this row in anyway?' and one of them looked at me and said: 'What's a key?' I laughed and gave up. I couldn't help but think that if the Prince's Trust was funding a band that didn't even know what a key was, we were all in trouble. We went ahead and did the day anyway and they were bloody useless. Abominable. I'm sure the Trust has done a lot of good, but this time they'd come unstuck.

FRANCIS: Around that time, in the early Eighties, Alan Lancaster was telling us that our financial affairs had come unstuck as well. He thought we were being ripped off. I didn't believe him. I could look at other bands and see that they were being ripped off, but I refused to believe that we might be in the same position.

RICK: The early Eighties were a nightmare for me. We were still recording and touring, still releasing singles. 'She Don't Fool Me' came out in June 1982 and a live version of 'Caroline' in November, plus a three-LP set 'From the Makers Of . . . ', but my own personal life was a mess.

After Heidi died, I plummeted even deeper than I'd been before. I was doing more drugs, costing about a thousand pounds a week. I was drinking heavily also, putting on a lot of weight. I'd invite lads from the local pub to the house from time to time. Six or seven of us would lock ourselves away in the billiards room and we would invariably end up with fighting. I was in a bad way.

When we were due to tour, the management would phone Marietta and say: 'Can you pull him together? Try and tell him he's got gigs to do.' She'd lay that on me and it would sober me up a little. I'd get myself together, although I was still looking bloated. I wasn't happy with myself, so then I'd have another drink to make me feel better. It was a never-ending downward spiral. If I had any discipline at all, it was the fact that I didn't take drugs or alcohol before I went on stage.

One morning I came downstairs, just about to set off for London on another three-day binge, when Marietta said: 'Can I talk to you for a second?' I said: 'What is it now?' and she told me that she was divorcing me. She was serious about it and she'd already started proceedings. I told her not to be silly, and went off to a snooker club in Soho thinking that she wouldn't go ahead with it.

When I realized that she meant what she said, I also realized that I still loved her, so I asked her to give me a little time. I said that if she hung in, I'd change, I'd stop what I'd been doing, but she said that she couldn't take any more. I then became Mr Nice Guy, but she wouldn't stop the divorce proceedings, and there was no way back.

I ended up by giving her the house and the studio, and I moved into a cottage. It was all dismal, awful.

FRANCIS: I started drinking when we were recording in Montreux in 1981. Everyone went to a fantastic Mexican restaurant and there were all these margueritas on the table. John Coghlan – this was before he kicked in the drum set and walked off – kept saying: 'Try one, have a marguerita,' – so eventually I did. Down it went and it was delicious. I put the glass down, drank another, another, another . . . I drank six straight off. Normally, whenever I had a drink – and I didn't drink much at all because I never liked the taste before – I'd have a headache within forty minutes or so and feel really dreadful. That time, though, even with all those margueritas, I felt fine. No hangover whatsoever.

My life got out of control. When I wasn't drinking, I was tooting, when I wasn't tooting, I was drinking. I thought if I was going to drink, I had to get pissed. There was no middle ground.

When we went to Monserrat in 1983 to record the album which became 'Back to Back', a combination of factors caused ill will between Rick, Alan and myself.

RICK: We went into Monserrat as a band and we came out split. There were drugs about, and for the first time all that closeness between Francis and me, our ability to look across the room at each other, see an expression and know exactly what the other one was thinking, had gone – vanished.

FRANCIS: One of the causes for the split was the fact that I thought our music could become slightly more melodic, more across the board; whereas Alan always had to have the 'tough' stuff musically. As far as he was concerned, we couldn't do anything wimpy or unmanly. He'd already objected to 'Rockin' All Over the World', and when we were recording 'Marguerita Time' in Monserrat, he clearly didn't want to do that either, so we had a falling-out.

RICK: Another problem might have been the fact that I was starting to sing some of the lead vocals. Before, they had been shared out between Francis and Alan. But the reason for my joining the group in the first place was to have another 'voice' in the band. I began by singing harmony, but gradually I'd sing the lead here and there.

FRANCIS: When Rick sang the lead vocals on some of the singles – oh dear, that was it.

RICK: After a while the vocal partnership became Francis and me, not Francis and Alan. So what was there for Alan then? Francis and I seemed to get more attention, we were the front men. And Alan hadn't been singing any of the songs. It must have mentally annihilated him.

FRANCIS: When we actually recorded 'Marguerita Time', it was late in the afternoon and Alan said: 'Oh, we can do that thing of yours – "Marguerita" – quickly now.' He was under the impression that we were just knocking it off when we did it. As far as he was concerned, it wasn't going to make it to the album and there was no pressure. So he did the bass in a laid-back way, which, funnily enough, was exactly the way I wanted it.

RICK: He made his classic statement about not being able to face his family if we released 'Marguerita Time'.

FRANCIS: For Alan, it wasn't a 'man's' bass. I remember from when we were younger exactly what that means, but that's how you feel when you're a kid. You're supposed to grow a little.

RICK: I was in the wrong at the time, I must admit, because I still felt, even though I liked 'Marguerita Time', that it wasn't heavy enough. I was still up the heavy rock road. But if Francis hadn't started writing material which was going to broaden our fan base, I don't think we could have come through this far. If we'd stayed the way we were, I don't believe we would have survived. Then, though, I wasn't sure about it all. So Francis and I had our first dispute.

And there was another argument going on when Alan wanted to sing the lead on his song 'Old Rag Blues'. Two versions were done of it and the record company chose the one Francis sang, so Alan must have felt rebuffed.

FRANCIS: I was jockeying for Alan's song to come out as a single, I was pushing for it, but Alan was fighting me all down the line because he wanted to sing it. I thought, Fine, you can fight me, but if you do, the record company won't put out 'Old Rag Blues', and it has nothing to do with me. I've done what was best for your song.

RICK: At the same time, I'd written a song, 'Too Close to the Ground' which I thought *I* should have sung, but it ended up with Francis singing it. I was gutted. At this point, the three of us, the key members, had all dug our heels in and everything was coming to a head. There was a terrible feeling in the control room. I remember thinking, There's Francis in there, singing my song. Let him fucking sing it and I'll just sit here outside.

FRANCIS: I didn't know anything about that then.

RICK: I couldn't stand all the pressure. How the feeling had turned so bad.

FRANCIS: *I* was pissed off that 'Too Close to the Ground' never came out as a single. Brian Shepherd and I both agreed that we should release 'Old Rag Blues' first, then 'Mess of Blues', then 'Marguerita Time' for Christmas and in early January, 'Too Close to the Ground'. But 'Too Close to the Ground' never came out as a single. It was a really good blues song and I thought with that order of play we'd get some credibility. I still don't know why it was stopped.

RICK: There was a complete lack of communication between us. Before, we'd always known what was going down, but at that point we'd stopped phoning each other, we'd stopped communicating.

FRANCIS: I can't remember any specific meeting after Monserrat when we decided to stop touring, but we all decided that the End of the Road tour in 1984 would be our last one. People had said that it's impossible to sell records without doing tours, but I didn't agree with that. As soon as we made that decision, we all relaxed a little.

I remember during that End of the Road tour, we were somewhere in Germany and I said, just before the encore: 'Give me a drink.' I was heavily into tequila then, but it was the first time I'd ever had a drink when I was playing. After we'd finished the encore, I swung around and said: 'You bastards, it sounds so good. No wonder you've been drinking all this time. Why didn't you tell me before?'

It got to the point where we were doing six or seven encores and it became a game – the audience knew we weren't finished, they knew we had to come back and do 'Bye Bye Johnny' to end the set. We'd get drunk and walk off and come back and say: 'What the fuck shall we do now?' We thought we were being wildly entertaining, but we weren't. It took me a while to realize that it only *seems* great when you've been drinking.

RICK: John Coghlan used to have a pint beside him the whole time, constantly recharged. He'd be drinking all the way through the set. Your co-ordination goes when you drink on stage. That's especially true for a drummer.

FRANCIS: Our last gig on the End of the Road tour, at the Milton Keynes Bowl on 21 July, should have been incredible. When I look at the video of it now, though, I'm embarrassed. It's diabolical. The best thing about that performance was the fireworks at the end.

RICK: It was supposed to be our last gig – what a way to go out – on a real low. The set was getting away from us and we weren't giving 100 per cent. When I think back, I realize that it was pretty nasty of us to say: 'Fine, we're stopping now,' without any explanation to the fans. No letter, no nothing. It was a bit unkind.

The touring may have stopped after the Milton Keynes concert, but the complications within the band were multiplying. Rick found himself in a financial mess, Alan Lancaster came back and forth from Australia, and the future was looking less certain for the survival of Status Quo as it was.

Francis's and Liz Gernon's daughter, Bernadette, was born on 3 August 1984.

FRANCIS: I was at Bernadette's birth. I liked Liz very much. We got on very well together, and I've always loved children. Liz and I never lived together. Most women who came to my house couldn't come to terms with the fact that I had my mother and sometimes my aunt living with me.

I said that I'd never lie to Liz – and I didn't. Until I met Paige Taylor in 1986. I was on a promotional trip when I met these two birds who looked like models – and in fact they were. Paige was a little over twenty and I fell for her. Or, to be honest, one part of me fell for her.

I lied to Liz for a few weeks, but one night I told her about Paige and that was that. I had thought that Liz might continue working for us – she was brilliant at her job – but Paige didn't go for that idea at all and eventually Liz moved to Canada. I haven't seen my daughter since she was three or four, but Simon and Nicholas and Kieran – my children with Jean – all live with me now, and I believe that Bernadette will come to me at some point in the future. I remember when Rick got divorced from Marietta and he didn't see Richard for a long time, he was very upset. He said: 'I've lost my boy.' And I said: 'Rick, you never lose your children.'

RICK: After my split from Marietta, I thought that I had lost Richard, and I was in a very bad way emotionally. Financially-speaking, I was also a disaster.

One day the bank called me in and told me that I had no money left. I said: 'How can I be broke? I've been working non-stop.' The manager said: 'Yes, but you've spent a fortune and blown your money.' I couldn't even afford the rent of the cottage I'd moved into after Marietta and I split up. I had been living there with Debbie Ash, a dancer with Hot Gossip, but I had to move out because I couldn't afford it.

Debbie told me that I could come and live with her and her daughter at a flat in London her father owned, and I thought, Great – that solves something, at least. I was down to a couple of hundred pounds, and I had a huge overdraft on top. I could barely manage to pay for food for the three of us.

When Debbie and I came to a sudden end, I found myself with nowhere to go. All I had to my name was a Range Rover. I packed all my stuff in it, drove to the office and went and cried my eyes out to Colin Johnson. I said: 'Look, I've got one key. That's all I've got left. One car key.' Alan Lancaster was claiming that we'd been ripped off to the tune of millions, but nobody really knew what had happened. All I knew was that I didn't have a roof over my head.

I checked into the Holiday Inn in Chelsea. They knew who I was, so they didn't ask for any money initially, and I started to look around and try to find a flat in town. I'd been in a beautiful mansion and now I was wandering around bedsits – really grim places. I'm claustrophobic anyway and the idea of living in a cramped space was horrible to me. Finally I found a flat in Battersea which looked out over the river and was cheap enough for me to afford – just – so I ensconced myself there. I had an ashtray that I've always kept my loose change in, but at this point it became my lifeline, because loose change was all I had.

Any money I made from the End of the Road tour was taken up paying off some of my huge overdraft. From time to time I would scrape the odd money together to get drugs – even when things were that bad, I'd still buy the wretched stuff. And I had a brief affair with Debbee Ashby, a Page Three girl.

My cousin Sue called me one day and said that she'd received a letter from Patti – a girl I'd gone out with for a while when I was eighteen or so – who had been great fun. Sue said that I should give her a call in Australia, so I phoned her up. She'd been living in Australia for ten years and she told me she was coming home. I said I'd meet her at the airport.

By that point I couldn't pick her up in my car because things had got even worse. I'd been banned from driving and I didn't have a car any more. I'd been to the Hard Rock café one night and I was pissed out of my brains. I'd parked my car right outside and as I left, three policemen at the door asked me for my autograph. I said: 'Sure,' and signed autographs for their kids and then, like an idiot, I walked one step forward, two back, three sideways and fell into the car, right in front of them.

The next thing I knew, I was driving along and I saw the police following me. I thought, I know my way around Shepherd's Market and the back streets of Soho, so I can get rid of them, shake them off. I was driving a GT Volkswagen Golf and I turned left up a one-way street into a road marked no entry. It was a dead end. I didn't even have my lights on. I stopped, the police van pulled up behind me, and I had to laugh. I wasn't thinking of the consequences at that stage, I just wound the window down, held the keys out to the policeman and said: 'Nice evenin', Sergeant.'

I was arrested and driven to the police station in their van. They told me to walk in a straight line and I staggered all over the place. They took a statement, that was it. I was done.

Patti and I got back together after all those years, and after a bit, I told her that she might as well move in with me. We settled down in Battersea, but things got worse instead of better. I wondered whether we'd made the right move by living together. Neither of us had any money and I didn't see how I was going to go forward any more, what the future could possibly hold.

After the End of the Road tour, the band went to the studio to complete the live album of the gig. 'The Wanderer' was released as a single in November 1984, and it went to Number Seven in the charts, then the LP '12 Gold Bars' reached Number Twelve in December.

But the outlook was very bleak indeed. I could see that Francis didn't want to work, but I didn't know why. Alan would come back and forth from Australia, but we weren't doing anything constructive, the band was falling apart at the seams. I was broke, Francis and I weren't speaking, there seemed no prospect of the band functioning the way it had before, and Alan kept claiming that we'd been ripped off. All I can say is that I'm glad I didn't know then that it would get much worse before it would get better.

9

The 'End of the Road' tour was, effectively, the end of the road for Status Quo as a functioning band. Although they had agreed to keep on recording together, Alan Lancaster had gone back to Australia and Rick and Francis weren't the frien s they had been for so long. Both decided to go out on their own and make solo albums, a move which might have worked, but served only to add to their problems.

RICK: Phonogram gave me a hundred grand to do a solo album. It ended up costing one hundred and ten – it was called 'Recorded Delivery' – so it cost me ten grand, which I didn't have. At that point Alan had disappeared to Australia, poor old Spud (John Coghlan) had long since sunk into a vat of Tennents Pilsner and Status Quo was almost dead.

I had visions of my album being a hit, and putting a band of my own together, starting out again in the clubs. I was assigned to a new guy at the record company and he played it to a couple of people and they apparently said: 'Well, it's all right, but who is it?' They didn't recognize my voice. It was turned down flat.

FRANCIS: I had always wanted to do something with Bernard Frost, because I liked working with him. We'd written a lot of songs in Ireland, so in 1985, Bernie and I did an album – it was called 'Flying Debris', and two singles were released from it. They made it into the charts, but suddenly disappeared. Perhaps it wasn't in anyone's interest for Rick and I to go solo.

I think people thought that if Rick and I had a success with our solo albums, that would be the end of Status Quo. Actually, I didn't have that in mind at the time – I thought if my album did well, it would strengthen Status Quo's position as a whole. But it's like The Stones – when Jagger or Keith Richards do solo albums, it's not the same as the group doing one together. The public and everyone else likes the idea of a group, they also like the idea of Rick and I doing everything together. If you don't do that, you're destroying something, a sort of myth.

RICK: After my album was turned down I thought, That's it. I've had it. I'd lost everything: my daughter, my wife, my house, my money – the taxman was after me for huge sums of money which I didn't have. It was all gone, and Quo seemed to be gone as well.

I was sitting with Patti in Battersea one evening and we'd had quite a few drinks. I said something to her and got up to leave. I went out, walked half a mile or so along the Thames, sat down and just looked at the water. I was at rock bottom and I thought to myself, I only have to jump in there and my problems are over. All sorts of thoughts went through my head. One of them was that if I drowned, I'd know how Heidi had felt. My dad, who had been in the Navy, consoled me when Heidi died by telling me that drowning was the best way you could go. He said that at first you black out and then everything becomes colourful and it's quite nice. I had always hung on to that image, because then I could believe that Heidi hadn't suffered. So I figured that drowning was the way I should go, too.

Then I started to think, Well, if I do throw myself in, I'll probably think it's a mistake, try and swim for it and make it back to shore. I'm a good swimmer. So what's the point of doing it? My mind was going round and round in circles.

Whatever I had said to Patti before I left the flat must have made an impression, because after I had gone she phoned Colin Johnson and told him to get to our place quickly – she said that she thought I was about to do something very stupid. Colin arrived to find me on the river-bank. He sat down beside me and I was crying; he chatted to me, calmed me down. Eventually we walked back to the flat and I cried the whole way home.

I saw myself being bombarded from every side, and I felt I didn't have a friend in the world. Francis and I were hardly talking to each other at this point. We had drifted apart because of the drugs and the drink. My own personal life was bugging me, I didn't see how I could get back on my feet again. I couldn't see any way out. I went out with the intention of killing myself, but when it came to actually doing it, I couldn't. If I had really wanted to, I would have gone down there and thrown myself straight in. I wouldn't have just sat and thought about it.

After the failure of their albums, both Francis and Rick were at a low ebb. In need of money, they were persuaded to do personal appearances at night-clubs. This was a far cry from packed-out shows at Birmingham and Wembley and the nadir of Francis's and Rick's career.

FRANCIS: I think various people did believe that it was all over for us. You can tell when people make a run for the exit, when they think they're on a sinking ship. And that's what people thought at the time – that Status Quo was a sinking ship. When we went to do those personal appearances, all we actually did was sit on bar stools and answer questions from people. Women would throw their knickers at us and we'd sign them.

RICK: We'd go to discos and clubs and we'd be advertised outside: Francis Rossi and Rick Parfitt from Status Quo will be here to answer your questions. We'd turn up for three-quarters of an hour and the punters could ask us any questions they liked. We'd be up there like lambs to a slaughter.

FRANCIS: At the time, I didn't think it was so bad, but looking back I think it was disgraceful. It was putting us in a position that was basically saying: They've had it, they're finished.

RICK: We were desperate, though, desperate for money. That's the only reason we did it.

FRANCIS: I wasn't in as bad a shape financially as Rick, but I had to take out a mortgage on my house at the time. We'd get a couple of grand a night for these appearances, which was pretty reasonable considering we'd be pissed witless most nights. We were drinking very heavily in those days.

RICK: I wasn't. I'd cut down to about a bottle of scotch and two bottles of wine a day.

Although Rick had reached the bottom, he'd stopped on the right side of ultimate despair. What he was missing was the band and the music, vital elements in his life. Despite the End of the Road tour, and the wilderness year which followed, not everyone thought that Status Quo was dead. Bob Geldof contacted their agency and asked whether they'd appear for the Live Aid concert he was planning at Wembley on 13 July 1985. Alan Lancaster agreed to come back from Australia to play, so the nucleus of Quo was back together for an afternoon.

FRANCIS: When we were first approached by Bob Geldof to open Live Aid I wasn't keen as the band was completely unrehearsed. However, when we met Geldof in the Phonogram offices, he said:

'It doesn't matter a fuck what you sound like – just be there.' It was his honesty that changed my mind.

RICK: We certainly weren't worried about putting ourselves back on the map at that point. That's not how we saw it. It was strictly for the right reasons.

FRANCIS: The best part about Live Aid – or as I call it, Livid: Feed The Welsh – was the punters. You could sense how hyped up they all were. I was very happy about opening it because I wouldn't have wanted to hang around all afternoon waiting to play. The best band of the day, in my opinion, was Queen.

RICK: It was a fantastic day because everyone was on the same level, no-one was there to outdo the others. We all knew we were doing it for one reason – to help. The atmosphere onstage and backstage was fabulous. After we'd finished our bit, I stayed around for a couple of hours, then caught a helicopter back to Battersea with David Bowie. I went home, picked up Patti, got changed and later on took the helicopter back again. I waltzed back on stage to join in with 'Feed the World' at the end – it was incredible.

FRANCIS: Later on, when we did 'Feed the World' for the *Top of the Pops Christmas Show*, I remember a load of us were standing on the stage and Rick and I were put in position, which was all fine. Jim Diamond was next to us, and suddenly Bananarama came pushing through and one of them was crunching down on my foot.

RICK: Did that happen to you as well? One of them was stamping on my feet, too.

FRANCIS: I thought – sod this – if you want to stand here, go ahead. I'll go back. I felt that I'd done my piece, they knew I was there, I didn't have to push myself in front.

When a picture was being taken for the video of that song, some-one told me to get a chair and stand on it. Sting and everybody were up at the front and I went to the back. Rick decided he wasn't having any of this being in the back business and he went right up and moved Sting aside. Sheer embarrassment stops me from doing that. I figure if they want to be up there, they must be better than me, but Rick says they fucking ain't and he goes for it. I used to knock him and tell him he shouldn't do it, but when I see really huge stars doing it, too, I think, Well, fine, why shouldn't he?

RICK: At one of the Prince's Trust charity concerts we did at Wembley, when all the big names you've ever heard of were there, everyone had joined Paul McCartney on stage for the final song. Bryan Adams and I were at the back, playing away like we do. The chorus came up and Bryan and I were looking at each other and laughing. We thought, What the fuck are we doing here? We're just filling in. There's Knopfler, there's Clapton, there was the cream of the world's guitarists standing in the line-up at the front. Reggie was on the side tinkling away on the piano.

Bryan and I exchanged another look – we were both thinking the same thing: let's inch our way forward. So we did.

We edged our way up to the microphone where Paul Young and George Michael were singing and I was getting an elbow in the ribs from Paul. Everyone was grappling for the microphones, but I thought, If I'm on stage I want to be in the thick of the action. If people are jockeying for position, I'll jockey for it, too. That's just the way I am.

Despite their huge success at Live Aid, the happy public reunion between Rick, Francis and Alan was short-lived. The seeds of discontent planted at the recording session in Monserrat had grown into less-than-pretty flowers. Alan was still pressing for his heavier music, Francis was reluctant to continue working with him on that basis, and Rick was caught between them both, unsure of where his future or the band's lay.

FRANCIS: Alan was constantly back and forth from Australia in those days, but he came to England at odd times, when there was nothing specific going on.

RICK: He'd say he was unavailable for some things – like the video of 'Rockin' All Over the World', and certain other PR things we were supposed to do. He'd also show up at other times, when there was absolutely nothing to do.

FRANCIS: He'd stay in a hotel, just hanging loose, and he'd say: 'I know Rick will come out with me,' and they'd go off together.

RICK: It didn't take a lot to talk me into a night out in those days.

FRANCIS: I'd think, That's funny, they're going off together – what's going on here?

RICK: It was one of those triangular situations, which was made worse by the fact that Alan was convinced we were being ripped off. Francis said, 'No way,' and I wasn't sure. This started in the late Seventies and continued on, but back in the early stages, we weren't looking at the money – our interest was the band.

FRANCIS: We had lots of money then, but not what we should have had. That's where it seems Alan was right.

RICK: Eventually Alan convinced me to go to lawyers and solicitors with him to find out what was going on, but each time we did, doors were slammed in our faces.

FRANCIS: At one stage, when this was all reaching boiling point between the three of us, Alan drew up a kind of constitution. It stated that no decision could be made without the three key members of the band agreeing to it. I knew what that meant. If I agreed to it, then my position would change. I'd been instrumental in forming the band in 1962, everything had gone along fine for a while and then, according to this constitution, I was suddenly supposed to go from being leader of the band and the lead singer to being one of the *three* key members. Not two, but three.

If it had been Rick and myself as the two key members, I would have said fair enough, but when you have three people in an equation like that, it means you can't fart without a discussion. What if Rick and I were to agree about something and Alan didn't? Where would we be then? It wasn't going to work, especially because I knew he'd say no to some of the slower songs, ones like 'Living On An Island', or 'Dirty Water'. At the heart of it all was this disagreement about what direction our music should take. And that kind of disagreement can't be solved without someone either giving in completely or leaving.

RICK: I didn't know what Francis wanted. I knew that there was something wrong, that he and I weren't communicating, but we weren't good enough buddies at the time to talk about it. I was caught between him and Alan, and as far as I could see, Francis didn't want to work any more, full stop. I couldn't understand why that was the case, I didn't see that the problem was Alan's presence in the band.

FRANCIS: Alan wanted to do a cheap album in Australia. He was convinced that we could do one for sixty grand. This was unlike him, because he had always been a perfectionist about recording, so I couldn't understand why he was trying to do something on the cheap. Basically, I think he wanted us all to move out to Australia so he could work from home, as it were. He was into a real estate scheme at the time, and he was trying to convince Rick and myself to lend him a huge amount of money to invest in old people's homes in Australia. We turned it down because I'm never sure about rock musicians suddenly becoming businessmen in an entirely different field.

I knew that if I backpedalled at all, if I agreed to this constitution or to this Australian recording venture, Alan would, of course, stay in the band and all the problems would still be there. Nothing would have been solved. What I didn't know at the time was what would happen if I said to Rick that we could have the band without Alan. I didn't know where Rick stood or how he would react.

RICK: I wasn't sure what I could say to Francis because I didn't know why he didn't want to work. Money was running short and Alan kept saying to me: 'Francis doesn't want to work.' I said: 'I know he doesn't, but why doesn't he?' Alan then suggested that he and I go on together, without Francis. We could go on the heavy rock road, the way he thought it should be. At that point I was really mixed up, but I figured, Francis may not want to work, but I *have* to.

FRANCIS: Alan then came to me and said: 'If you really don't want to work any more, you know Rick and I will go out and do Status Quo Mark Two.'

RICK: I didn't know he'd said that to you.

FRANCIS: I had a feeling that Status Quo Mark Two wouldn't be acceptable to anyone. I also thought, OK, if it is, I've lost nothing, really. I sat back and held on to see what would happen. I didn't say anything to Rick at the time, because I wasn't sure what I could say. People get between you, that's what always happens.

RICK: All I could think was that the band had to go on and that Francis didn't want to. Alan took the idea of Status Quo Mark Two to Phonogram. I had warned him against this because I knew his approach would be all wrong. He could be absolutely right about some things, but the way he went about it would sometimes really put people's backs up. I'd seen this when we'd gone traipsing around the lawyers' offices about the band's finances. He'd barge in shouting and I'd think to myself, This is really not the way to do it.

But Alan went ahead and told Phonogram that Francis wasn't going to work any more and that they better get their fingers out and concentrate on the two of us.

FRANCIS: Phonogram said: 'No way – if you can get Rossi and Parfitt together, fine. Without Rossi and Parfitt, forget it.'

RICK: It was sad because Alan had only been doing what he thought was right to guarantee the band's future. That put me in a very difficult position. I didn't want to hurt Alan and I didn't want to hurt Francis. I sensed that Alan had suffered in the past on the publicity side of things because the fans recognized Francis and me, people wanted to talk to Francis and me, it was just the way it happened, even though Alan had been a founder member of the band and I hadn't. I think it must have hurt him badly.

I had to choose between them, which wasn't just a question of choosing between friends, but also choosing between different styles of music. I had been leaning to the heavy rock sound, Alan's sound, but when I thought about it, I knew that Francis had a flare for songs, that his idea of broadening the base of our music was the right idea.

I figured maybe we'd had our heavy time and we should branch out because branching out meant going forward. Also, I actually liked different types of music myself. I like songs which have a country flavour – I grew up singing songs like 'Down The Trail of Aching Hearts', an old Hank Williams' number. I've always had an eclectic taste in music. I loved 'Marguerita Time' and I loved 'Rockin' All Over the World', which Alan hated. I saw the way forward, the future was with Francis. At last I was sure this was how it was meant to be.

But then I had to tell Alan that it wasn't going to work between him and me. That wasn't easy.

FRANCIS: And that's how it all ended up in court. In 1985, just after we'd done Live Aid, he sued for the right to use the Status Quo name. He took out an injunction to stop us working without him under the Status Quo name. He didn't want Rick and me to continue using it without him.

When it actually came to court, and the case was being heard, Rick and I were sitting having a cup of tea together in the court cafeteria and all of a sudden Alan came in. He sat down and said: 'I warned you two. No hard feelings. I did warn you I'd do this.' And I said: 'Yes, no hard feelings. It's in the court's hands now, whatever they decide will be it.' As far as I was concerned, if we'd lost, I would have said: 'Fair enough.' When it went against Alan, he went fucking mad.

RICK: He didn't think he'd lose.

FRANCIS: He had grown up in a very tough, macho environ-ment. He'd had to fight all the time. He didn't like the idea of losing. If he made a mistake on stage, it didn't happen – it was someone else's fault. That's why he said: 'No hard feelings.' He was convinced he was going to win. Two days later – wow, did he have hard feelings! But he had forced the issue. He'd forced the issue in the first place by going to Phonogram with the Status Quo Mark Two idea, and he forced it again by taking us to court. When you force things like that, you either lose or win, it's as simple as that.

After the court case was over and Alan Lancaster had officially left the band, Rick and Francis were nominally back together, but still without any specific direction. Every year from 1973 until 1985 they had had a top twenty hit, but in 1985 that amazing run broke. With Alan and John Coghlan gone, the original band had halved, and neither Rick nor Francis knew which step to take next to put themselves back on track. They still had the name Status Quo, but the two years they had spent unsure of each other required an immense impetus which would recreate the old ties between them and forge new ones.

10

Necessity is the mother of invention. Francis and Rick won the court case, but that didn't dispel the tense feelings which had built up between them. They didn't walk out of the court and rush to the nearest recording studio to start again. However, they were still under contract to Phonogram; Status Quo were signed up to produce another three albums, and the record company executives thought it was time to get to work.

Knowing this to be the case, Rick called Francis and asked him round to talk through the possibilities. What kind of album could they do? Who might work with them? All these issues had to be ironed out before they could fulfil their commitments.

RICK: I hadn't spoken to Francis for quite some time, but once I got the call from the record company demanding an album, I asked him to come round so we could sit down and talk about it. We started discussing everything that had gone on, and for the first time I realized what the problem had been. He hadn't wanted to work with Alan any more, and he had thought I'd been on Alan's side. That cleared up a lot for me. I thought, At last – it's going to work again.

I suggested that if we were to make a new album, it might be a good idea to use John 'Rhino' Edwards who was a great bass player and Jeff Rich – a terrific drummer – as well, of course, as Andrew on keyboards. Jeff and Rhino, both ex-members of the Climax Blues Band, had worked with me on my solo album. Francis said: OK, although he wasn't keen on the idea of working with people he didn't know, particularly guys who had already worked with me on my own project. I said: 'Let's just try it out, and if it doesn't work, it doesn't work.'

When we got into rehearsals, it was very refreshing. Francis soon felt at home with Rhino and Jeff, and he and I were getting along well for the first time in years. There was a different vibe between us. We had enough material for the album, and Francis had found a song called 'In The Army Now', which was a minor hit in Holland for the Bolland Brothers, but hadn't made an impact anywhere else. He latched on to it and played it to me in his car. I had reservations about it.

Rhino and Jeff were so enthusiastic that they fired Francis and me up again. They brought us back to life, because the music was really pumping – it had that 'here we go again' written all over it. During rehearsals, Francis or I would say: 'Just try this,' and we would drift into 'Big Fat Mamma' and then we'd naturally go into 'Don't Waste My Time' and 'Rockin' All Over the World'. It sounded stunning. All of a sudden the fire was alight again. We said: 'Bloody hell, this is good.'

FRANCIS: When we first got together with Rhino and Jeff, we wanted to show them what we were all about, so we played the 'End of the Road' video for them. We started to watch it and it was excruciating – we hadn't realized until then how bad we'd been. We were supposed to be showing them how ener- getic we were, how great we'd been on stage, and it was like watching dead people. It was very embarrassing, so we told them to disregard it completely.

RICK: I find it depressing watching the 'End of the Road' video – not only for the fact of how unenthusiastic we looked, but also because it brings back the bad memories.

A few months later, we talked about doing some shows again. We hadn't been on stage for a long time, and, of course, never with Rhino nor Jeff. It was an awesome thought, really like starting all over again. But we were excited by the prospect. We delivered a single, produced by Dave Edmunds – 'Rollin' Home' in May 1986, which went to Number Nine in the charts. Then we released the LP 'In The Army Now' that September, which was produced by Pip Williams. The 'In The Army Now' single was a massive hit – it went to Number Two in October 1986, and the band was up and running again. It was as if someone had taken an old banger out of a barn, polished it until it was gleaming, fired it up – and – it started. I couldn't believe it.

FRANCIS: Before Jeff and Rhino joined, they knew about us, but they weren't about to let either of us try to come across as big time rock stars – that wouldn't work with them. What amazed Rick and me was that they have 100 per cent enthusiasm – whether it's a rehearsal or a pisshole gig, they'll give it everything.

RICK: We put a set together, and just to be on the safe side, we thought, Let's go in by the back door, let's test this out and see if it actually works as well as we think it does.

So we went to the Middle East to try it out. You play to ex-pats, an audience of maybe one thousand, fifteen hundred people. It was a good earner and a perfect rehearsal for the new band. We were nervous at first, but then we got out on stage, the adrenalin was pumping and it was fantastic. This line-up was seriously good.

FRANCIS: What makes it work so well now is that nobody gets the hump. No-one says: 'Oh, you said something in the dressing-room I didn't like, so I'm pissed off tonight.' We used to have that the whole time. Now everyone gives it their all.

We made a decision that has to do with the development of the band since Rhino and Jeff joined. We know it's very easy to go up on stage and think, Fuck it, especially if it's a poxy sound, if the acoustics aren't right. When that happens we look around at each other – I look at Rick, we both look at Rhino and we know we're not enjoying it because the sound is bad. Instead of letting that get us down, we'll do anything to get each other up. We'll talk to each other on stage. I'll say to Rick something like: 'How's your motor? Have you sold it yet?' or 'What are you doing after the gig? Going straight to bed?'

RICK: People are fascinated by the fact that Francis and me have a natter on stage. We'll talk about anything. I'll say something to Francis and he'll bat it back. Sometimes it's a huge relief to have a chat. If there's a problem, we all lift one another up.

FRANCIS: The original band would have brought each other down. We know that if you're out there feeling bad and you aren't getting any help, if nobody up there with you is trying to get you back up, all it does is get worse. You can't do that to an audience.

RICK: The speed at which we play on stage as opposed to playing on a record is phenomenal. If we tried to play 'Whatever You Want' or 'Caroline' at the speed it is on the albums, it would feel like slow motion.

It depends on the acoustics in the hall; if the sound on stage is good, we can really set the place alight. Some nights we'll come off and say: 'That was good tonight, it's been no effort at all.' People look at us, think, Bloody hell, they're forty whatever and they're leaping around like youngsters.

When the gig isn't acoustically right, it's affectionately described as being like dragging a Morris Minor uphill with a rope tied to your bollocks. On nights like that, we say: 'It was a bit Morris Minor, wasn't it?' If the sound isn't right, the Thespian comes out in you.

FRANCIS: Whatever happens in a gig, there is this belief that the show must go on. There are times I've played when I've had 'flu, times when I've gone round to the side of the stage, chucked up and gone straight back – all of us have done that.

If you want to, turn me on to.
anything you really want to
Turn me on to your love your love. 1
If the night-time, is the right time
anytime of yours is my time
We can find time for love for love. 2

Come on sweet Caroline
You're my sweet Caroline
You know I wanna take you
I really wanna make you. 3 7
Come on sweet Caroline
You're my sweet Caroline
take my hand
Together we can rock.n.roll.

When I'm thinkin of you sleepin.
I'm at home alone and weepin. 4
Are you keeping your love your love
So if you want to turn me on to
anything you really want to 5
Turn me on to your love your love

Solo 6

CAROLINE   Ross Young

Second draft of 'Caroline', written in studio.

RICK: We went for twenty years without cancelling a gig – we only do in a dire situation – when someone has something a bit more terminal than a cold or 'flu.

FRANCIS: It's remarkable when you've got 'flu – you can feel like a sack of shit all day long, you get to the gig and think, I'll take it easy tonight, but when you get on stage, you get pumped up instantly.

RICK: Even with exhaustion, which does catch up with you on tour, we have this running joke. Someone will come in before the show and say: 'I'm knackered, I'm going to pace myself tonight,' and we all nod seriously and say: 'Of course you will.' We know that eight bars into the set, whoever it is who is pacing himself will be flying around the stage, steaming through the set.

FRANCIS: Can you imagine walking on the stage and saying: 'I can't go on, I've got a cold – here's my doctor's note.'?

RICK: Sometimes before the show, you may not feel that you can give 100 per cent, but the second the lights go down and you hear the roar of the audience, you feel the vibes of ten thousand people hitting you. Any aches or pains are forgotten.

You always have to be aware on stage because there are a lot of guitar necks swinging around. Francis and Rhino do a thing where Francis swings round and Rhino ducks; if he doesn't, he's had it.

FRANCIS: We were doing 'Roll Over, Lay Down' once and I was above Rick's head with the guitar and he lifted his head up too quickly or I didn't get away quickly enough and – smash, right in the face. There was blood all over the place. The punters loved it.

After their triumphant comeback with 'In The Army Now', and their successful trip to the Middle East, Francis and Rick were ready to start touring again, both in Britain and overseas. Colin Johnson had left

and Alan Crux was now managing them, along with Iain Jones. The British tour in the summer of 1986 had gone down very well, but then Alan Crux suggested that they do a gig in Sun City, South Africa, in October 1987. The band agreed – with the stipulation that they play to integrated audiences. A storm of protest awaited them on their return.

FRANCIS: When we got there, we saw posters on the walls of other people who had played there – loads and loads of very big names. We did ten shows to mixed audiences; we had a black crew, black people working with us, but when we got back all hell broke loose.

RICK: Alan Crux came out with us and then left us to do the gigs while he went on safari. I wonder sometimes what was behind his idea to send us there. But we thought, because we had stressed that we'd play only to a mixed audience, that we were giving entertainment, we weren't being prejudiced.

When we came back – my God, we were completely murdered by the Press. We were blacklisted throughout Europe, banned from playing in Sweden, everywhere we went we had a rough ride with the media.

Had the audience been whites only, then fine, we would have deserved to get our knuckles rapped. The after-effects stayed with us for a long time. Our fan club in Holland dropped us completely – it was a bit like the time when John Lennon got such stick for saying The Beatles were more popular than Jesus. It was a nightmare.

FRANCIS: Eventually we wrote a letter of apology to the UN, saying that we regretted doing it and that we'd never do it again. And then umpteen bands like The Christians said that they would never play on the same stage as Status Quo. A few months later, they supported us in Switzerland.

I kept wondering about it all; were people actually saying that there aren't any problems here in Britain, that the black people

S T A T U S   Q U O
======================

Status Quo, having seen first hand the progress for equality and
reform in Bophuthatswana, do not feel the need to make
any personal comments to justify them playing in Sun City.

It is known however that the band has purchased a mini bus for
the Temogo School for mentally nandicapped in Mogwase and
arranged for all South African record royalties to be donated to
a Bophuthatswana charity for children in need. They also met
with the chief officer for Bophuthatswana to see first hand the
programme which trains citizens of the Country to manage all
major industrial concerns within Bophuthatswana, and are
extremely impressed and encouraged by what they have seen.

The band certainly do not feel that by refusing to play in Sun
City that this will help the coloured cause in any way and do not
believe in sanctions that are likely to affect peoples jobs, both
black and white.

It should also be noted out that Francis Rossi took his Asian
girlfriend with him to Bophuthatswana, so to suggest that the
band is racist or in support of apparthied in any way would be
absurd.

here are really taken care of and the only place they aren't is South Africa? Is that what they believe?

Alan Lancaster used to say that just because you're good in your field, you shouldn't think you can go wandering into any other field and try to take over. That's why I was surprised when he got involved in real estate and old people's homes. Rock stars and movie stars sometimes do that – they think, I'm good at this, so I can be good at everything else, too. I can tell the Government how to run the country. I can change the world. Everyone should follow my example.

Celebrities take on a mythical image. I know people who think it's wonderful for big rock acts to do charity benefits. The fact is, when we do a charity show, all we do is perform for twenty minutes or so. The punters are the ones giving the money, all those people out there watching us are the ones who are actually contributing. They think we're so charitable when in fact they're the ones who are.

Live Aid made over fifty million pounds – a lot of money, which was terrific. But I wondered afterwards why the major oil companies didn't sit down together and say: 'Look, these little schmuck rock stars have made dickheads out of us, why don't we all just blank the advertising on petrol for six months and give the money we would have spent on that to charity?' That would be an outrageous amount of money. It didn't happen and it probably won't, but it would have been nice to see.

People criticized us when we did Sun City, but no-one said a bad word when we played in Russia the next year. Everyone knew there was repression in Russia in 1988, but it was absolutely OK for us to play there. That never made sense to me.

In August 1988, when Status Quo went to Russia, it was still a communist country. The Berlin Wall was standing and the KGB were still in force in Moscow. Quo were hugely popular there, but when they arrived, they found it a depressing and sometimes bewildering experience.

RICK: The idea of going there to see first hand what life was like in a strictly communist country fascinated us. We stayed in a hotel with some five thousand rooms. I like watching television, but the thought of watching Russian politics for three weeks frightened the life out of me. So I had a television, video machine and speakers all set up in a flight bag and I took a caseload of videos. I gauged it so I'd have two films per night to watch.

FRANCIS: We were there for a little over three weeks in a monstrosity of a hotel. We figured out that the KGB colour-coded their shoes each day so they'd recognize each other and wouldn't waste their time watching fellow KGB blokes.

We played in the huge Olympic hall which was cut in half – one side was for Torvill and Dean, the other for us.

RICK: Apart from the fact that it was falling down, it was a nice venue to play. Seventeen thousand people each night for seventeen nights. Before the first show, we thought, This is right up our street. The lights went down, we opened with 'Whatever You Want', we got to the end of it and there was nothing. Silence. There was a huge gap and then a polite ripple of applause.

I looked at Francis and thought, This is going to be a fucking nightmare. But I knew we'd be thinking the same thing: Plough on, we'll get 'em. Second song in, much the same. At that point I knew it was going to be hell. There were a whole load of dignitaries down at the front in their uniforms.

The first slow song we did – 'Dirty Water' – Francis motioned to them all to join in, and there was a little bit of response. There was a signboard left over from the Olympics and we asked the people who were looking after us to put 'You sing with us' up on the board in Russian – and we thought, Brilliant, we've cracked it!

Francis was singing and pointing to the board and they cottoned on and all started to sing along. Suddenly it tore the place apart – they went berserk. It was Francis Rossi and Status Quo from then on – he'd got them all singing, hadn't he? Everywhere we went after that there were posters with big pictures of Francis and the rest of us were just dotted around. We gave him a bit of a hiding for that.

In the evenings we'd go over to a Western hotel which took hard currency. When you finished a gig, there was nowhere else to go. We'd have a few drinks there, but for the most part we stayed in our rooms.

Nothing worked there. Everything was at least forty years old. We had ex-politbureau cars called Seagulls. Two days out of three, they'd break down. If we were in the middle of a street, the driver would get out with a bottle of water, pour some in somewhere and the fucking thing would start again. There we were sitting in the back of these limos, completely embarrassed because we were surrounded by people in broken-down Ladas. And they've probably had to wait ten years to get the Lada.

FRANCIS: If it started to rain, the limo would stop in the middle of the street again and the guy would get out, go to the boot, unlock the boot, lock it again and then come and put the windscreen wipers on the car. If you didn't lock the wipers away, they'd be stolen.

RICK: The Russian audience were particularly fond of 'In The Army Now'. I'm not surprised.

In December 1989 Status Quo went to Nassau to record the album 'Perfect Remedy' with producer Pip Williams who had been working with them fairly consistently since recording 'Rockin' All Over the World' in 1979.

By this time neither Colin Johnson nor Alan Crux were managing the band and Iain Jones, who had worked with them for many years in various capacities, took up the mantle of manager and quickly realized that the band had serious financial and contractual problems that needed urgent expert attention.

In a desperate effort to resolve these matters he approached David Walker who, apart from being an astute businessman and creative

*manager, was Chairman of The Handle Group of Companies and
had worked with Quo indirectly for a number of years in his capac-
ity as manager of Pip Williams.*

*Francis and Rick were delighted when Iain brought David to Nassau
where it was agreed that they would join The Handle Group. Little did
they realize at the time that this would be the start of the most successful
and enjoyable period of their careers.*

RICK: Nassau was seen as a trip to lighten us all, to go somewhere
refreshing and a little exotic. If there's a choice between recording
an album in England in the winter when it's raining and horrible
or being in a studio which is on the beach, overlooking the sea,
we know which one we want. So we said: 'Yeah, let's have some
of that – it will make a great change.'

FRANCIS: I agreed to go out there, although I must admit I prefer
to be able to record somewhere which enables me to get home
every night.

RICK: I went out early with Patti for a Christmas holiday, and it
was monsoon time. There was nowhere for us to stay when we
arrived – there was supposed to be a beautiful beach house and
that turned out to be a shack with flapping windows, the whole
bit. It was awful; we had no food, no shops were open – it was
a total disaster. But Patti and I sat through it – no television, no
nothing.

Then the band came out with their wives, girlfriends and kids,
although Francis came on his own. The setting was beautiful.
The weather finally turned nice, and we had barbecues in the
evenings. We had a private swimming-pool to ourselves – it was
an idyllic scene. But there was work to be done. It was difficult
to switch from lazing around on lilos and scuba diving to getting
up to go to work in the morning.

It was all a bit of a wrench, but we knuckled down to it –
and it was fairly productive – especially compared to Monserrat,
the only other exotic location studio we'd been to. David Bowie

came into the studios with the Tin Machine to record their first album. We got on all right with them and saw them periodically. Everyone was mingling.

We got into a routine; we all had bikes and would have a long bike ride in the morning – anything from thirteen to eighteen miles, so we were getting fit. After that, we'd take a quick dip in the sea and then start work at ten o'clock, even if the sun was blazing. We'd eat at the studio complex – the food was pretty crap – conch stew, conch steaks, everything conch, so we rebelled against that and changed the cook. At six every evening we'd have a barbecue, and when that was finished, we'd sit on the end of the jetty and look up at the sky. It was the typical tropical scene – a beautiful beach with palm trees and the sunsets were something else. It was paradise. We were there for nearly three months. Everybody was so brown, you couldn't get any browner.

David Walker appeared about two-thirds of the way through, bearing good news. We were still frayed at the edges owing to what had happened before. The financial situation was not good. David lifted our spirits in a big way. He said: 'We'll get out of this, don't worry,' and shortly thereafter, David was finding money that we didn't know existed, he was clearing everything up. Within a relatively short time, I'd cleared my overdraft with the bank, and had money again. No-one was breathing down my neck any more.

The appearance of David Walker came as a great relief to Rick and Francis. When he took over the band's affairs, Quo was in dire financial straits, owing money to the Inland Revenue, banks and their record company. Walker couldn't understand how, after twenty-plus years of success, selling something like one hundred million records, not to mention their recent hits – 'In The Army Now' and 'Burning Bridges' – Quo could possibly be in such a position. As a result, he started looking into various matters, and recovering money owed to them. Thorough investigations which Walker instigated have thrown up a number of major questions, some of which have yet to be resolved. Lengthy discussions on past financial matters are still going on.

With Andrew, Rhino and Jeff, Francis and Rick now had the perfect band with the right sound and without any lurking resentments or bad feelings. What had started with a phone call to sort out an obligation to Phonogram had ended in the rebirth of a rock legend.

11

As the end of the Eighties drew near and the band continued to gel, both Rick's and Francis's lives began to straighten out. The excess of drugs and drink, which had started in the late Seventies and had carried on, had caused only destruction and despair. They'd lost their friendship, they'd lost money as a result of their excessive behaviour and they recognized that what they had first believed to be adding to their lives had, in fact, done exactly the reverse.

FRANCIS: Rick and I both got ourselves into the drug lifestyle. I knew what it was like, I said I'd never do it, and I went ahead anyway.

I used to get up in the morning, take a shower and feel quite good because I'd had only one line before the shower. Then I'd have breakfast and start again. I was doing coke, sulphate, dope and downers. What I noticed most of all was the effect it had when I got up on stage. Usually, as soon as you walk on, the audience goes crazy and you get a real rush. But when you do coke, that rush goes. Whatever that adrenalin does to you on stage, you don't get it with toot. You stand up there thinking, Yeah, right, and the thrill goes out of it all.

Initially you think coke is really lovely, then you get wired and wound up. Something worries or frightens you. When that used to happen, it reminded me of the times I'd done something wrong at school on a Friday and I knew I had to see the headmaster on Monday morning. All weekend I'd be sitting thinking about it and dreading it. With coke, the night comes and you know you won't be able to sleep. You're lying in bed grinding your teeth and you think, Why am I doing this? It outstays its welcome.

I was caught with some coke in my possession in the early Eighties. I was presenting an award to U2 in Ireland one New Year's Eve and it was quite a wingding over there. When I got back to Heathrow, I went to the place where I'd parked my car in the Terminal One garage. I saw that someone had smashed the car window and I thought, shit, but the speakers were there, the radio was still in place and whoever had smashed the window hadn't taken the usual stuff. Suddenly I remembered I'd left a little bit of coke in the glove compartment – a line, one toot. It was in a little green wallet along with my credit cards. I looked inside and saw that it had gone, so I thought, OK, that's what they wanted.

Then I turned round and saw the wallet on the back seat and I thought, That's strange. The cards were there, the coke was there. I thought, I'm a lucky boy. When I drove out and paid the parking ticket, the man at the cashier's booth said: 'Excuse me, sir, your car window's been smashed.' I said: 'I know that, don't I? I'll deal with it when I get home.' He said: 'Well, that policeman over there would like to have a word with you.'

Oh, I see, I thought. So I went over to the policeman and he asked: 'Is this your car?' I said: 'Yes, it is and the coke's mine, too.' He went quiet. I asked him what the matter was.

And he said: 'You just told me the cocaine is yours.' The conversation then went like this:

'Of course it's mine.'

'But I hadn't asked you.'

'That's what you were *going* to ask me, wasn't it?'

'Of course.'

'That's what you pulled me over here for – you're not interested in my window. You know there's something in the car you want to bust me for.'

'You're a funny man, aren't you?'

'Why?'

'You've admitted it and I haven't asked you.'

'What do you want me to do, deny it and then you can question me and we can play a game for ten minutes? Yes, it's mine. It's my credit cards, my car – what do you want me to say?'

So then he busted me. I was interviewed by two guys from the serious crimes squad – not the drug guys – and the whole time I was being interviewed I was saying: 'Yes sir, no sir, yes sir, no sir.' I could see one of them writing it all down and I said: 'Oh, it looks like I'm taking the piss with the "Yes sir, no sir" business.' He said: 'Well, you are, aren't you?' I said: 'No, this goes back to school – I was taught to say sir or ma'am or madam and I still do. That's just the way I am. I don't have a problem calling someone sir.'

They brought me back to my house to search it and the moment they walked through the front door, they knew exactly where everything was. They said: 'Take us to the music room first' and I thought, How do they know I have a music room? They went directly to my bedroom, they went straight to the side of the bed I slept on, but by this time they were calming down a bit. They asked to have a look at the studio; I wondered how they knew I had a studio?

Some months later I got to court and I was shitting myself. I thought: They've got me. I'm in big trouble. I was sitting there with the lawyer and there were some Press about and in came this policeman. He shook hands, said: 'I'm the prosecuting officer, I'm sorry, mate, you should have been let go.' I said: 'It's no problem.' So I stood in court and they read out what I'd been caught with. It was about nought nought nought point 1 per cent of a gramme of powder, of which nought nought nought nought point 1 per cent was actually cocaine. I thought, I'll kill the guy who sold me that. I knew he was selling shit.

I got done for six hundred pounds. The same cop came up afterwards and said: 'I'm sorry, that's heavy.' But I was relieved. I've always thought that if you do something wrong and you get caught, you have to admit to it and pay the price. That's the way I was brought up and that's why I admitted straight off to the policeman at Heathrow that the coke was mine. There's no point in lying and trying to dodge about. If you do something wrong, or against the law, you take the consequences and don't moan about it.

After my divorce, I went off everything. So I started suddenly going apeshit in my thirties. I used to come back to my house and try to get back to reality and then I'd think, Oh no, let's play for another day. In those days Rick and I were both wild, and that contributed a lot to the bad feeling between us. Rick would get quite aggressive when he was drinking whisky, and I couldn't see any way of getting through to him. Besides, I was out there myself, I wasn't functioning normally.

After Heidi's death, Rick couldn't motivate himself to do anything. I guess he drank so much and did so many drugs to forget. I couldn't help him then. Unless you've actually lost someone that close to you, I think it's impossible to help.

As time went by, I realized that I was getting out of control and I wasn't enjoying it. When I was drinking, I'd spend most of the next day getting over it. My stomach felt awful, it was affecting my throat, and I decided, when we were in Moscow, to cut back. I thought I'd have a drink on the encore and that would be it. I wouldn't drink through the night.

I did that and then two days later, I took it further. I decided not to take a drink on the encore either, because after the show the night before, I'd had a shower and I felt terrible. That's the point when I said to myself, Stop this. I stopped drinking after the show as well because I wasn't interested. I won't say I'll never do it again, because that's a dangerous thing to say.

I came off the coke in much the same way. I just kept saying to

myself, I'll have a toot later, not now. After a recording session in
Nassau in 1989, I went back to my room at about ten o'clock and
thought, OK, I'll have a toot now. Then I thought about it some
more and realized I didn't want to. I had no interest in staying up all
night and being a wreck the next day, I just wanted to go to bed and
get some sleep. So I did. And that was the end of my coke days.

Anytime after that when I've thought of having a toot, believing
that I could have just a small one and get away with it, all
those memories come flooding back, and I think, No – I don't
want to be wired, I don't want to be wound up. I didn't like
the way it took over my life.

Sometimes people don't like hearing that you've cleaned up.
They'd much rather believe that you're out there doing wild things
because you're supposed to be a wild rock 'n' roll man. They want
everyone to be like Keith Richards. In a sense, then, you're living
their fantasy life for them. If you're a normal bloke with a normal
life, then where's the fantasy? They've been ripped off.

I know one star who is so miserly, so tight, that if his fans
knew the truth about him, they'd be insulted. They wouldn't
like to think of someone so famous buying second-hand goods.
A fan would probably say: 'Here I am, struggling away and you're
living the life I get only in my dreams and you're being a stingy
bastard – what's wrong with you?'

When people meet us, they say: 'You're really ordinary, aren't
you?' and I look at them and say: 'Yes.' Of course we are. I can find an
excuse for someone like Michael Jackson not to be ordinary given
the life he's led from childhood, but most people *are* ordinary.

Two girls who come to see our gigs a lot came to one last year
and asked if they could come back to the room afterwards. We said:
'Sure, if you don't mind the fact that we're just going to be sitting
around playing cards.' They said: 'No problem,' and came back to
the room and stood, watching us play cards. Then they asked: 'Is
this all you do?' I've never seen two people so bored in my life.

We told them that this was as exciting as it got, this was the
highlight of our day. And they thought we were taking the piss.
Three-quarters of the way through the show, Andrew, Rhino, Jeff
and I are looking forward to our game of cards, and Rick is looking

forward to his tea; why should it bother anyone else? I don't see the point in being wild and crazy for other people's benefit.

RICK: Francis and I cleaned up at about the same time. After we got together with Andrew, Rhino and Jeff and re-formed, I started to become sensible again. I had a responsibility and a sense of purpose. It wasn't a case of trying to be good for just a few hours any more, it was long term, because the band was back. And the band was better than when we'd actually started, better than any of us could have imagined.

We had thought that if we could get it back firing as much as it did before, then that would be great, but this band knocked spots off the old one. It was brighter, punchier. As a result, I began to be brighter and punchier, too. After a while, I didn't need the coke any more. With the new group, I had a direction again.

Getting off coke wasn't difficult for me. As soon as I stopped, I found I didn't want it any more. What did affect me very badly, though, was a sleeping-pill called Rohypnol. It's morphine-based, a substitute for coming off heroin, a fact which I didn't know at the time it was prescribed for me. When Debbie Ash and I split up, I had problems sleeping. We'd had a serious romance, spent all our time together and I'd even thought of settling down again with her and her daughter Candie, whom I was very close to. The break-up, when it came, was difficult, and I went to a doctor to get something to help me sleep.

Rohypnols are very powerful indeed and you become very, very dependent on them. I've since discovered that they're banned in America, Australia and Japan. In Europe you have to be fully checked out before a doctor will prescribe them for you, but in this country they're still available, though not for long, I hope.

The band called them 'donkeys', because they could put out a donkey. Most people are totally knocked out by half a tablet, but I was taking three at a time at one stage.

I would take a couple of hundred on the road with me, bags full of them because I was anxious about being anywhere without them. Once I did run out, though, when I was in Guernsey, and I had a dreadful night. It was terrible. But I didn't make the connection then; I thought I'd just had a rough night, I didn't realize it was because I hadn't taken a pill.

Taking them made me feel blurred during the day. People would say: 'You're a bit drowsy, a bit slow,' and I'd say: 'No, I'm not.' I was very protective about them. But they affected my memory as well. We'd be on tour and I couldn't remember where we'd been the week before. I was living in a cocoon of Rohypnol.

I knew I had to come off them, but I had no idea how brutal that would turn out to be. I decided to go cold turkey on holiday in Spain. A doctor had warned me that stopping dead like that would be difficult, but I wasn't prepared for the horrors.

One night was particularly gruesome and I wrote about it later: Feeling tense. Palpitations. Pupils dilated. Dry throat, lump in the throat. Shaking. Anxiety. Bad moods. No humour. No laughing. No smiling. Attacking words. Very little sleep. Very little taste. Sex drive down 50 per cent. Bad dreams of people bleeding and going mad on drugs. Feeling sick. Dreaming of smells you can't describe. Waiting to return to normality, but not knowing when. You don't like the light. You don't like talking to anyone. You can't see people. You don't want to look in mirrors. Change of personality. Aching all over.

After living through this hell, I know that it's a better idea to come off something as powerful as that gradually. What does seem strange is that giving up cocaine was so much easier than getting off a pill prescribed for me by a GP.

The late Eighties not only brought an end to Francis's cocaine and alcohol use, but also saw the finish of his relationship with Paige Taylor, whom he had met in 1986. They had been engaged for a short time, but Francis's heart actually lay elsewhere. After the trip to Russia, he determined to take action and pursue the woman he loved.

FRANCIS: I first met Eileen in 1974. I was in New York, visiting my cousin Patrick – who's a poof, a lovely bloke – and his mother.

Eileen was a friend of Patrick's so I saw her then and I thought she was fabulous. At the time, though, we didn't connect. I thought she was far too nice for me.

Eleven years later, in 1985, she and Patrick came to stay here in my house and I thought she was even lovelier. I saw her sitting by the fish pond with my sons, Nicholas and Kieran, who were thirteen and six at the time, and I could see how relaxed she was with them. I couldn't get over how natural and nice she was.

When I came back from Moscow, I heard that she had got married. I called Patrick and asked why she had done it. He told me that she'd been crying, that she hadn't wanted to get married and I said: 'Then why did she do it?' He said: 'I don't know. What did *you* get married for in the first place?' I couldn't answer that.

I said to my mother: 'I'm going over to the States, and if I can, I'm bringing Eileen back with me.' The feeling I had for her wasn't like the feeling I'd had for any other woman I'd met or known. I thought I'd loved people before, but this was different.

I went over and arranged to meet for breakfast. Patrick said he had a headache, so we were alone. She seemed really sad to me, but I thought, How the fuck am I going to say this? How am I going to get her to come back with me? She's bound to say: 'No, I've just got married.' But I went ahead anyway. I said: 'What about you coming to live with me, and if it works out, it's great, if it doesn't, it's fine, too.' She said: 'Yes.' I said: 'Great – more coffee?'

It was as simple as that. I floated everywhere afterwards. I had really expected her to say no, but I knew I had to try. She'd been under pressure from her parents to marry and she'd even been crying walking down the aisle. Her husband wasn't really interested in her as a person, so it wasn't as if I broke up a happy marriage.

After Eileen said yes, everything has changed. I've been walking on air ever since. I keep telling her that I got the best deal, that she got the rough end. I just look at her and giggle to myself. I didn't think, Ooh, I'll get that one. I just looked at her and thought, Isn't she wonderful? She used to teach deaf and dumb children in New York, but if someone said that to her, she'd punch them. She'd say: 'They're not dumb, we are.' Yes, my love, I think, fair enough.

People must get tired of me saying how wonderful she is,

but I don't care. My whole life has changed. Now I'm actually looking forward to growing old with her. I'd like us to go to Brighton and be that old couple sitting on the beach with a blanket around them. And everyone else can say: 'Oh, look at them, look at that old couple!'

Francis and Eileen were married in a Register Office on 19 June 1991. They have two sons, Patrick and Finn. Eileen is expecting their third child at the end of 1993.

Rick remarried as well, on 5 July 1988 and Patti gave birth to their son Harry on 20 June 1989.

RICK: Patti and I had lived together for quite a while, and one night I said: 'Look, do you fancy getting married?' She asked me if I was serious and I said I was, even though I didn't do anything dramatic like go down on bended knee.

When the day came, we had a great time. We didn't have a honeymoon because I was working, but on our wedding night we went out and stayed at the Sheraton at Heathrow – it's affectionately known as Tequila Palace. We decided to go there, celebrate and afterwards come home and settle down.

When Harry came along it was the first birth I'd seen and I was absolutely thrilled – that was a fantastic experience. I didn't throw up, faint or anything like that – I remember it very vividly and always will.

About two and a half years after Harry was born, the relationship between Patti and me started going downhill. We didn't have anything to say to each other, which was odd in a way because we'd always been such good mates. I hope we still can be friends in the future, but when we got married things became difficult. I find a marriage certificate something of a taboo, I guess. It's a symbol and it means that you're handcuffed to each other: you're together and you're supposed to be happy together.

Eventually I had a couple of affairs and I tried to lie about them, but I can't tell lies. Telling a lie is like living with a poison inside you, and I couldn't live with that poison. It made me feel ill. I told her it was apparent that our relationship was coming to an end and the only thing to do, really, was to separate.

I need space. I need freedom. I need my own time. I'm certainly half to blame – more than half – but I can't stand finding myself in a situation where someone's asking me where I've been, why I didn't call, all that stuff. I'm a bit of a mental claustrophobic, so I feel stifled when that happens. Separating from Patti was a very hard decision, but I had to make it in the end.

I've never seen Francis as peaceful as he is now. He's happy in his house with his whole family around him – and we're different in that sense, because I need to be able to lock myself away when I feel like it, just be on my own. It's taken me a long time to realize that.

Harry spends every weekend with me and I think it's important for kids to know that their parents can get along, even if they have split up. I didn't see Richard for a long time, but I don't blame Marietta for keeping him away, because she knew what a state I was in back in those wilderness years. Richard had witnessed some of my awful behaviour and he was frightened stiff of me.

But three years ago, Marietta phoned me out of the blue and said: 'Look, I think it's about time Richard saw you and you saw Richard.' He was fifteen going on sixteen and I hadn't really seen him for about six years. I had written a beautiful song called 'Richard's Song', but I hadn't been a part of his life. When Marietta suggested that I see him, I said: 'Great!' and Patti was very understanding.

Marietta then said that she'd like to have a chat to me about him before he and I met, so I went and had dinner with her in town. We had a good talk and everything was OK.

I was so thrilled to see him again, I couldn't believe it. I wanted to tell everyone: 'This is my son.' In the days when I'd sobered up and saw life more clearly I realized how much I missed him.

Now, after all these years apart, he's living with me. I'm incredibly proud of him, his personality, everything about him and it's fantastic to be a part of his life again.

12

By 1989, Francis and Rick had both reached forty and their lives were becoming, if not exactly settled, at least a little calmer. Status Quo as a band was reaching an audience which spanned all age groups, appealing to fans from seven and below to seventy and above.

Francis's push to broaden the base of the music and Rick's own ability to appreciate other styles as well as heavy rock has made Quo one of the few bands able to survive the test of time.

Perhaps part of the secret of their success is the special relationship they have with their fans. They know what their audiences want, what they like and they never hesitate to give it to them.

FRANCIS: I know what it's like to *be* a fan sitting watching a group you like. I went to an Eagles concert once. Reggie, Townsend, Daltrey, all sorts of stars were there and we were all gobsmacked. The place was packed and I had a really good seat on the ground, but I *still* couldn't make out quite who was on the stage, so how could anyone else with less good seats?

People were shouting out, requesting various songs, and I thought, Fuck that! *I* want 'Already Gone'. When they finally played it, I was so happy that I went home stupid, thrilled. That night I thought, Well at our concerts, there must be some poor sod out there the way I was tonight, waiting for 'Caroline' or 'Down, Down', and he wants to go home happy.

I know musicians who won't play their old hits, they say: 'We like to stretch our audience.' Dickheads. I don't think it's fair to change the melody of a song either. I saw Paul Simon doing that a while back and I thought, Hey, if you're bored with singing the song, *that* bored, then just don't do it.

Lots of bands used to release an album, go out on the road, and only sing songs from that album, no others. Pink Floyd used to do that. In my opinion, if an audience wants to hear specific songs, even if you've played them millions of times, it should get to hear them. To send an audience home happy is what it's all about.

RICK: If I go to see the Stones, I want to hear 'Brown Sugar' and 'Jumpin' Jack Flash', I don't want to hear the album tracks that I don't know. We're in the position where we can play an hour and forty-five minutes of hits and that's what we do. That's what the fans want to hear. That's what they love. If we drop anything out, they get upset.

We listen to the fans, we often chat to them, and they tell us that they don't want us to change the set. We adjust it slightly, but you can't take any of the major songs away. They let you know when you get it wrong. You can tell by their expressions, the way they look at you from the audience. You feel guilty if they're looking at you and they're clearly upset. We don't want to let them down.

During the bad times, we'd neglected our following, we hadn't thought about our fans. But, of course, loyal as they are, they were still there when we came back and we're now filling Wembley for three nights on the trot. All credit goes to them for hanging on in there and coming out in droves again. Playing at Wembley or any big, packed-out gig is incredible. When the lights go down, and a roar goes up, it's just a fantastic feeling.

FRANCIS: When we split up and I thought we weren't going to gig any more, I had to admit that I missed being 'him', the Francis Rossi I am on stage. I used to go into the studio and say: 'Am I like "him" yet?' and someone would say: 'Yeah.' I'd think, Oh, all right, then. When most people go to work they might get a few, 'good mornings' from people, but when I walk on stage, people scream. I missed all that. I love to see people enjoying themselves, I love to leave an audience knackered.

As I see it, we're musicians *and* entertainers. I like to get a thing going with the audience, I like to play with them.

One time about two or three tours back, we were playing at Wembley just before Christmas and we were into the encore. I was just about to get into 'A Whole Lotta Shakin' Goin' On' when I saw some bloke in the audience getting up to leave. I stopped and said: 'Hallo – where are you going? Don't think you're getting out of here before the rest of this lot so you can make it to the car-park first.' It was just someone I decided to pick on and he sat right back down.

After the show, David Walker came back to our dressing-room and said: 'I'd like you to meet my mum, Bella.' I said: 'Fine, nice to meet you.' Then David said: 'And this, by the way, is my stepfather, Jim.' There he was – the guy I'd picked on. He was an American and he turned out to be a lovely guy. He said: 'I felt just like a naughty boy at school, so I sat down as fast as I could.'

Another part of the Quo magic is the songs they have written themselves. Both Francis and Rick are prolific songwriters. Francis has collaborated with Rick, with Bob Young, with Bernie Frost and others to produce a phenomenal amount of classic recordings and Rick has worked with a variety of people as well to release a string of hits.

FRANCIS: I usually compose the tune first, I don't often start with the lyrics. Occasionally the lyrics can come just like that, off the top of your head. Last year when we did 'Mysteries From The Ball', every line was completely off the top of our heads.

RICK: It was in the vein of 'Matchstick Men', the lyrics were really far out. Francis and I didn't know what it meant, actually. *Ice is afloat on my wings*, could be the god Isis afloat, or it could be ice is a float. We were freaking out, writing down anything that came to us. And we were drinking only water.

FRANCIS: Sometimes you have to really grind to get the lyrics out.

RICK: The worst thing that can happen to you is if you're writing the lyrics and you have a great line that ends in something like 'orange'. Try to get a word that rhymes with 'orange'. You can get yourself into a hell of a mess unless you keep it simple. If you find yourself with one line that really works, you might tie yourself up in knots and sit for four days trying to come up with the next one which works with it.

FRANCIS: On the 'Rock 'Til You Drop' album, there was a track called 'All We Really Want To Do'. I was messing about with it at the end of the day, and I had come to the chorus and to remind myself where I was for the next day, I said to myself: 'All we really want to do is pollywollydoodle all the day.' I knew the following morning that I couldn't actually use pollywollydoodle, so I came up with something similar which fit. 'All we really want to do is what we want to do and do it all the day'.

RICK: If you've got a working line in your head, it's easier. You can base everything else around it. If you have a basic melody but no lyrics, it's difficult to start, but at some point it will become apparent. A line usually comes into your head which you begin to sing and that's the starting-off point. Songs can become very precious to you.

FRANCIS: If it's your song, you don't want anyone else to touch it.

RICK: It's almost like having a beautiful car. You take it out for a drive, but you don't want to leave it anywhere. Your soul is in it. If you believe you've written a great song, you think, Wow, this is wonderful. When you go in to record it, it's a bad feeling, really, because you want it done exactly your way. You think, If the others don't play it the way I want, there's going to be trouble.

FRANCIS: It's so valuable and you want everything to be perfect; no-one else is listening to it in that way except you. If it's Rick's song that's playing, I sit back and think, Yeah, that's lovely. Meanwhile he's sitting there biting his nails.

We try not to get *too* precious about songs. I always maintain that after the first love song was written, every subsequent one was a copy; after the first rock song was written, every subsequent one was a copy – and on and on. When you think about the lyrics of love songs, we're all saying the same thing: I can't help falling in love with you; I'm your puppet; I will always love you; you light up my life; you're my everything. Those heart-rending lyrics don't come easily to me. I can't imagine singing: 'Baby, you're the only one for me.'

RICK: You have to do what's suited to you. I thought that Bryan Adams song 'Everything I Do, I Do For You' was a particularly brilliant song. If we had done it, it would have been highly boring. We've attempted songs in that vein, but it doesn't work for us.

FRANCIS: Perhaps if we'd written it, it might have worked.

RICK: It would have needed a hell of a lot of producing, though. It would have had to have been overproduced.

FRANCIS: I heard that Bryan had done the demo for that song and that they had him in the studio for over forty hours trying to put the vocal down the way it had been on the demo. Finally they just sampled it from the demo – they should have gone with the demo in the first place.

A lot of the time, if you know you're only doing a demo, you relax, and because you relax it ends up sounding great. We should probably use those demos when it happens like that, but we're all show-offs and performers and think it's not for real until the fucking red light comes on in the studio.

RICK: When you get into a recording studio and you've got forty-eight tracks and every piece of equipment available on the leading edge of technology, you tend to want to use it all. A lot of the time, you don't really need all that equipment, but it also depends on how far the producer wants to take it.

Pip Williams, who was our producer for years, sometimes got carried away because he was a perfectionist. Once I was making a video of everyone recording and I videoed Andrew doing a take on 'Burning Bridges' – it sounded absolutely wonderful, spot on.

FRANCIS: It was Andrew's first pass at it and it was just right.

RICK: Pip spent all that day and the best part of the night trying to get him to do it again. We don't like to cause any animosity in the studio, so we didn't ask why.

FRANCIS: When you ask the guy to do it over and over again, eventually he loses the feel for it. Also, producers or record company executives often feel that they *have* to mess around with a song. When we had recorded two or three tracks for the 'Just Supposin' ' album, we played one of them to the record company and a guy there said I would have to remix it. I said: 'Fine.' Then I made a copy of it, without changing a thing, and sent it to him. 'Great,' he said. 'That remixing makes all the difference.'

RICK: Once you're in a studio, you can't afford to be sitting around for four or five hours doing nothing. You get bored if it's taking hours to get another person's bit down. All of a sudden the producer might turn to you and say: 'Right, you're on now, Rick.' If you've been sitting around doing nothing, it's like being woken up first thing in the morning and told to get to the football pitch and play a game straight off.

FRANCIS: It can take a day or two just to set up the drums. And then, when you start recording, you might have to break for half an hour to cue the snare drums. Once that's fixed, back you go, and then the snare drum goes off *again*. After two or three days of this, the producer asks: 'Do we have any drum samples?' You think, Wait, hang on a minute. What was the point of spending all this time on the drum kit when all you have to do is push a button, link it to the right machine and you can have any snare drum bit you want to use? The technology is getting so advanced, soon there won't be any humans involved.

RICK: I have nothing against drum machines. I like playing against them on a demo.

FRANCIS: But Rick and I will actually push ahead of the drums on the beat. A producer would say: 'No – hold back', but that's part of our magic. But it's impossible to define what *really* makes up the magic. To try to pin it down is a mistake.

I went up to my son's, Simon's, room the other night and he was watching a show on TV; it turned out to be something the band had done for the BBC last year, a live performance. I watched myself and then I went back downstairs and started to sweat. My heart sped up because I was back there on stage, playing.

Generally, I don't like to look at clips of myself. If I do, I think, Imagine standing like that or doing that. What a twit! And I swear to myself that I'll never do it again. Then when I actually go back on stage, my legs splay out and that's it. I've done it again. I can't help it any more. I believe, though, that if I study myself too much, if I actually knew what the success formula was, and was conscious of doing it the whole time, I'd start to manipulate it. And that would mean I'd lose it. I go by instinct. We all do.

In February 1991, Status Quo received the Brit Award for an Outstanding Contribution to the British Music Industry. They weren't accustomed to winning awards and even less accustomed to dressing up in black tie for formal occasions. What should have been a normal, ordinary award ceremony, however, became something else altogether. They'd surprised people four months before with their twenty-fifth anniversary at Butlin's, and they had a surprise in store for the Brit Awards, too.

RICK: We knew we stood a reasonable chance of winning the Outstanding Contribution Award, even though the Stones were up for it as well.

We hadn't thought much about awards before – those were for other people, other bands. We'd never been worried by that. But it was a real honour. Then we heard that they wanted us to play at the Brits. It wasn't just a case of picking up the award and going; we were supposed to do a medley of our hits.

That posed a problem because we don't like performing in front of our contemporaries. When you look down and you see McCartney, Elton John and Eric Clapton sitting there and there's us who are supposed to have only three chords in our repertoire anyway, you can get a little thrown off.

So we thought – in typical Quo style – we'll make it a laugh. The team said: 'Look, we'll do some pyrotechnics and we'll make it look fabulous.' The lighting was all brilliant and fireworks would be going off. It would look terrific.

But we knew that when we actually received the awards, we had to wear dress suits and bow-ties. The show was planned so that it would segue straight from receiving the awards to playing. We were supposed to play in our dress suits. Then Francis came up with this idea: why don't we have Velcro dress suits on top of our stage gear, then rip off our suits when the time comes to play. Brilliant – solved it! Not only do we have our denim underneath, but nobody's ever done this before.

FRANCIS: When we were out in California, we'd been taken by leisure suits, we thought they were great. I'd had an idea for our tour. I thought, Let's do the encore in leisure suits. We'll come out on stage in leisure suits, rip them off each other and we'll have our jeans underneath. I figured the audience would love it. So when this Brit thing came up, I went back to that idea. Come out in Velcroed tuxes and then rip them off. It was extremely difficult to walk around that night because we were fully clothed underneath.

RICK: When we got up to receive the award, we were nervous because when you get out of your seat you think the Velcro's going to rip – the trousers were Velcroed right up the back of the legs and the back of the jacket. The only giveaway was that we had white stage pumps – I suppose everybody thought, Typical fucking Quo – no style, they wear dress suits and ruin it all by wearing pumps. Nobody had a clue that we were going to rip the suits off. When we did it, the place went wild. There was rapturous applause, and everyone was in hysterics.

FRANCIS: I hate the idea of making a speech at an award ceremony. The only thing I want to do is say: 'Thanks' and get away. Again, just because I can perform on stage singing songs and playing the guitar doesn't mean I'm a natural speechmaker. I get nervous, but then occasionally I see Reggie make a speech, and I know he's nervous, too, but he looks totally calm and composed. I admire that.

RICK: Shortly after that, we were honoured at the World Music Awards in Monte Carlo. That was a crazy time. Everybody turned up, the whole party gang. It was a real rave. I sat next to Kylie Minogue and I said: 'Hallo, good evening.' She said: 'Hallo.' So I said: 'How are you doing, all right?' She replied: 'Fine, thanks.' That conversation wasn't exactly taking off. You get the vibe when someone doesn't want to talk to you.

There was a mystery woman on my left who was a mystical type of woman, very interesting. She believed in reincarnation and I had a pleasant conversation with her. Kylie had Prince Albert of Monaco on her other side, so I suppose she was doing all right. Ringo was there and Cliff was performing as well; it all ran incredibly late because Elton decided he wanted to go on at a certain time, so everything was pushed back. It got to two o'clock and we still hadn't performed. It was unlike Reggie to pull a wobbly like that. We didn't get on till half-past two and Cliff was fuming, but then we went on to a club and we really raved. Needless to say Francis didn't go. He doesn't like parties.

When we met Prince Albert, he told us that he'd been a lifelong Quo fan and had secretly flown to one of our gigs the year before. He told us that he could play the piano – badly – but that he intended to have a serious go at mastering his guitar technique.

I enjoyed Monte Carlo, I enjoy those kinds of dos and I like to go for it. Generally on tour you don't go to raving parties, but in a situation like that you can have fun. I came back with a hangover – like you do from Monte Carlo.

FRANCIS: I'm not what anyone would call a party person. The only party I've ever had at my house was when I was married to Jean. She pushed me to have a New Year's Eve party, so I finally agreed. People turned up at eight and by half-past nine, she was upstairs crying her eyes out, asking me to turn them out of the house. They'd made a mess of the place and were totally abusing it. I know there can be decent parties – the Butlin's Anniversary party was great – but when I'm at an award ceremony or something like that, all I'm thinking about is when will it all be over so I can get back to my hotel room, or preferably, if possible, back home.

Ripping their formal clothes off at the Brit Awards was an example of the humour underlying the band's attitude towards life. Francis and Rick especially have built up a relationship which is full of good-natured ribbing and fun. Over the years they have developed what amounts to their own language – they can sit in a room together, and have a conversation which no-one else in the world would understand. And it doesn't have to be a short conversation – if they wanted, they could carry it on for hours,

leaving any listener totally in the dark. They know that humour makes the hard work and the long hours a little lighter.

RICK: Rhino and Jeff thought Francis and I were pretty wacky at first, I think, but after seven years, they know just about all the slang we use. It's not your normal cockney rhyming slang because it's linked to our pasts, and also what happens to us on tour. Sometimes we use words to replace other words without rhyming them. If I say 'Yuri Gagarin' for example, it actually means 'egg'. It doesn't rhyme with anything, it's just what we happen to call an egg.

And some of the rhymes we do use wouldn't make much sense to anyone else. If you want to sit in the front of a car you say: 'Let me get in the Brunt.' Derek Brunt is a bloke I used to go to school with, and because it was such bad rhyming slang, so off the wall, it stayed. It stuck.

FRANCIS: We can get very complicated. I can say 'twist' for example, and that means 'clout', because of 'twist and shout', but we won't tell people what 'clout' means. Only a very clever, intuitive person could find that out.

RICK: Over the years, you build up thousands of things like that. Francis and I are so attuned these days that if we haven't seen each other for months, I can come up with a new slang word I've thought of while we've been apart and he'll latch on to it right away, I don't even have to explain it. Sometimes we'll have rhyming slang on top of rhyming slang. 'Kettle' means 'watch': kettle and hob . . . fob . . . watch.

FRANCIS: We can get very basic and play with names: Scott Problems. Willy Makeit. Hugh Miliated. Mr and Mrs Perglue and their daughter, Sue. We can have fun with all that.

RICK: We once had a bus driver who would say after anything we said that might remotely have a sexual connotation, 'she

So there I was standing at the bar in the battle, having a quiet Forsythe and a butcher's about. I saw the most gorgeous creamy sitting on a yogi in the little jack, having a laugh with her china. She had bacons up to her Gregory, blue mincers, a long blonde barnet and a set of barries that made me go weak at the biscuits.

It so happened that I had a rake of bangers in my sky, and I wondered if she'd like to come for a meal. I hoped that she wouldn't pork the Jeremy because a complete Queen's Park was asking her out. But she said she was Hank, so off we went to find a restaurant. She had the Lillian, I had the Greg. Afterwards, I got the jack, left an Ayrton for the baked and got in the jam.

As we were driving back to her cat and mouse, I was wondering whether I was going to get a Howard of her barries, because, after all, I was *still* a Queen's Park to her and anything south of her loaf was a bit risky. So we had a chat and a bit of how's your father and said goodnight. I then returned to the rub a dub dub and got Mozart on a few pigs.

Quo Slang.

cried'. We might be upstairs in the hotel and say: 'It's time to go down', and he'd say: 'She cried'. Francis and I thought, Oh God, what a pain in the ass, but as it went on we got to love it. It was so bad that we started to do it ourselves. We knew it was corny and awful, so we turned it round and used it. Other people could look at us and think, That is *not* funny. But if it's funny to us, sod everyone else.

Someone will say something at the beginning of a tour which will trigger someone else off and we'll use it throughout the whole tour. You've only got to get three or four of those phrases and keep applying them relentlessly, and they become funnier each time. That's the key to getting through a tour. I don't know if other bands do it. I know a band like Queen have had some pretty wild times, but I don't think they had a particularly great time on the road. You read about the Stones sitting up all night playing guitars in their hotel suites, but I don't know if that's amazing fun.

I came up with the worst album titles for us in the world the other day. I pictured the record sleeve with 'Quomosones' written over the top and 'Jeans' underneath, or a picture of the sky with a hole in it with 'Quozone' written across it.

People don't realize how tough it is to get through tours – the only time you're apart is when you're asleep. And you're talking about a marriage of five people, not two. You spend more time with the band than with your wives. If we couldn't laugh, I don't know where we'd be.

13

Francis and Rick might believe that the people who are the true charity workers are the punters who pay for the tickets to see benefits, but they have done more than their share of charity fund-raising over the years. They've worked for the Prince's Trust, Live Aid, Band Aid, Nordoff-Robbins and, in April 1991, they even went back to gaol for a good cause.

RICK: One of the prison officers at Pentonville had asked a few prisoners to put a band together, but they had virtually no equipment. They had established a workshop and asked us to open it for them. We went down there and it was awful. There was wire everywhere, electric fencing.

FRANCIS: Two of the inmates were showing us round the cells. They were younger than us and they had on their blue overalls.

I was looking round the cell and noticed a picture on the wall. 'Who's that?' I asked and one of them told me that it was his wife. 'Cor!' I said. 'What are you doing in here, then? She's stunning.' He said: 'Oh, you get used to it. I'm only in here for fourteen years this time.'

I had to ask him why he kept coming back when he had a wife and family, why he kept breaking the law. Apparently, he worked on the assumption that if you do fourteen or fifteen jobs and get caught for one of them, you're ahead of the game – quids in.

RICK: You get a really uneasy feeling being in there.

FRANCIS: You go past cells and you hear the blokes saying: 'Fucking bastards.' And we thought they were going to like us.

RICK: We went into the workshop and there were about one hundred inmates all sitting there. A couple of remarks were thrown at us.

FRANCIS: Remarks like: 'I'll kill you.'

RICK: Unbeknown to us – we hadn't been primed – we were expected to get up on stage and make a speech. So I got up and said that we were knocked out to be there . . . we declare your workshop open. At that point the prison band took over and played 'Rockin' All Over the World'.

FRANCIS: They had this problem: members of the band would keep getting out, being released, so they were changing round the whole time. They probably had to ask a guy how long he was going to be in for before they'd let him play.

RICK: Afterwards we sent them a keyboard and a few amplifiers. The whole thing did bring back our experience in Vienna, though.

On 30 June 1990, Status Quo joined an all-star line-up for a charity concert at Knebworth. The concert was for the benefit of Nordoff-Robbins

The Wild Side of Life? (© George Bodnar)

Nassau: Fun in the Sun.

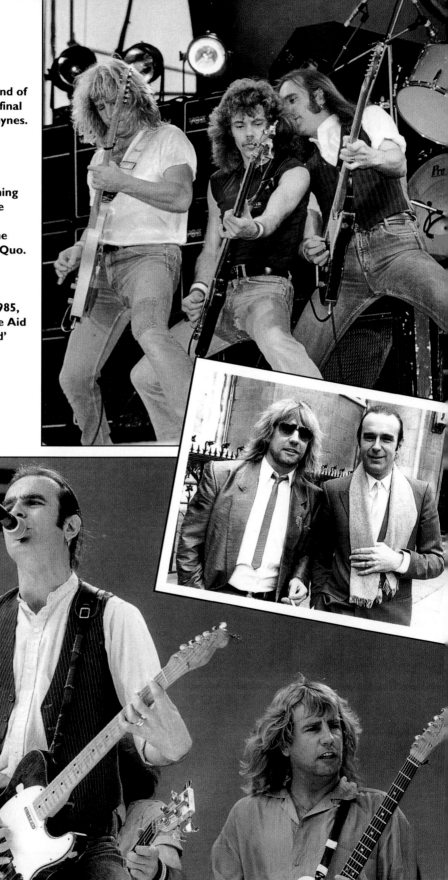

Rick, Alan and Francis at the End of the Road, their final gig at Milton Keynes. (© *Joe Bangay*)

Insert: Rick and Francis outside court after winning their legal battle against Alan Lancaster for the name of Status Quo. (© *The Press Association*)

Below: 13 July 1985, opening the Live Aid 'Feed the World' concert. (© *Syndication International*)

The Royal Seal of Approval: with Prince Charles at the Prince's Trust Concert,1982 (© *News Team International*); with the Queen in Berlin, 1992 (© *Simon Porter*); with Fergie at the Nordoff-Robbins Centre, 1991 (© *Richard Young*); and with Diana at the Live Aid concert in 1985 (© *The Press Association*).

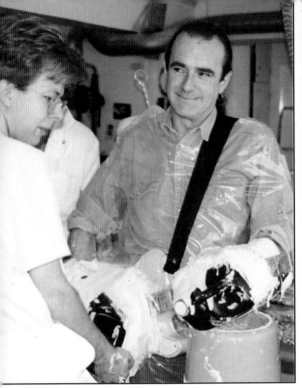

Francis and Rick modelling for Madame Tussaud's Rock 'n' Roll Hall of Fame. (© *Simon Porter*)

'Can we have your autograph?' (© *Dave Hogan*)

Giving the punters
whatever they want.
(© *George Bodnar*)

Francis and Rick undress at the Brit Awards. (© *London Features International*)

Francis and Rick in Pentonville – a narrow escape. (© *George Bodnar*)

Back to the Future: Butlin's 25th anniversary. (Above and below: © *Joe Bangay*, right: © *George Bodnar*)

(Left © London Features International, below: © Joe Bangay)

Still Rockin

Somerwest World
Congratulates
STATUS QUO
on their
25ᵗʰ ANNIVERSARY

THE STATUS QUO GUITAR

Rick rediscovers The Highlights.

DO NOT ENTER
"ROCK LEGENDS"
ASLEEP.
THANK YOU.

Rock 'Til You Drop.
(Photographs ©
George Bodnar,
below: © Joe Bangay)

STARFLIGHT

Status Quo
'TIL YOU DROP

ROCK 'TIL YOU DROP
WEMBLEY ARENA
SEPTEMBER 21st. 1991

FOR THE GUINNE...

B Britannia

PREMIER

Not another idea, David.
(© George Bodnar)

Clockwise from top: Francis with
Finn; Nicholas gives Kieran and
Patrick a ride; Bernadette at the
piano; Francis relaxing with Simon;
Francis working with Kieran.

Rick with Harry; Richard; Harry.

Music Therapy. Status Quo, who are the Music Therapy Silver Clef Winners performed for an hour. When the concert was originally announced at the end of 1989, one hundred thousand tickets were sold within forty-eight hours. Televised and broadcast to sixty-five countries, the gig raised six million pounds which helped pay for a new music therapy centre in London. A double, live album from the event entitled 'Knebworth' was released five weeks later.

RICK: I really enjoy working for Nordoff-Robbins. It's been a long-standing charity in the music business because it's such a good one. I went to one of the music therapy sessions with the kids. They're autistic children and it's amazing to watch what music can do for them. You stand behind a mirror – a one-way mirror – and you see the therapists sing the children into the room, incorporating each one's name into a song. It's incredible to see what happens to these kids, who are usually curled up in a corner completely unresponsive, when they hear their name in a song.

The therapists are brilliant. They encourage the kids so much. Within half an hour I saw a kid who had come into the room open up, respond. He was playing the cymbals and beating the piano, loving it.

The old centre was in Camden and really run down. We thought we could give a concert and raise enough money to build a new centre. All of the musicians taking part made it clear that it was the audience which was paying the money and building the centre, we were just strutting our stuff. The goal was to earn six million pounds in a day and we did.

Once a year there's a do when we all get together and have a really good lunch. We all know we're there to raise money; there are charity auctions and things are sold for outrageous prices.

A couple of years ago there was an elephant up for auction. I'll never forget it. Rod and Reggie started competing with one another. Rod went to five grand, Reggie went to seven. Rod went to ten. It was only a little decorative elephant, maybe worth a few bob. But neither of them was going to give in. The place was in hysterics. Reggie went up to fifteen, Rod to seventeen. In the end they bottled out at twenty grand. I can't remember who won, but it was a hell of a lot of fun.

There's a guitar that goes around every year. Whoever buys it keeps it for a year and then gives it back to be re-auctioned and each year it goes up in value. It's signed by Hank Marvin, Stevie Ray Vaughan, Mark Knopfler, Eric Clapton, all sorts of great people. We bought it for ten grand one year.

After we'd raised the money from the Knebworth concert, we went to the opening of the new centre and it was wonderful to see this sparkling new building. I think everyone who was involved would have loved to have been there if they could.

Rick and Francis were effectively immortalized in May 1991 when waxwork models of them made for Madame Tussaud's Rock Circus Hall of Fame were revealed to the public.

RICK: On the first day's sitting, a photographer shoots a picture of you for the exact pose your dummy model will have. Dickhead here, and I say it myself, takes on a smiling pose, a grin – and that's how the picture came out. It meant that, from that moment on, when they were doing all the modelling, I'd have to be smiling.

They are so meticulous, they even strip you down to your knickers. They pinpoint your head, your nose, your cheekbones, so that they have the exact dimensions, the exact angles. You stand for half an hour in the pose you've taken, have a five-minute break and then adopt that pose again. So in every session, I had to smile in just the way I did in the first picture. No matter how long it all took, I had to be laughing.

I had geezers running round with rubber gloves on their heads doing chicken impressions so that he could get another picture of me laughing in exactly the same way. I used to think of the most ridiculous things to make myself laugh. It's very hard to laugh all the time, and this was even harder than it might have been, because all the laugh lines on your face have to be the same – if they aren't, it doesn't work. So not only did I have to laugh constantly, but I had to laugh in a specific way.

FRANCIS: We were standing on this circular stand, they were spinning us about and taking pictures from every angle. They're really looking at you, examining you closely and that's a little unsettling, too. Then they put this mould in your mouth to get your teeth perfectly – it's just like being at the dentist.

RICK: They hand you a guitar and then put the neck of the guitar through a box. Then you put your hand in the box and they fill it to mould it. It takes at least fifteen minutes to get your hand out, and you begin to wonder whether you'll ever get it out again, whether you've lost it for good. The actual sessions were painstaking. They take a snip of your eyebrow. And when it comes to your hair, they have to match it strand for strand. Actually, the thorough job they do is quite incredible. They're not mucking about, they're doing it properly.

FRANCIS: Afterwards, when the model is finished and you see it, it's weird to look at yourself from behind.

RICK: I found it very strange to walk around the back of myself, because normally you never see your whole back view. Now we know what we look like from behind. As long as no-one comes and sticks pins in us, I guess we're all right.

FRANCIS: It's funny to be in a position where people can recognize you on the street. You forget that you've got this face that people know. The other day I was in an American diner near my house and I said something. The guy behind the counter said: 'I knew it was you.' As soon as someone says something like that, I have to think, How do I look, do I look too old, do I look like *him*?

Rick and I were at a gig a while ago, when we walked out on the stage to watch the crew taking the stuff down and these girls came up, obviously up for it, and one went: 'Oh.' I said: 'What?' and she said: 'I thought you were taller and more . . . ' 'More what?' I asked. 'What do you mean?' People have this vision of you and if it doesn't correspond exactly, they're disappointed.

I went out with my ex-wife to a restaurant once and I heard somebody say: 'He's only come out to be recognized.' That couldn't be further from the truth. If you're in a restaurant you can hear people whispering; this whispering goes round and then you feel them staring at you. It's fucking embarrassing to have people stare at me when I'm eating.

RICK: When you're eating, you're halfway through your meal and someone comes over to ask you for an autograph, you think, Why couldn't they have waited until I've finished? The majority of people who ask for autographs are fine, but then you get your 'gallons'.

'Gallon' is a nickname we have for a certain type of person. In that movie *Airplane*, there's a guy who's talking so much that the Indian chap sitting beside him tips a gallon of petrol over himself and threatens to set himself on fire. If someone is talking to you too much, is a pain in the ass, won't go away, he's a gallon – gallon of petrol. In the end you have to blank someone like that out, because otherwise they'll sit down with you in a restaurant, anywhere. They'll move in on you and you can't get away.

We've got what we call 'gallon alerts' now and 'gallon passes'. A gallon pass is a box of Swan Vestas put in a laminated ticket pass. We say to anyone who is being a gallon, when you come along to the gig, wear this around your neck, it will get you anywhere. All the crew and all the security know about gallons and if they see someone with one of these passes, they know their job is to keep him or her away from us. The gallon thinks, 'Oh, great. I've just been given a special pass', when it actually means they won't be able to get anywhere near us.

When you don't get recognized, though, I suppose you have to start worrying. It's very flattering really when you're in the street and you hear someone say: 'Oh, that's whatsit from whatsit.' Funnily enough, people will come up to me and say: 'I've been a Quo fan for years, Francis.' Right: they've been a Quo fan for years and they think *I'm* Francis.

FRANCIS: I was with Reggie once somewhere and someone asked him for his autograph and he said: 'I'm not Elton John.' You could see this guy getting more and more brought down, because he knew it *was* Elton John. But Reg just kept on going: 'No. I'm not Elton John.' Being recognized like that and asked for your autograph can take you differently on different days, depending on what mood you're in.

RICK: I think we've all done what Reggie did at one point or another. I took my son Harry to Longleat a little while ago; we were in the restaurant and a guy sent his girlfriend over to talk to me. She had a northern accent and she said: 'My boyfriend asked me to come over because he thinks you're from Status Quo.' So I put on a northern accent myself and said: 'No I'm bloody not and I keep getting mistaken for that geezer and it's starting to make me sick.'

You do get to a point, if it's a hot day and you're stressed or whatever, when you think, Oh no, please leave me alone. It happens very rarely. 99.9 per cent of the time, I'm only too happy to sign autographs. I'd much rather be semi-famous than not famous at all.

FRANCIS: If someone asks me for my autograph I agree, or I make a joke and say: 'I knew it was me all along' – anything to stop the embarrassment. I used to like to go to fairgrounds, but I can't any more. It starts with the odd person and then it spreads like wildfire – they come looking for you.

One person asks: 'Please sign, just one, for me.' Then someone else does, and I think I'll just do three or four. Suddenly there are all these people queuing up and by the time I get to the end, I hear someone say: 'Who *is* he, anyway?' How can they ask me for an autograph when they don't know who I am? I'm standing there shaking giving autographs. If I'm at work, fine, I'm used to being Jack the Lad at work, but if I'm not, it can be nerve-racking.

RICK: One guy came up to me on a boat and said: 'I know you from somewhere.' I said: 'Probably because I'm in Status Quo.' He said: 'No, that's not it. No, you're not', shook his head and walked away.

When I was young, I had pictures of stars up on my wall, and I'd think, 'Oh, will it ever happen to me? And when it does, you've got to appreciate it, you can't turn around and tell people you won't sign autographs. I've actually seen a huge star do that; he was standing there, and only three people were waiting for his autograph and he refused. That's not on to me. It's those people who have put you there in the first place. You should never forget that.

FRANCIS: Occasionally, being someone people recognize can be a little frightening. There was one woman who used to come round to my house all the time. I'd talk to her for a few minutes, but I'd never let her in. The next thing I knew, I got umpteen letters, saying things like, I've been on your yacht, I've been on your plane, I've been talking to you on the telephone. All these absurd stories. But she was so persistent and so convinced all this was happening that even my mum began to believe there was something to it.

One night she came round at about eleven o'clock and just stood in the garden looking through the windows. I thought, Uh-oh, a nutcase, and called the police. They found her in the garden and then they came to me and said: 'She says this, she says that – is it true?' I don't have a yacht. I don't have a plane. She'd made up everything, and I had to convince the police that she was lying after *I'd* called *them*.

She used to send me tapes of herself singing songs. And one evening my family and I were sitting around talking about that Phil Collins cover of 'You Can't Hurry Love'. The next morning a copy of that single came through the letter-box, so she must have been listening in somehow, she must have had her ear to the front door, which was a weird thought. Eventually she disappeared.

There was another girl who used to come to every single gig we did, she saw every show on the tour. She always wore dark clothes and she had dark curly hair and she was very quiet. I'd talk to her a little, but it began to get out of hand. I had to keep her away from me because she always went straight for me. At one gig, we got out of the bus, we checked security – I had told them to make sure to keep her away – and I kept my head down as I went into the building. As soon as I got in and put my head up – *whap!* She'd landed on my back, wrapped her arms around my neck. She was a strong little thing – it was hard to get her off. There wasn't anything freaky about her, but she certainly knew how to make her presence known.

With such a high public profile, Rick and Francis are inevitably invited to appear on numerous television chat shows. An appearance on Terry Wogan's Wogan *on 28 August 1991 turned out to be completely different to what they expected.*

RICK: The *Wogan* show was awful. Some interviewers put you at ease immediately and you can put them at their ease – even if they have any reservations about you or they haven't done their homework properly. That didn't happen with Terry.

FRANCIS: We'd known him for years on and off, and this was one of those things that was supposed to be good for our career, to do the 'sit down and chat' routine. I thought it was going to be reasonable. We started talking – Rick and I can do it when we get going, we are capable of taking whatever he throws at us and playing with it and handing it back, but he wouldn't let us.

RICK: Francis and I can hold the fort, no problem. Wogan didn't have to carry us. But it was very much *his* show – Gloria Hunniford was wonderful when we did her *Sunday, Sunday* show. When she asked us a question, she'd let us answer it. But Wogan would ask us something and we'd be halfway through our answer – Francis and I would be building up one of our ping-pong patter routines where we're batting it backwards and forwards and eventually it becomes funny – when suddenly Wogan would butt in and change direction. He'd be on to something else and we hadn't finished our point. It wasn't a question of time running out. We're professionals, we understand about that. There was plenty of time.

I thought we'd be all right because I always quite enjoyed his show, but I sussed then and afterwards that he changed tack so often it made it difficult for his guests. You couldn't make it flow.

FRANCIS: I think that's why he lost the show.

RICK: Clearly, with us, it just didn't gel – maybe he didn't understand where we were coming from. Our sense of humour, if you leave us to it, will come across. I'd been looking forward to doing the show, but from one minute in, I thought, Uh-oh, this isn't working. When you're doing live television you can't suddenly barge in and say: 'Hold it, hold it! We haven't finished our point!'

FRANCIS: Any time we tried to be a little witty, he shut us down. His mike was slightly louder than ours, too. This was just before the show went off the air. I found it really off-putting at the time because it could have been good.

I enjoyed the Michael Aspel show we did, though. Aspel was good. He went on about the three-chord thing, how Quo plays only three chords and I said: 'I don't know why everyone keeps banging on about this three-chord thing.' Dawn French was on with us and she turned and asked: 'So what's "Caroline", then?' and I said: 'Three chords.' Then she said: 'What was "Down, Down"?' and I said: 'Three chords', and it was really funny, very good.

RICK: It was a nice little bit of roasting. We like things like that. And Michael Aspel is good at letting things flow. He asks amusingly mysterious questions sometimes, but it's lighthearted. We enjoyed ourselves, so I suspect that the viewers did as well.

On 22 September 1991, Status Quo made rock history. Showing stamina and style, the band played four gigs over the UK in twelve hours – the Sheffield International Centre, Glasgow SE and CC, Birmingham NEC and Wembley. Thanks to generous sponsorship from John Nelligan at the Britannia Music Club, the proceeds from the four shows – in excess of £250,000 – were split between Nordoff-Robbins Music Therapy, the Brits School for Performing Arts and local children's charities co-ordinated by the four radio stations which co-promoted the event: Capital FM, Hallam FM, BRMB and Radio Clyde. In order to accomplish this feat, they had to race from city to city on a schedule so tight that every minute counted.

FRANCIS: Rick and I weren't sure when David Walker came up with 'Rock 'Til You Drop' as an album title. What we didn't know at the time was that he also had this idea of doing four shows in one day as a promotional exercise to launch the album. We knew we needed a song and we both envisaged some heavy-metal, up-tempo rock number, but Andrew Bown had the 'Rock 'Til You Drop' song and we liked it because it went against expectations. The title made you think it was going to be a hard-rock song, when actually it has a nice, slower beat. So we agreed to have 'Rock 'Til You Drop' as the album title.

RICK: The idea blossomed and Andrew came up with the song and we thought, Fine. Then David asked whether we thought we could do four gigs in one day. Rather than do the usual thing and put up posters on walls to advertise the album, he wanted us to go out on a limb and do something completely different. That way we would achieve massive media exposure, promote the album, raise money for charity and get into the *Guinness Book of Records* – all in one go.

David's good at coming up with original, slightly off-the-wall ideas like that. He'd been the one who suggested that we have our twenty-fifth anniversary at Butlin's and he came up with the idea of the Absolutely Quo campaign. He'd seen that there had

been an 'Absolutely Queer' poster campaign in California 'outing' supposed famous gays and lesbians, so he decided we should 'out' closet Quo fans. There were posters printed up, saying Absolutely Quo and we outed people such as John Major and Jonathan Ross, people David was convinced were secret head-banging Quo fans.

The 'Rock 'Til You Drop' idea sounded a little naff at first, but then we thought it might be fun, so we told him we thought we could do it. We also told him we thought he was stark-raving, fucking mad.

FRANCIS: Deciding to do it was the easy part. Putting it all together was a logistical nightmare and took a full nine months to achieve. David set up an operations centre at Handle with Iain Jones supervising everyone in the office to organize the schedule on a minute-by-minute basis. Our production manager Peter Hillier had to organize four separate stages, four identical sets of equipment and four different road crews. The four venues must have thought that our promoter Maurice Jones and our agent Neil Warnock were completely nuts when they said that they wanted to book each venue for an hour at off the wall times.

RICK: Simon and Christine Porter, our publicists, had to be everywhere at once on the day, so Christine was following us with plane and helicopter loads of national media from around the world and Simon was arriving at each gig slightly before us to organize everyone before we arrived. Just on the flying side, there were over 100 take-offs and landings.

FRANCIS: Nobody left a stone unturned to make the event happen. In the two weeks leading up to the day Iain and Simon were working twenty-hour days, adjusting the schedule a fraction here, a fraction there to make up time. Our road crew, as always, were wonderful and worked their balls off for this one.

Quo had over two hundred and fifty people working on the day to make it happen. They needed 60 drums, 200 amplifiers, 62 guitars, 165 cymbals,

12 miles of cable, 50 cameras, 200,000 watts of power, 2500 lights, 8 helicopters, 5 jets, 20 limousines and 16 police escorts.

RICK: Chris Tarrant flew around with us to make a documentary on the event. He's a complete nutter and one of our oldest friends. He turned up on the day dressed as Biggles and was in a state of collapse by the end. We felt satisfied that we had got our own back for all the times he threw custard pies into our faces and tipped buckets of beans over our heads back in the old 'Tis Was' days.

FRANCIS: On top of all this David decided that we should launch 'Rock 'Til You Drop' a month before the event in a hangar at RAF Northolt. We had four stages, one in each corner of the venue, complete with backline and lighting rigs with each venue name and time of playing above the relevant stage. Chris Tarrant then announced the event to the assembled media, flying around like a madman from stage to stage. It was only then I realized that he was obviously as mental as we were.

RICK: We arrived for the launch in two Second World War Spitfires – an incredible experience. We then used the stages to rehearse for the day itself by playing on the exact stage and working with the crew which would be at each venue. We had only three members of our own crew at all four venues – Peter Hillier, Mike 'Bunny' Warren on sound and Pat Marks, our lighting director. Although the stages were all identical, the sound was slightly different on each one. We rehearsed solidly for almost three weeks to get everything right for the day.

FRANCIS: Suddenly, somewhere along the line, we thought, Who's going to come out to see us at two in the afternoon in Sheffield? And we knew we didn't want to charge people money for a promo like that, so we decided to put the ticket price at six pounds and give the proceeds to Nordoff-Robbins.

We wanted to make sure that the audience was getting value for money, so we had competitions and we gave away our guitars after we'd played them on stage, and we tried to make it all fun for them.

I didn't really think it was going to work, but we did remarkably well. Rhino and Jeff gave it their all, the way they always do, even at two in the afternoon.

When we were in the helicopter on the first leg of the trip from Northolt to Sheffield, we had to take evasive action because of another plane too near to us. We did a quick dive.

RICK: There was nothing to worry about, really. It was only a 747 on our starboard side travelling at about four hundred miles per hour – there was easily eight feet to spare.

FRANCIS: I was worried about Sheffield, because we were playing in the new venue there, but seven or eight thousand people turned up in the afternoon. We could have done it with three thousand, but it was fantastic to have that many people. We thought, Blimey, you've turned out. Thanks! That was wonderful.

RICK: We were relatively match fit and we thought, This is going to be a doddle. We played for an hour, went straight back on the helicopter, straight on to the jet, jetted up to Glasgow, did the gig there – and we even had three minutes to spare when we got to Glasgow. Other than that we had absolutely no time – it was dash, dash, dash.

FRANCIS: We had had to start off at the BBC at eight o'clock, so it was a long day.

RICK: If something had gone wrong, or if we had kept an audience waiting, it would have been awful. We managed to complete the whole event, with only forty-nine minutes to spare.

FRANCIS: I was starting to lose it on the way back from Birmingham to Wembley. I fell asleep on Rick's shoulder.

RICK: It felt just like old times. There we were, cuddled up together on an aeroplane.

FRANCIS: When we got into the helicopter in Birmingham, there was some nut standing right up against the glass looking at us, saying he wanted to ride with us to London. He was staring like a madman, shouting: 'You bastards won't take me to London!' We had no idea how he had managed to get on to the tarmac.

Someone finally got him away – we couldn't move with him standing there; if we'd started up, the helicopter would have lopped his bloody head off. He was the type you wouldn't want to meet in a dark alley. You couldn't tell what he was going to do.

RICK: The day had been non-stop. The mental and the physical pace was incredible. By the time we got to Wembley, the crowd was so fabulous that we got our energy back, but halfway through the set, we did begin to feel drained. I think we were in shock by the end of it. We came offstage and we'd just sat down, when David came in and said: 'Come on, you have to get back on. Norris McWhirter is going to give you certificates for the *Guinness Book of Records*.'

Then I noticed that my mother was backstage, all dressed up. My cousin Sue was there as well, and I said: 'What are you doing here?' They said: 'Don't you know?' and I said I didn't have a clue. Apparently they were going to do a *This Is Your Life* on us. But it never happened.

FRANCIS: I wouldn't have wanted to be part of that anyway. I would have hated it. It was after midnight, we'd just done four shows all over the country; the prospect of going to sit on a stage and do a television programme wasn't for me. We would have been there until two in the morning. And they might have brought in John Coghlan and Alan Lancaster.

After the court case, Alan said to someone in the Press: 'Everything will be fine as long as I don't come within three feet of them' – 'them' being Rick and me. We knew exactly what Alan was trying to say. He considers himself to have a three-foot reach for a punch, so the idea was, if we get too close, he'll clobber us. Although I have to say three feet is a very long

CERTIFICATE

GUINNESS BOOK OF RECORDS

AS A FINALE TO THEIR 25TH ANNIVERSARY

YEAR, STATUS QUO PLAYED FOUR MAJOR UK

VENUES IN 11 HOURS 11 MINUTES

ON THE 'ROCK 'TIL YOU DROP' TOUR ON

21 SEPTEMBER 1991. THE EVENT COVERED

SHEFFIELD, GLASGOW, BIRMINGHAM AND LONDON.

DONALD McFARLAN   NORRIS McWHIRTER

reach for a guy his size. So if Alan had been brought on, who knows what might have happened.

RICK: Apart from that, if the two of us were sitting there, they'd have had to say: 'Rick Parfitt and Francis Rossi: These are your lives!' I can imagine some old teacher of Francis's coming on whom *I've* never seen in *my* life. Perfect! And what would they have done with that red book? Ripped it in half?

As it turned out, we never did the show. David Walker had insisted that it be a show about the band, not our personal lives with wives and children and the whole bit, but the *This Is Your Life* people were heading in that direction. They wanted it to be about Francis and me, not the history of Status Quo as a band, so it got scrapped at the last minute, which was just as well considering how tired we all were.

FRANCIS: Our first manager, Pat Barlow, was there because of the *This Is Your Life* bit, which I was very glad about – not only because it was nice to see him, but also because we found out that he hadn't been paid money he was owed from way back when. He'd been owed three or four thousand pounds when he stopped managing us. As far as we were concerned, he'd been paid. He hadn't been, though, and naturally he thought Rick and I were responsible.

Rick and I felt awful. We didn't know anything about it and we felt dreadful. Of course we said that we'd pay him straight off, but as soon as he found out that we hadn't known about it, he said: 'Oh no, don't worry.' That's the kind of guy he is. We insisted and said: 'Give it to your grandchildren or something, but please take it.' He's a beautiful person. His wife was a beautiful person, too. Someone screwed him in our name – that's what happens a lot in this business.

We take more chances now than we used to with the old band. We could have looked complete fools with the 'Rock 'Til You Drop' or the 'Anniversary Waltz', but they worked.

Some time ago we were supposed to be doing a deal with Perrier. We had this song from 'Rockin' All Over the World'

Some time ago we were supposed to be doing a deal with
Perrier. We had this song from 'Rockin' All Over the World'
which they wanted for their ad – they were going to do Status
Queau, which was a good concept, because that's what Perrier is all
about – status water. For some reason they dropped out at the last
minute – it was a brilliant ad, so I don't know why. We were upset
because by then we were committed to going with a single which
fit their campaign – 'Can't Give You More' with its chorus 'eau,
eau, eau, eau' – which we wouldn't necessarily have gone with.

RICK: We'll do commercial link-ups like that as long as it's
something creditable, not silly. As long as we think it's fine,
then if it backfires, it's our fault. If it's successful – fantastic, if
it's not, you take the rap for it. But the chances are anything will
work if you do it properly, if you give it 100 per cent.

*In August 1992, Status Quo were invited by Radio One to headline their
twenty-fifth anniversary celebrations at a massive 'Party In The Park' at
Sutton Park in Birmingham. Quo played a blistering forty-five-minute
set to 125,000 people and presented a celebration birthday cake to Radio
One DJs past and present. The band was introduced on stage by Alan
'Fluff' Freeman, a fitting tribute from one of Francis's and Rick's oldest
friends and staunchest supporters throughout their career. A live album
of the event 'Live Alive Quo' was released in October, coinciding with
an invitation for the band to play at 'The Last Tattoo' in Berlin, in the
presence of Queen Elizabeth II. Perhaps an unlikely Status Quo fan,
the Queen proved to be gracious and welcoming.*

FRANCIS: Because the Berlin Wall had come down, the military
was changing the British troop positions, moving soldiers out, so
we were there for the last tattoo. After we'd played, the Queen
said to me: 'You're really quite good, aren't you?' and I thought,
That's nice, but what do you mean by the 'quite'?

RICK: She said to me: 'These aren't quite the conditions you're
used to playing in, I imagine.' I said: 'No, ma'am. We're not used

to having the audience so far away.' She sat right by the front and later she said: 'I thought you did extremely well.' She was very nice and a lovely looking lady, actually. She has stunning eyes.

FRANCIS: We put a few noses out of joint among the high-ups in the military there. They put us in a line with all the top-ranking Army people who were dressed up in their sashes and their spurs. At first we were in the middle of the line, then one of the chief aides came and said: 'Status Quo, follow me,' and we were moved to the front of the line.

You expect the Royals to use their privileged position when they can, but we were on a plane trip to the West Indies once, on the way to Monserrat, sitting in First Class, when a stewardess came up and asked us if we'd like to move. Princess Margaret had come aboard and First Class was full, so she didn't have a seat. We said: 'No, we didn't want to move,' and we saw Princess Margaret later, sitting in the economy section – in one of those seats the stewardess has which you can put a curtain around. She hadn't made a fuss about it, there was no big to-do. I thought that was very reasonable of her.

When we met Fergie at a Nordoff-Robbins fund-raising event, we thought she was a right fun girl. I think she's been given a hard time and I feel for her.

RICK: We know that Princess Di is a Quo fan, and I remember being impressed when we saw her at the Café Royale. There was a Capital Radio lunch for the Save a London Child campaign. After they'd done the line-up, which is normally quite stiff, we all sat down to listen to some talent contest, and Di took her jacket off. She seemed very relaxed and it was lovely to see her looking so much at ease. She was sitting at a table with Roger Daltrey on one side and Bill Wyman on the other. We were a little miffed about that – we would have liked to sit beside her.

FRANCIS: That's all right. Daltrey and Wyman are older than us. Age before beauty.

14

On stage, Rick and Francis are the perfect hard-rocking duo; their voices and their actions complement each other and have done for twenty-eight years. Offstage, they can create the same magic together, trading banter and decades of shared experiences.

A key to their ability to get on so well and last so long is the fact that they are both strong individuals who have different tastes, different enthusiasms and different styles of living. They are not carbon copies of one another; if anything they are like opposite sides of a coin. Their lives, when they are not touring or recording, are spent in pursuit of their own kinds of happiness.

FRANCIS: In 1974 I bought the house I'm living in and moved in in 1975. I loved it then and I love it now. It's on part of an estate which was once owned by a father and son. The father lived in a house near by and the son lived in what is now my house. As the years went by, plots have been sold off, but originally the whole area was owned by those two. The son put real love into this place and I'm trying to do the same.

I've added on to the house and I've built a studio which I had soundproofed with four and a half tons of lead. I've always wanted to have a studio like it, and I enjoy working there. I'm very much a homebody. The last time I came back from a tour, I stayed in this house for three months, I didn't even go outside the gates.

People might be surprised by the things I like doing. I can get off on cleaning the cooker or clearing out a drawer. When we had that big storm in October 1987, my sons and I got out the chain-saw and spent days getting rid of all the mess, clearing up; we loved it.

My sons all live with me, and we've turned out to be a musical family. The other night I was in the studio; Nicholas was in the control room working with his band; Kieran was rehearsing with his band in his bedroom and Simon was rehearsing for something he's doing. Even Patrick and Finn, who are young, go around playing imaginary guitars, strumming away. The idea of a family all involved in music has always appealed to me.

I used to lie awake at night worrying that my children would get ribbed at school. I knew they'd be targets for some not-so-nice comments, because they had me for a father. An uncle of mine once told me that when people pull, you push – when they push, you pull; and I've never forgotten that. So I told my kids that they shouldn't get upset or react to any comments. If someone says: 'Your dad's a prick, isn't he?' they should just say: 'You should try *living* with him.' If they say: 'He can't play the guitar to save his life, can he?' the reply should be: 'No – I'm still trying to teach him.' If you react or get defensive, that means that whoever is giving you a hard time will keep going, but if you agree with him, even take it one step further than he has, it's like pulling the rug from under his feet. He can't do anything.

I've thought occasionally that my job has been unfair on my children. Because of the kind of business this is, life at home has to revolve around me: Dad's got a gig, Dad's got a rehearsal; things like that. And I've missed a lot because of all the touring. I've been away for half of Finn's life, for example, and I don't think that's fair on him. I was away for most of Simon's life, most of Kieran's life. And I was in Nassau when Patrick was born. I've been at the births of my other children, though, and it does make me cry.

When I saw Nicholas being born, it was wonderful. I remember cutting the cord; it was a close run thing, however, because the day he was born, the band had to catch a boat to go on a European tour. Luckily, the timing was right, and I cut the cord, ran out, called my mother-in-law to tell her the baby was a boy – which she refused to believe, because she was convinced he was going to be a girl – and we just managed to catch the boat. Eileen had a Caesarean when she had Finn, and I watched that, too. I'm not squeamish about those things at all. I found it fascinating.

When I'm at home I have a daily routine. I work in the studio in the morning, take a break for lunch, go back in the afternoon, and then do my exercises. I like to keep fit. I can outrun anyone these days. I went vegetarian a while ago which has helped me feel much better. I used to think veggies were a pain in the ass, but if you don't go on and on about it, it's fine. It suits me. I've had acupuncture as well and I'm interested in homeopathic medicine.

I remember Alan Lancaster saying once: 'You've got to do something about that,' and I said: 'Something about what?' 'Your body,' he answered. And he was right. I used to have a piece of toast for breakfast, not eat until six in the evening and then have whatever I liked. And in the days when I was drinking and doing coke, I was really messing up my system. I think I've got off lightly because I'm still alive. My personality changed then as well. When I was doing coke, I became a social animal. I was out there doing anything, going to all sorts of places, and that's not me.

People sometimes ask me if I believe in God, and I say: 'Yes,' because I do, although I couldn't sit down and explain exactly what it is I believe in. It's just a knowledge I have, a feeling. If someone says: 'How can you believe? You can't prove God exists,' I answer: 'Yes, but you can't prove he doesn't either.' I think they're afraid to admit to themselves that there might be a God. When I get really involved in a conversation like that, I add: 'Fine, if there's no God, I'll come over and rape your daughter. And then I'll kill her.' And the person will look shocked and say: 'Oh no, you can't do that!'

So I say: 'Why not? If there's no God, what difference does it make?' 'Because it would be wrong,' is the answer I always get. 'If there's no God, why would it be wrong? All that I would be doing is just breaking a man-made rule.' 'But it's wrong,' the person will protest. 'You just know it would be wrong. It's the feeling you have.' 'Exactly. It's the feeling you have,' I answer, and that sums it up for me. People do know the difference between right and wrong, there *is* a difference between right and wrong, and as far as I'm concerned, that feeling, that knowledge, stems from God.

I always used to think that I'd be dead by the time I was forty-five, and that thought didn't bother me. But now my ambition in life is to get old. I didn't think forty was going to be as good as it was, and growing older has just kept getting better. People talk about the good old days, but for me, the good old days are now.

The other night I heard about someone dying at eighty-one and I thought, Shit, that's not long enough. I want to watch that magnolia I've planted grow. I used to see those old boys playing bowls and think, You must be joking. Now I think, Oh, that looks nice.

RICK: When I've got leisure time, I like to spend it leisurely. When I had my studio, I'd work, but not all the time like Francis. I relax a lot – almost to the point of laziness. When I'm in the mood, I take time out to write, but I can't sit down and force it.

I like to get away, I like to change the colour completely and do something totally different. I loved learning how to fly. Now I've let that drop, but I'd like to take it up again seriously. I used to have a boat as well, and being out on the water is heaven for me.

Because I can get claustrophobic sometimes, I love the open space and the faraway horizon on the ocean. I sold the boat, but I'd like to have another one down in Southampton so that I could go out on the Solent. But it has to be a power boat – I don't like sails. It must have an engine, go fast. I'm still a kid when it comes to that sort of thing: batting along in the air or on the sea – as long as I'm steaming along, I'm quite happy.

I've always loved sports as well. I've played some cricket matches for the Lord's Taverners and that's a nice way to spend a day, although in the last match I played, I was called on to bowl and that was something of a disaster. I'm a fast bowler, of course, but I hadn't bowled since I left school, when I was captain of the cricket team. At the Lord's Taverners match, I thought, No problem, I'll remember how to bowl, it will all come back to me. Although our side was a showbiz side – people like Chris Tarrant and Bill Oddie play for the Taverners – we were up against semi-pros that day. I remember Alan Lamb's brother was playing against us.

I came up to bowl and I hadn't bothered to measure the run-up, as I was sure that I could perform as I did thirty years ago, so I let the ball go and it hardly reached the batsman. By the time it got to him, it was trickling along the ground. I thought, God, this wicket's longer than when I was a kid. Of course it wasn't. On my second ball, I reckoned, I'll really give this one some. It ended up going past the batsman's ear, I literally threw it at him. It was wide, of course, seriously wide. I never did find my length or line. I was probably hit for thirty off each over. But I scored eighteen, which wasn't bad. I'm playing again soon, much to everyone's misfortune.

Cars are my passion. From a very young age, I've had a love affair with them. As a boy, I used to look at the wheels, the shiny hubcaps, and be completely fascinated.

I liked to get inside a car and see how the bonnet looked; it always seemed bigger from the inside. It was my idea of sex when I was nine or ten, it used to turn me on. My dad's first car was a Standard 8 with a little Union Jack on the front. The registration was DHO 455 which I really wish I still had. If anyone's got it, I'd buy it in a second. I loved all the little gadgets, the little indicator arms which would come out at the side like flaps. We'd buy parking lights to clip on to the window, and we'd put a little oil stove under the engine at night to keep it warm.

When he first took me out in the Standard, my dad turned to me and said: 'Look at that, son, thirty miles an hour.' Thirty was really pushing it back then. By the time I was twelve I was a complete car freak.

The first car I had was a Standard 8, like my dad's but a newer model. My mother bought it for me for thirty-two pounds. It was creamy, smooth, so I nicknamed it a Creamord.

I told my mother when I was fifteen that it was my ambition to have a Jag by the time I was twenty-one. I bought one when I was nineteen. That was after 'Matchstick Men' came out. I had a Jag, Francis had a Jag, Alan had a Jag, but theirs were blue and mine was maroon. My father ended up smashing it because it was too powerful for him, and that was the first time Francis saw me cry.

My first really wonderful car was a Mercedes 280SE, silver, twin-head vertical lamps. That was a beautiful car. I smashed that one up the night before I was flying to Germany to marry Marietta in her village.

My Porsche 911 was my all-time favourite car. I really knew that car and it knew me – we used to talk, chat. We were a fairly potent team.

I always wanted to be a racing-car driver, but strangely enough, I haven't been around a track. I enjoy go-karting, though. I've had so many cars through the years, but I feel passionately about all of them. I can't help it – wherever I go, a car will plonk itself in front of me and say: buy me.

I know my love of cars will last for ever, it won't go away. It's part of my character. So is my need for independence. It took me two marriages and three children to discover that I'm not cut out to be a married man. It may be selfish, but I *have* to have my independence. I found I didn't have that in marriage. I've always been afraid of letting people down. If I let myself down, I can handle it, but I don't like letting other people down. Within a marriage I found the temptations were too great for me – not necessarily the temptations of other women, but my desire to do what I wanted to do when I wanted to do it.

It's much better for me to be on my own, a free spirit. I come and go as I please now. And if I'm pissed off, I can shut myself away, which I love. I don't have to answer to anyone, and no-one has to cope with whatever mood I'm in. I'm an up-and-down person, my moods vary a lot and to impose those on someone else seems unfair to me.

These days I live life the way I want to, whereas before I lived a lot of my life for other people. That was my own choice – but I've realized that I have enough problems looking after myself. I don't want the responsibility of looking after someone else on a full-time basis. There's too much fun to be had, and I've got to have fun, because I think fun should be part of life. Other people can have fun in different ways, they can be happy in much more settled lives, and I respect that. But the only way for me is to be on my own, be free. I need to make my own decisions which won't affect anyone else directly. Then, if I make a mistake it's down to me – I don't hurt anyone else or put anyone else in an awkward position.

Now that I've recognized what makes me tick, and what's best for me, I have better relationships with the people I'm close to. I'm much happier now than I've been for years.

15

*After twenty-eight years together, Francis and Rick are used to criti-
cism; they know that certain critics label them a 'three-chord' band
with no musical diversity and they know how to answer those jibes,
both thoughtfully and humorously. The fads and trends in the music
world don't affect them. But they've also had to deal with the sad
fact that, over the years, various people have tried to split them up
and cause trouble in their friendship. However, because their friendship
goes back so far and has been so strong, they know where they stand,
with each other and with themselves.*

FRANCIS: Anyone who really listens to our music will know
that we have more than three chords. If you look at the singles,
you could say that some of them are the same, but if you look at
'Rock 'n' Roll', 'Proposin'', 'Marguerita Time' or 'Living On An

Island', you'll see they're not the same at all. And if you listen to all the album tracks, you'll hear a lot of different songs.

Record companies, when they see a success, go with it. They release the singles they think will appeal most to the public. That doesn't mean those are the only kinds of songs we do, it simply means that those are the ones which sell the most. When we released 'Living On An Island', people asked why we'd done something so different. You can't win.

RICK: There are seven chords in that one.

FRANCIS: Everything UB40 has done has the same beat, but no-one says to them: 'Why do you do reggae all the time?'

RICK: And every rap record is exactly the same. I heard a rap single the other day and counted one chord in it – the opening one.

FRANCIS: *I* heard a *Spitting Image* piss-take of rap recently and the lyrics were: 'No lyrics, no lyrics.' That sums it up perfectly for me.

RICK: A lot of thought must go into some of those rap lyrics. And we thought, Down, down, deeper and down was boring.

FRANCIS: If the critics are right about us, that means that we're wrong to play the music we play and the people who come to see us, in ever-increasing numbers, are wrong as well. A lot of the people who come to our concerts go to see other acts. They'll see Dire Straits or the Pet Shop Boys, Motorhead, Guns N' Roses – their taste is quite diverse. So presumably, they're fine when they go to see the other bands, but suddenly turn into dickheads when they come to see us.

RICK: In the early Eighties it was very unfashionable to come and see Quo. Then, around 1989, 1990, we started to feel trendy again. It was 'cool' to see us.

FRANCIS: When we used to play in Sheffield, we'd be playing to around two thousand people. But the year before last we went there and nine thousand people turned up. Last year we played to eleven and a half thousand – with no album or single out. So we must be doing something right.

RICK: Three chords.

FRANCIS: Three chords that people like. People think you've sold out if you do something commercial. With my Italian background, I grew up listening to opera. I'd listen to the great arias – 'Nessun Dorma', 'La donne mobile', and those have commercial choruses, they're catchy, they appeal to people. They're not complicated, but they're what the public wants to hear.

UB40 came back on to the music scene and into the Number One slot this year with 'I Can't Help Falling in Love With You'. That was a very clever move – they found an old favourite to cover in their reggae style. That was the song which Roy Lynes used to sing when The Spectres were at Butlin's, the only one we did which got applause. And all sorts of people have covered it. Andy Williams, whoever – people who kids today would think were definitely uncool. But UB40 do it and it still appeals – that particular song is an old Italian one, in fact. It has been around for ever and will remain that way because it has a lasting appeal. That's why I wonder sometimes about rap. Will people be humming rap songs in twenty years? Will groups then be bringing back cover versions of rap classics?

I used to say in interviews that I liked Abba, and no-one could believe it. I couldn't stand looking at them, but I thought they had some great songs. I like Roxette and that's frowned upon too. It's not 'musically correct'.

The whole thing with rock 'n' roll, if we say it started in the late Forties, early Fifties – the idea of rock was to let your hair down and let rip. Well, somewhere along the line, we've lost the point, because we intellectualize about it and become élitist about it. I've read things journalists have said they can see in the music, and I think, What the fuck are you talking about?

I saw a band in America who have been around a long time and the lead singer was doing an interview. He was asked: 'Are you still doing the same stuff you started out playing?' and he said:

'Yes, we're still a rock band.' He didn't elaborate, he didn't need to.

RICK: That sums it up.

FRANCIS: But each time we're criticized, we tend to fall for it. We try to explain, justify ourselves. But that's exactly what we want to say: 'Yes, we're a rock band.'

RICK: In the early days, the criticism stung us, but now it's become a bit of a joke. 'The three-chord lads are back,' and all that. We can laugh about it now, although I think it has worn a bit thin.

FRANCIS: I did get angry when a guy reviewed a gig we did at Wembley years ago and all he could say was that Rick and I were passing dandruff back and forth to each other. He didn't say a word about the crowd – who had gone apeshit that particular night. They like to build people up here and then they love to knock them down. It's the politics of envy.

In the early days, we were the most unlikely band to succeed. And then, when we did succeed on the pop scene, we were the most unlikely band to switch gear and succeed in rock. And when we re-formed, we were the most unlikely band to hold on to our success.

RICK: And we're still the most unlikely band to be there after twenty-eight years.

FRANCIS: Since the beginning, people have tried to split Rick and me up. I know that the desire to come between us is motivated by jealousy, but I can't understand why. I can't spend twenty years reading about me and him being a pair of dickheads who can't play, who are in a lousy band who play the same music all the time, and then figure out why anyone would be jealous. We've been told that we're a pair of wankers and then they try to split us up.

If we were Lennon and McCartney, OK, I might begin to understand. But why us? As far as I'm concerned, we're just these two blokes who have been together a long time and who have had a lot of hit records. But we're the most knocked band ever.

RICK: You could call us a knock and roll band.

We've been asked so many times in interviews, Why does it all sound the same? I'd say that the records aren't the same, but the *sound* is. I don't know exactly how we get that sound, but we intend to keep it. If someone were to go to the chairman of Coca-Cola and say: 'Listen, everyone loves Coke, but it's exactly the same. Each Coke I drink tastes the same, why don't you change it? Throw away that secret formula you have and go for something different,' I think I know where the chairman would tell him to go.

The music we play is basically simple, but not everyone can play it like we do. It has to come from the heart – if you don't play it with fervour and gusto, it will sound like crap. You have to *feel* it, and you have to give it 100 per cent – more, if you can. If you don't, it doesn't work. If there's any secret to our success, that's it.

Some people think, Oh, let's start a band and we'll play like Quo – it will be dead easy. A lot of people have tried to do that and failed because there's something in the way we play it that no-one else can copy.

The music takes you over and you find yourself playing with boundless energy. The music inspires us to play like that – that's why it works so well. The energy is phenomenal – the music raises you and holds you up there, and the audience are up there with you. You never stop running or leaping. At forty-four, I wonder sometimes where I get the energy. I thought I would have slowed down by now, but I get out there and it's kicking and there's nothing like it in the world. It's the best high going.

Our set makes demands on us. It says, in effect, If you want to play me, take me on, you've got to kick ass and play me well. As we can still get goose-pimples playing after so many years, when it's on the money like that, we've got to be doing something right.

As long as our attitude remains like that and we don't get complacent, we'll stay in there. I wouldn't like to slow down and think, Hang on, this ain't like it used to be. As it is at the moment, there's no stopping us.

FRANCIS: People ask us if there's anything left. We still think we're going somewhere, building something.

RICK: We'll last through 1995 at least. We might even hit 2000. But if we do, we'll probably be on a cruise ship. I like the thought of us lasting thirty years. Over the last eighteen years, we virtually haven't stopped. We've been touring on and off throughout every year apart from 1985, and lately we've upped the pace. I tend to think we're going to work our balls off next year, and after that Francis and I will sit down together, have a chat and discuss what we're going to do. The thought of touring is awesome, but once it gets rolling, you go: 'Yeah, we're away.' You get fit while you're touring by the very nature of what you're doing. As long as it's still fresh and the adrenalin flows, we'll keep going.

Looking back, I sometimes wonder what would have happened if we hadn't split up, if Francis and I had had the equivalent of a happy marriage for twenty-eight years without any hiccups. I'm not sure, but I don't think it would have been as interesting.

To be able to get back together, though, had a lot to do with our beginning. During the Butlin's days, we'd spend all our time together, talking about anything. After a while, we were so close that with just a glance I could tell what he was thinking, and vice versa. And then, of course, we developed our own language.

FRANCIS: I daresay that as the years passed, John Coghlan and Alan Lancaster must have found it a serious affront – the way Rick and I would be together. When Rick joined the band in 1967, he was my ally; although I liked the others, there was something about Rick which was closer to me. If I were sitting beside him and our knees touched, he wouldn't jump away – if I touched Coghlan, he'd move like hell. Anything too tactile or too personal was too much. I'm not saying that people shouldn't move, but it's tiny little things like that which count in friendship.

RICK: We used to sit over at Francis's house and design cars – we were both mad about Mini Coopers, so we'd sit there drawing them, talking about them, just hanging out. I'd never known a friendship like that before.

FRANCIS: It was the same for me. That's how I felt.

RICK: Lots of people for various reasons have wanted to wreck our friendship. People have tried and just about succeeded. We had some wilderness years when we weren't getting along. But we know that if we stay together and we're strong, then the band is strong.

It must be pissing a lot of people off that we're back up there and still on top, still kicking ass. For a while, in the mid-Eighties it was as if we were swimming underwater. It's a great feeling when you come up for air.

FRANCIS: No-one can get to us now, or affect us, really, because we believe in what we do. We know we're fucking good no matter what anyone says. It's as simple as that . . .

EPILOGUE

The two men in their forties checking into the hotel in Minehead in October 1990 may have seemed like unusual guests in their long hair and jeans. They may have looked more like rock stars than typical businessmen, but then Francis Rossi and Rick Parfitt have never been typical rock stars, either.

They've never been willing to rest on their success, or take it for granted. Throughout their career, they've performed anywhere and everywhere, on a gruelling, relentless schedule of gigs which would have exhausted anyone less committed to the music. And in the midst of all this hard work, they managed to have fun. Fans going to a Quo concert can't sit still – they respond to the energy and the passion up on stage, and they keep coming back for more.

The spirit of Status Quo is contagious, it's why the Butlin's Ballroom was shaking at the twenty-fifth anniversary celebrations, it's why they still shake packed-out concert halls whenever they play and it's why in September 1993 twenty-five thousand people flocked to see Francis and Rick switch on the annual Blackpool illuminations.

From the moment when Francis and Rick were given their first guitars, they have dedicated themselves to music. And they've always been willing to take risks. They're the young boys who got out on stage as soon as they could, wherever they could, and they're the teenagers who decided that having hits in the charts wasn't enough if they couldn't play the music they wanted to play.

Francis and Rick sacrificed success in the pop world for the chance to go in a different direction and be themselves. They weren't going to bend to fashionable trends – even if that meant playing to an audience of three people at 5 a.m. So they put on their jeans, got out on stage and got down to business; in their case, the business of rock 'n' roll. While other bands came and went on the music scene, Status Quo remained firmly in place, knowing that they could only be comfortable playing the music they believed in.

What they communicate in the music has a lot to do with their characters. They've never, despite the success they've had, been hooked on glamour. They don't see themselves as being above anyone else; they're two men who wanted to be musicians, who like what they're doing and who aren't conceited or prima donnas. People meeting them are surprised at how normal and friendly they are.

Even other rock stars have been surprised. Mark Owen from Take That, says: 'What we liked so much about meeting them was just how friendly and down-to-earth they were. They have been in the business a long time and we are complete newcomers compared to them. But they treated us with respect and that really knocked us out. They weren't at all like big shots looking down on us as just a bunch of kids. They couldn't have been warmer and more encouraging. They were really nice geezers and I'm sure that's why they have survived for so long.'

From the first meeting at Butlin's in 1965, Francis and Rick forged a friendship which has carried them through to the Nineties, one which adds to the spirit of the band because it's a shared love of their work and a shared sense of humour.

They know now where they've been and where they're going, and are happy in their different lifestyles. In their mid-forties, they've reached a stage of contentment, but they're not complacent – the original spark is still there. The true spirit of Status Quo lies in the hearts of the band; they aren't happy unless they're giving 100 per cent. And when they give 100 per cent, the audiences don't just appreciate the effort, they go wild.

As Cliff Richard comments: 'You know what you're going to get with Quo – solid, reliable rock 'n' roll – and to stand in with the Quo army is a great experience.'

As well as giving their all to audiences each time they perform, Status Quo have raised huge sums of money for charities over the years. Although they don't like to take too much credit for their efforts, others recognize the hard work, time and money Quo have donated to good causes. Perhaps the most eloquent thank you on behalf of these charities comes from Prince Charles himself: 'I shall never forget a particular Status Quo concert in 1982 when I was first introduced to the members of the band, all of whom seemed to be contemporaries of mine. Apart from the fact that I became prematurely deaf after that concert, I shall always be deeply grateful to this most enduring of groups for their immense generosity to my Prince's Trust. Their subsequent contribution to worthy causes has been in the order of millions of pounds and so many people have very good reason to be grateful to them.'

Twenty-eight years after their first meeting, Francis Rossi and Rick Parfitt are still going strong. Together, they have created rock history, giving music fans a string of hit songs and decades of hard-rocking concerts. But they aren't about to sit back and bask in their past achievements. Status Quo is a band which loves a challenge, a group of guys who raced all over the country in a day, rocking till they almost – but not quite – dropped. The combination of Francis Rossi, Rick Parfitt, Andrew Bown, John 'Rhino' Edwards and Jeff Rick is unstoppable. Their audiences keep expanding, taking in all age groups, reflecting a vitality which is amazingly fresh.

DJ Alan 'Fluff' Freeman, who was one of the twenty-fifth anniversary party revellers, says: 'Having played their records from the very start, I'm extremely pleased to find that twenty-eight years later they're still drawing enormous crowds and giving as much family entertainment as possible. It's never over until Status Quo finish playing.'

In October 2015, the Butlin's Ballroom might just be rocking to the sounds of a fiftieth-anniversary gig. Book the tickets now. It's sure to be one hell of a show.

APPENDIX

STATUS QUO – THE FACTSHEET

- **STATUS QUO'S** total worldwide record sales exceed 100 million units.

- **STATUS QUO** have recorded 44 British hit singles – more than any other band.

- 22 **QUO** singles have reached the British Top Ten.

- **QUO's** first hit single was **'PICTURES OF MATCHSTICK MEN'** which reached Number 7 in January 1968.

- **FRANCIS ROSSI** and **RICK PARFITT** are the only original members of the current **QUO** line up. Keyboard player **ANDREW BOWN** joined in 1976. **JOHN 'RHINO' EDWARDS** (bass) and **JEFF RICH** (drums) both joined in 1986.

- **QUO** have made more than 100 appearances on BBC TV's 'Top of the Pops' – more than any other group.

- **QUO** have spent over 380 weeks in the British Singles Chart – the sixth highest ever.

- **QUO** have had more hit albums in the British Albums Chart than any other band, apart from The Rolling Stones and The Beach Boys.

- **QUO'S** 1990 **'ROCKIN' ALL OVER THE YEARS'** album has sold over 900,000 units in Great Britain, attaining triple platinum sales status. The album spent over six months in the British Albums Chart, including ten weeks in the Top Ten. Worldwide sales exceed five million.

- In 1982 **QUO** became the first contemporary band to play to Royalty when they performed a sell out charity show attended by **HRH PRINCE CHARLES** at the NEC in Birmingham. All proceeds were donated to the 'Prince's Trust' – the first major fund raising event for the charity.

- In 1981 **QUO** became one of the first recipients of the coveted **SILVER CLEF AWARD**, presented annually by the Nordoff-Robbins Music Therapy Trust for outstanding services to British music.

- In 1985 **QUO** opened **LIVE AID** with the song which was to become the event's anthem **'ROCKIN' ALL OVER THE WORLD'**.

- 1986 saw **QUO** playing three major shows in different countries within a twenty-four-hour period. Using a variety of private planes and boats, the band played in Britain (Knebworth), Switzerland and Denmark.

- In 1988 **QUO** played a record-breaking series of fourteen sell-out shows to over 300,000 people at the giant Olympic Stadium in Moscow.

- **QUO'S** 25th anniversary celebrations in 1990 at Butlin's in Minehead became the media event of the year. Over 300 press, radio and TV representatives from throughout the world teamed up with holiday-makers to see **QUO** perform a special show in the Butlin's ballroom!

- **QUO'S** 25th anniversary Number One single **'THE ANNIVER-SARY WALTZ'** featured the band performing excerpts from sixteen classic rock 'n' roll songs. Totalled together, the original versions spent a staggering total of 292 weeks in the British Singles Chart.

- 1990 also saw **QUO** appearing at the massive Knebworth charity show. Broadcast to a worldwide TV audience of 200 million people, the event raised over £6 million for the Music Therapy Trust.

- September 21st 1991 saw **QUO** enter the Guinness Book of Records when they successfully completed their most ambitious project ever by playing four British shows in 11 hours and 11 minutes. The **'ROCK 'TIL YOU DROP'** event saw **QUO** play sell out shows at Sheffield Arena, Glasgow SE&CC, Birmingham NEC and Wembley Arena.

- **'ROCK 'TILL YOU DROP'** raised £200,000 for children's charities. The marathon event took a year to organize and involved four stages, 60 drums, 200 amplifiers, 62 guitars, 165 cymbals, 12 miles of cable, 50 cameras, 200,000 watts of power, 2500 lights, 250 crew, 8 helicopters, 5 jets, 20 limousines and 16 police escorts.

- **QUO'S RICK PARFITT** and **FRANCIS ROSSI** saw double during 1991 when they unveiled waxworks of themselves at Madame Tussauds Rock Circus wax museum. The waxworks are now included in the exhibition's 'Rock Legends Hall of Fame'.

- 1991 also saw **QUO** presented with the most prestigious award in British music when they were awarded the **BRITS AWARD** for **'OUT-STANDING CONTRIBUTION TO THE BRITISH MUSIC INDUSTRY'**. The band collected the award in typical **QUO** style by ripping off their dinner jackets to reveal jeans and T-shirts hidden underneath. Britain's biggest selling daily newspaper The Sun described the stunt as 'the highlight of the entire show'.

- **QUO** made it a double celebration later in 1991 when HSH Prince Albert of Monaco presented the band with the **'OUTSTANDING CONTRIBUTION TO THE ROCK INDUSTRY'** award at the World Music Awards in Monte Carlo.

- In 1991 **QUO** 'went inside' for a day when the band opened a music workshop for inmates at London's Pentonville Prison.

- The summer of 1991 saw **QUO** co headline Britain's biggest stadium tour of the year when the band played eight sell-out shows with Rod Stewart. Over 260,000 people attended gigs at Celtic FC in Glasgow, Manchester United FC, Gateshead Stadium in Newcastle, Ipswich Town FC and Wembley Stadium.

- In August 1992 **QUO** headlined the Radio One 25th Anniversary Celebrations, playing to 125,000 people at the **PARTY IN THE PARK** at Sutton Park in Birmingham.

STATUS QUO – THE DEFINITIVE
SINGLES COLLECTION

7″ SINGLES AS THE SPECTRES

9/66   I (WHO HAVE NOTHING)/Neighbour, Neighbour (Piccadilly 7N.35339)

11/66   HURDY GURDY MAN/Laticia (Piccadilly 7N.35352)

2/67   (WE AIN'T GOT) NOTHIN' YET/I Want It (Piccadilly 7N.35368)

7″ SINGLES AS THE TRAFFIC JAM

6/67   ALMOST BUT NOT QUITE THERE/Wait Just A Minute (Piccadilly 7N.35386)

7″ SINGLES AS THE STATUS QUO

1/68   PICTURES OF MATCHSTICK MEN/Gentleman's Joe's Sidewalk Cafe (Blue Pye 7N.17449) {some b-sides had 'Gentleman Joe's Sidewalk Cafe (Minimum 75c)'}

3/68   BLACK VEILS OF MELANCHOLY/To Be Free (Blue Pye 7N 17497)

7/68   ICE IN THE SUN/When My Mind Is Not Live (Blue Pye 7N.17581)

1/69   MAKE ME STAY A BIT LONGER/Auntie Nellie (Blue Pye 7N.17665)

7″ SINGLES AS STATUS QUO

4/69   ARE YOU GROWING TIRED OF MY LOVE/So Ends Another Life (Blue Pye 7N.17728)

9/69   THE PRICE OF LOVE/Little Miss Nothing (Blue Pye 7N.17825)

3/70   DOWN THE DUSTPIPE/Face Without A Soul (Blue Pye 7N 17907) {later pressed on Red Pye, Black Pye, Precision and PRT}

10/70   IN MY CHAIR/Gerdundula (Blue Pye 7N.17998) P/S

6/71   TUNE TO THE MUSIC/Good Thinking (Blue Pye 7N.45077)

11/72   PAPER PLANE/Softer Ride (Spiral Vertigo 6059 071)
{later pressed on Silver Vertigo}

2/73   MEAN GIRL/Everything (Blue Pye 7N.45229)
{later pressed on Turquoise Pye and Red Pye}

7/73   GERDUNDULA/Lakky Lady (Red Pye 7N.45253)

8/73   CAROLINE/Joanne (Vertigo 6059 085)
{b-side shown as written by Lancaster and on some copies
credited as Lancaster/Parfitt}

4/74   BREAK THE RULES/Lonely Night (Vertigo 6059 101)

11/74   DOWN DOWN/Nightride (Vertigo 6059 114)

5/75   ROLL OVER LAY DOWN/Gerdundula – Junior's Wailing
(Vertigo QUO 13) P/S

2/76   RAIN/You Lost The Love (Vertigo 6059 133)

7/76   MYSTERY SONG/Drifting Away (Vertigo 6059 146)

12/76   WILD SIDE OF LIFE/All Through The Night (Vertigo 6059 153)
{later pressed on Buff Vertigo}

9/77   ROCKIN' ALL OVER THE WORLD/Ring Of A Change
(Vertigo 6059 184) P/S

7/78   MEAN GIRL/In My Chair (Red Pye 7N.46095)

8/78   AGAIN AND AGAIN/Too Far Gone (Vertigo QUO 1)

9/78   PICTURES OF MATCHSTICK MEN/Ice In The Sun
(Red Pye 7N.46103) {later pressed on PRT}

11/78   ACCIDENT PRONE/Let Me Fly (Vertigo QUO 2) P/S

3/79   PICTURES OF MATCHSTICK MEN/Down The Dustpipe
(Pye Flash Backs FBS 2) P/S {yellow vinyl. Later pressed on black
vinyl and on PRT}

6/79   IN MY CHAIR/Gerdundula (Red Pye 7P 103) P/S

9/79   WHATEVER YOU WANT/Hard Ride (Vertigo 6059 242) P/S

11/79   LIVING ON AN ISLAND/Runaway (Vertigo 6059 248) P/S

10/80   WHAT YOU'RE PROPOSING/A B Blues (Vertigo QUO 3) P/S

11/80   LIES/DON'T DRIVE MY CAR (Vertigo QUO 4) P/S
{also issued in a black and white P/S}

2/81   SOMETHING 'BOUT YOU BABY I LIKE/Enough Is Enough
(Vertigo QUO 5) P/S {issued in a multicoloured P/S, Blue P/S and
Red P/S}

11/81	MEAN GIRL/In My Chair (Old Gold OG 9142)
11/81	ROCK N' ROLL/Hold You Back – Backwater (Vertigo QUO 6) P/S
3/82	DEAR JOHN/I Want The World To Know (Vertigo QUO 7) P/S
6/82	SHE DON'T FOOL ME/Never Too Late (Vertigo QUO 8) P/S
10/82	CAROLINE (Live at the N.E.C.)/Dirty Water (Live at the N.E.C.) (Vertigo QUO 10) P/S {also issued as a Picture Disc QUO P10}
5/83	PICTURES OF MATCHSTICK MEN/Down The Dustpipe (Old Gold OG 9298)
9/83	OL' RAG BLUES/Stay The Night (Vertigo QUO B-11) P/S {blue vinyl. Also issued on black vinyl QUO 11}
11/83	A MESS OF BLUES/Big Man (Vertigo QUO 12) P/S {also issued with a reversed P/S}
12/83	MARGUERITA TIME/Resurrection (Vertigo QUO 14) P/S {also issued on Blue Vertigo, White Vertigo and as a Picture Disc QUOP 14}
5/84	GOING DOWN TOWN TONIGHT/Too Close To The Ground (Vertigo QUO 15) P/S
10/84	THE WANDERER/Can't Be Done (Vertigo QUO 16) P/S {also issued on Blue Vertigo}
11/85	CAROLINE/Down Down (Old Gold OG 9566)
11/85	ROCKIN' ALL OVER THE WORLD/Paper Plane (Old Gold OG 9567)
5/86	ROLLIN' HOME/Lonely (Vertigo QUO 18) P/S {also issued on Blue Vertigo and Bronze Vertigo. Shaped Picture Disc QUO PD18}
7/86	RED SKY/Don't Give It Up (Vertigo QUO 19) P/S {also issued on Blue and Black Vertigo}
9/86	IN THE ARMY NOW/Heartburn (Vertigo QUO 20) P/S {also issued on Black and Green Vertigo. Picture Disc QUO PD 20 and some copies came with a free patch}
11/86	DREAMIN'/Long Legged Girls (Vertigo QUO 21) P/S {also issued on White Vertigo and Blue Vertigo. Some copies came with a wrap around poster QUOP 21}
3/88	AIN'T COMPLAINING/That's Alright (Vertigo QUO 22) P/S {also issued on White Vertigo and the Vertigo. Picture Box with Band History version QUOH 22}

5/88   WHO GETS THE LOVE?/Halloween (Vertigo QUO 23) P/S {Picture Box with Band History Part 2 version QUOH 23}

8/88   RUNNING ALL OVER THE WORLD/Magic (Vertigo QUAID 1) P/S with Sport Aid Leaflet {also issued on White Vertigo and Black Vertigo}

11/88   BURNING BRIDGES (On And Off And On Again)/Whatever You Want (Vertigo QUO 25) P/S {also issued on White Vertigo}

10/89   NOT AT ALL/Gone Thru The Slips (Vertigo QUO 26) P/S

11/89   LITTLE DREAMER/Rotten To The Bone (Vertigo QUO 27) P/S {with 'Perfect Remedy Tour' patch QUOP 27}

9/90   THE ANNIVERSARY WALTZ PART ONE/The Power of Rock (Vertigo QUO 28) P/S {also issued on White Vertigo. Some copies came with a misprinted sleeve. Silver vinyl copy in gatefold P/S QUOG 28}

12/90   THE ANNIVERSARY WALTZ PART TWO/Dirty Water (Vertigo QUO 29) P/S {also issued on Red Vertigo}

8/91   CAN'T GIVE YOU MORE/Dead In The Water (Spiral Vertigo QUO 30) P/S {also issued on Silver Vertigo and Black Vertigo}

1/92   ROCK 'TIL YOU DROP/Medley (Spiral Vertigo QUO 32) P/S {also issued on Silver Vertigo}

9/92   ROADHOUSE MEDLEY (Anniversary Waltz Part 25) (Radio Edit)/Roadhouse Medley (Anniversary Waltz Part 25) (Extended Version) (Polydor QUO 33) P/S

7″ DOUBLE PACK SINGLES

MARGUERITA TIME/Resurrection and Caroline/Joanne (Vertigo QUO 1414) Gatefold P/S

RED SKY/Don't Give It Up and Rockin' All Over The World/Whatever You Want (Vertigo QUODP 19) Gatefold P/S

IN THE ARMY NOW/Heartburn and Marguerita Time/What You're Proposing (Vertigo QUO DP20) Gatefold P/S

7″ UNISSUED SINGLES, SPECIAL PROMOS AND ODDITIES

1968 TECHNICOLOR DREAMS/Paradise Flat (Blue Pye 7N.17650) {planned release which was cancelled with only a few copies made}

1972 Children Of The Grave (Black Sabbath)/Roadhouse Blues (Phonogram DJ 005) {promotion E.P. 100 copies made}

1975 DOWN DOWN/Break The Rules (Lyntone LYN 3154/5) {flexi disc issued by Smith's Crisps}

1979 IN MY CHAIR (QUO 1 SFI 434) {flexi-disc issued to promote the single and the 'Just For The Record' album}

1981 ROCK N' ROLL/Hold You Back (Vertigo QUO JB 6) {jukebox version}

1982 JEALOUSY/Calling The Shots (Vertigo QUO 9) {planned release which was cancelled with no copies made}

1985 Interview with ROSSI and LANCASTER (QUO 1) Picture Disc

1985 Interview with ROSSI and LANCASTER (part 2) (QUO 2) Picture Disc

1985 Interview with ROSSI (QUO 3) Picture Disc

1985 Interview with ROSSI (part 2) (QUO 4) Picture Disc

1986 UNKNOWN/Unknown (Vertigo QUO 17) {planned release which was cancelled with no copies made}

1988 BURNING BRIDGES (On And Off And On Again)/Burning Bridges (On And Off And On Again) (Vertigo QUODJ 25) P/S {promotion single}

1989 I DON'T WANT YOU/It Takes Two – Almost But Not Quite There (Zonophone DLR 333) {bootleg single pressed on yellow vinyl}

1990 THE ANNIVERSARY WALTZ PART ONE/The Anniversary Waltz Part Two (Vertigo QUO DJ 28) P/S {promotion single}

1991 FAKIN' THE BLUES (Edit)/Heavy Daze (Spiral Vertigo QUO 31) P/S {planned release which was cancelled with only a few copies made. The 12″ version included the extra track 'Better Times'}

TWELVE INCH SINGLES

5/77 DOWN THE DUSTPIPE – Mean Girl/In My Chair – Gerdundula (Red Pye BD 103) {later pressed on PRT}

CAROLINE (Live at the N.E.C.)/Dirty Water (Live at the N.E.C.) – Down Down (Live at the N.E.C.) (Vertigo QUO 1012) P/S

OL' RAG BLUES (Extended Re-Mixed Version)/Stay The Night – Whatever You Want (Live at the N.E.C.) (Vertigo QUO 1112) P/S

A MESS OF BLUES (Extended Version)/Big Man – Young Pretender (Vertigo QUO 1212) P/S

THE WANDERER/Can't Be Done (Clear Vinyl Vertigo QUOP 16) Picture Disc

ROLLIN' HOME/Lonely – Keep Me Guessing (Vertigo QUO 1812) P/S

RED SKY – Don't Give It Up/Milton Keynes Medley (Vertigo QUO 1912) P/S {with wrap around poster QUO 191}

IN THE ARMY NOW (Military Mix)/Heartburn – Late Last Night (Vertigo QUO 2012) P/S with poster

DREAMIN' (Wet Mix) – Long Legged Girls/The Quo Christmas Cake Mix (Vertigo QUO 2112) P/S

AIN'T COMPLAINING (Extended Version)/That's Alright – Lean Machine (Vertigo QUO 2212) P/S

WHO GETS THE LOVE?/Halloween – The Reason For Goodbye (Vertigo QUO 2312) P/S

RUNNING ALL OVER THE WORLD (Extended Version)/Magic – Running All Over The World (7″ Version) (Vertigo QUAID 112) P/S

BURNING BRIDGES (On And Off And On Again) (Extended Version)/ Whatever You Want – Marguerita Time (Vertigo QUO 2512) P/S

NOT AT ALL/Everytime I Think Of You – Gone Thru The Slips (Vertigo QUO 2612) P/S

LITTLE DREAMER/Rotten To The Bone – Doing It All For You (Vertigo QUO 2712) P/S {gatefold P/S QUOX 2712}

THE ANNIVERSARY WALTZ/The Power Of Rock – Perfect Remedy (Vertigo QUO 2812) P/S {some copies were misspressed with 'live' versions of 'Little Lady' and 'Paper Plane' as the b-sides. Other copies were misspressed with 'The Power of Rock' on both sides}

CAN'T GIVE YOU MORE/Dead In The Water – Mysteries From The Ball (Vertigo QUO 3012) P/S

ROCK 'TIL YOU DROP/Medley – Forty Five Hundred Times (Vertigo QUO 3212) P/S {some copies had only the 'Medley' as the b-side}

CASSETTE SINGLES

NOT AT ALL – Gone Thru The Slips/same (Vertigo QUOMC 26)

LITTLE DREAMER – Rotten To The Bone/same (Vertigo QUOMC 27)

THE ANNIVERSARY WALTZ PART ONE – The Power of Rock/same (Vertigo QUOMC 28)

THE ANNIVERSARY WALTZ PART TWO – Dirty Water/same (Vertigo QUOMC 29)

CAN'T GIVE YOU MORE – Dead In The Water/same (Vertigo QUOMC 30)

ROCK 'TIL YOU DROP – Medley/same (Vertigo QUOMC 32)
ROADHOUSE MEDLEY (Anniversary Waltz Part 25) (Radio Edit) –
Roadhouse Medley (Anniversary Waltz Part 25) (Extended Version)/same
(Polydor QUOMC 33)

COMPACT DISC SINGLES

AIN'T COMPLAINING (Extended) – That's Alright – Lean Machine – In
The Army Now (Re-Mix) (Vertigo QUOCD 22)
WHO GETS THE LOVE? – Halloween – The Reason For Goodbye – The
Wanderer (Sharon The Nag Mix) (Vertigo QUOCD 23)
RUNNING ALL OVER THE WORLD – Magic – Whatever You Want
(Vertigo QUOCD 1)
BURNING BRIDGES (On And Off And On Again) (Extended Version)
– Whatever You Want – Marguerita Time (Vertigo QUOCD 25)
NOT AT ALL – Everytime I Think Of You – Gone Thru The Slips
(Vertigo QUOCD 26)
LITTLE DREAMER – Rotten To The Bone – Doing It All For You
(Vertigo QUOCD 27)
THE ANNIVERSARY WALTZ – The Power Of Rock – Perfect Remedy
(Vertigo QUOCD 28)
THE ANNIVERSARY WALTZ PART TWO – Dirty Water (Vertigo
QUOCD 29)
CAN'T GIVE YOU MORE – Dead In The Water – Mysteries From The
Ball (Vertigo QUOCD 30)
ROCK 'TIL YOU DROP – Medley – Forty Five Hundred Times (Vertigo
QUOCD 32) {guitar shaped case box}
ROADHOUSE MEDLEY (Anniversary Waltz Part 25) (Radio Edit) –
Roadhouse Medley (Anniversary Waltz Part 25) (Extended Version) –
Don't Drive My Car (Live) (Polydor QUODD 33) {limited edition
digipack. Part two with Roadhouse Medley (Anniversary Waltz Part 25)
(Roadhouse Mix) (QUOCD 33)}

LASER DISC SINGLES

11/88 AIN'T COMPLAINING (Extended) – That's Alright – Lean Machine
– In The Army Now (Remix)/Ain't Complaining (Vertigo 080 322–2)
5/89 BURNING BRIDGES (On And Off And On Again) (Extended
Version) – Whatever You Want – Marguerita Time – Who Gets The
Love?/Burning Bridges (Vertigo 080 620–2)

QUO – ALL THE ALBUMS

9/68 PICTURESQUE MATCHSTICKABLE MESSAGES FROM
THE STATUS QUO (Blue Pye) {stereo version NSPL 18220}
LP: NPL.18220

9/69 SPARE PARTS (Blue Pye)
{stereo version NSPL 18301}
LP: NPL 19301

8/70 MA KELLY'S GREASY SPOON (Blue Pye)
{original copies with a poster. Later issued on Red Pye and PRT}
LP: NSPL 18344 Cassette: ZCP 18344 Cartridge: Y8P 18344

11/71 DOG OF TWO HEAD (Blue Pye) Gatefold Cover
{later issued on Red Pye and PRT)
LP: NSPL 18371 Cassette: ZCP 18371 Cartridge: Y8P 18371

12/72 PILEDRIVER (Spiral Vertigo) Gatefold Cover
{later issued on Silver Vertigo. Later copies came in a single
sleeve}
LP: 6360 082 Cassette: 7138 042 Cartridge: 7739 009

9/73 HELLO! (Green Vertigo)
{original copies with a lyric inner bag and poster}
LP: 6360 098 Cassette: 7318 053 Cartridge: 7739 015

1974 QUO (Green Vertigo)
{original copies with a lyric sheet/poster}
LP: 9102 001 Cassette: 7231 001 Cartridge: 7739 018

2/75 ON THE LEVEL (Green Vertigo) Gatefold Cover
{with a lyric inner bag. Later copies were issued in a single sleeve}
LP: 9102 002 Cassette: 7231 002 Cartridge: 7739 024

3/76 BLUE FOR YOU (Blue Vertigo) Gatefold Cover
{with a lyric inner bag. Later copies came in a single sleeve}
LP: 9102 006 Cassette: 7231 005 Cartridge: 7739 029

3/77 STATUS QUO LIVE! (Green Vertigo) Double Album – Gatefold Cover
{picture inner bags. Later issued on Yellow Vertigo}
LP: 6641 580 Cassette: 7599 171 Cartridge: 7799 004

11/77   ROCKIN' ALL OVER THE WORLD (World Vertigo)
{with a picture inner bag}
LP: 9102 014 Cassette: 7231 012 Cartridge: 7739 036

10/78   IF YOU CAN'T STAND THE HEAT (Green Vertigo) Gatefold
Cover {with a lyric inner bag. Later issued on Yellow Vertigo and
copies came in a single sleeve}
LP: 9102 027 Cassette: 7231 017

10/79   WHATEVER YOU WANT (Green Vertigo)
{original copies with a lyric inner bag and merchandise leaflet}
LP: 9102 037 Cassette: 7231 025

10/80   JUST SUPPOSIN' (Green Vertigo)
{later issued on Yellow Vertigo}
LP: 6302 057 Cassette: 7144 057

3/81   NEVER TOO LATE (Yellow Vertigo)
{with a lyric inner bag}
LP: 6302 104 Cassette: 7144 104

10/82   1+9+8+2 (Yellow Vertigo)
{with a lyric inner bag}
LP: 6320 189 Cassette: 7144 189

11/82   FROM THE MAKERS OF . . . (Phonogram) Triple Album
{with information sheets. Metal box set PRO BX 1}
LP: PRO LP 1 Cassette: PRO M.C. 1

11/83   BACK TO BACK (Truck Vertigo)
{with a lyric inner bag and merchandise leaflet}
LP: VERH 10 Cassette: VERHC 10

8/86   IN THE ARMY NOW (Blue Vertigo)
{with a picture inner bag and merchandise leaflet}
LP: VERH 36 Cassette: VERHC 36

6/88   AIN'T COMPLAINING (White Vertigo)
{with an information inner bag and merchandise leaflet}
LP: VERH 58 Cassette: VERHC 58

11/89   PERFECT REMEDY (Yellow Vertigo)
LP: 842 098–1 Cassette: 842 098–4

9/91   ROCK 'TIL YOU DROP (Spiral Vertigo)
{cassette had six extra tracks}
LP: 510 341–1 Cassette: 510 341–4

| 11/92 | LIVE ALIVE QUO (Polydor)
{picture inner bag. Cassette had two extra tracks}
LP: 517 367–1 Cassette: 517 367–4 |

COMPILATION ALBUMS

11/69	STATUS QUO-TATIONS (Marble Arch) {stereo version MALS 1193} LP: MAL 1193
5/73	THE BEST OF STATUS QUO (Blue Pye) {later issued on Red Pye, Precision and PRT} LP: NSPL.18402 Cassette: ZCP 18402 Cartridge: Y8P 18402
6/73	GOLDEN HOUR OF STATUS QUO (Pye Golden Hour) LP: GH 556 Cassette: ZCGH 556 Cartridge: Y8GH 556
10/75	GOLDEN HOUR PRESENTS STATUS QUO – DOWN THE DUSTPIPE (Pye Golden Hour) LP: GH 604 Cassette: ZCGH 604 Cartridge: Y8GH 604
4/76	PICTURES OF MATCHSTICK MEN (Hallmark Marble Arch) LP: HMA 257 Cassette: HSC 268
9/76	THE REST OF STATUS QUO (Red Pye) LP: PKL 5546 Cassette: ZCPKB 5546 Cartridge: Y8PKB 5546
10/77	THE STATUS QUO FILE (Red Pye) Double Album {with information inner bags. Original copies came in a blue sleeve and later copies in a blue and white sleeve. Later issued on PRT} LP: FILD 005 Cassette: ZCFLD 005
5/78	STATUS QUO (Hallmark Marble Arch) LP: HMA 260 Cassette: HSC 322
10/78	THE STATUS QUO COLLECTION (Hallmark Marble Arch) Double Album Gatefold Cover LP: PDA 046 Cassette: PDC 046
6/79	JUST FOR THE RECORD (Red Pye) {first 10,000 copies were pressed on red vinyl} LP: NSPL 18607 Cassette: ZCP 18607
3/80	12 GOLD BARS (Green Vertigo) {later issued on Yellow Vertigo} LP: QUO TV 1 Cassette: QUO MC1

9/80	STATUS QUO (Pickwick) Double Album – Gatefold Cover LP: SSD 8035 Cassette: SSDC 8035
4/81	SPOTLIGHT ON STATUS QUO (PRT) Double Album LP: SPOT 1010 Cassette: ZCSPT 1010
9/81	FRESH QUOTA (PRT) {10″ mini album} LP: DOW 2 Cassette: ZCDOW 2
10/82	SPOTLIGHT ON STATUS QUO VOL.2 (PRT) Double Album LP: SPOT 1028 Cassette: ZCSPT 1028
6/83	TO BE OR NOT TO BE (Pickwick Contour) LP: CN 2062 Cassette: CN4 2062
7/83	WORKS (PRT) {10″ mini album} LP: DOW 10 Cassette: ZC DOW 10
11/81	12 GOLD BARS VOLUME 2 (and1) (Yellow Vertigo) Double Album Gatefold Cover {with a merchandise leaflet. Original copies only included Volume 1} LP: QUOTV 2 Cassette: QUOMC 2
10/85	NANANA (PRT Flash Backs) LP: PBLP 8082 Cassette: ZCFBL 8082
11/85	THE COLLECTION (Castle Communications) Double Album – Gatefold Cover LP: CCSLP 114 Cassette: CCSMC 114
10/87	QUOTATIONS VOL.1 – THE BEGINNING (PRT) LP: PYL 6024 Cassette: PYM 6024
10/87	QUOTATIONS VOL. 2 – FLIPSIDES, ALTERNATIVES AND ODDITIES (PRT) LP: PYL 6025 Cassette: PYM 6025
10/88	FROM THE BEGINNING (PRT) {picture disc} LP: PYX 4007
4/90	GOLDEN HOUR OF STATUS QUO (Knight) Cassette: KGHMC 110

9/90   B-SIDES AND RARITIES (Castle Communications) Double
        Album – Gatefold Cover
        LP: CCSLP 271 Cassette: CCSMC 271

10/90   ROCKING ALL OVER THE YEARS (Yellow Vertigo) Double
        Album – Gatefold Cover
        LP: 846 797–1 Cassette: 846 797–4

10/90   INTROSPECTIVE (Baktabak)
        {clear vinyl}
        LP: LINT 5003 Cassette: MINT 5003

12/90   THE EARLY WORKS (Essential) Five Album Box Set with
        booklet
        LP: ESBLP 136

1/91   NIGHTRIDING (Knight)
        Cassette: KNMC 10018

4/91   ICE IN THE SUN (Marble Arch)
        Cassette: CMA MC 108

10/91   BEST OF STATUS QUO 1968–1971 (Pickwick)
        Cassette: PWKMC 4080

10/91   BEST OF STATUS QUO 1972–1986 (Pickwick)
        Cassette: PWKMC 4087

RE-ISSUES

5/83   HELLO! (Yellow Vertigo)
        LP: PRICE 16 Cassette: PRIMC 16

5/83   PILEDRIVER (Yellow Vertigo)
        LP: PRICE 17 Casette: PRIMC 17

8/83   QUO (Yellow Vertigo)
        LP: PRICE 38 Cassette: PRIMC 38

8/83   ON THE LEVEL (Yellow Vertigo)
        LP: PRICE 39 Cassette: PRIMC 39

12/83   BLUE FOR YOU (Yellow Vertigo)
        LP: PRICE 55 Cassette: PRIMC 55

9/83   STATUS QUO LIVE! (Yellow Vertigo) Double Album –
        Gatefold Cover
        LP: PRID 5 Cassette: PRIDC 5

8/85	ROCKIN' ALL OVER THE WORLD (Yellow Vertigo) LP: PRICE 87 Cassette: 7138 095
10/87	PICTURESQUE MATCHSTICKABLE MESSAGES FROM THE STATUS QUO (PRT) LP: PYL 6020 Cassette: PYM 6020
10/87	SPARE PARTS (PRT) LP: PYL 6021 Cassette: PYM 6021
10/87	MA KELLY'S GREASY SPOON (PRT) LP: PYL 6022 Cassette: PYM 6022
10/87	DOG OF TWO HEAD (PRT) Gatefold Cover LP: PYL 6023 Cassette: PYM 6022
9/90	SPARE PARTS (Castle Communications) LP: CLAP 205 Cassette: CLAMC 205
9/90	DOG OF TWO HEAD (Castle Communications) LP: CLAP 206 Cassette: CLAMC 206
2/91	WHATEVER YOU WANT AND JUST SUPPOSIN' (Vertigo) Cassette: 848 087–4
2/91	NEVER TOO LATE AND BACK TO BACK (Vertigo) Cassette: 848 088–4
2/91	QUO AND BLUE FOR YOU (Vertigo) Cassette: 848 089–4
2/91	IF YOU CAN'T STAND THE HEAT AND 1+9+8+2 (Vertigo) Cassette: 848 090–4
2/91	PILEDRIVER (Vertigo) Cassette: 848 171–4
2/91	HELLO! (Vertigo) Cassette: 848 172–4
2/91	ROCKIN' ALL OVER THE WORLD (Vertigo) Cassette: 848 173–4
2/91	ON THE LEVEL (Vertigo) Cassette: 848 174–4

INTERVIEW ONLY ALBUMS

1986   INTERVIEW (MM 1221) Picture Disc
1989   INTERVIEW PICTURE DISC (Baktabak BAK 2110)

CASSETTE ONLY ALBUMS

2/81   THE MUSIC OF STATUS QUO VOL.1: 1972–1974 (Vertigo 7215 038)

6/82   100 MINUTES OF STATUS QUO (PRT ZCTON 101)

4/89   PRT C–90 COLLECTOR SERIES (PRT C90 3)

COMPACT DISC ALBUMS

1983
1+9+8+2 (Vertigo 800 035–2)
NEVER TOO LATE (Vertigo 800 053–2)
12 GOLD BARS (Vertigo 800 062–2)
BACK TO BACK (Vertigo 814 662–2)

1984
12 GOLD BARS VOLUME 2 (Vertigo 822 985–2)

1985
THE BEST OF STATUS QUO (THE EARLY YEARS) (PRT CDNSP 7773)

1986
MA KELLY'S GREASY SPOON (PRT CDMP 8834)
DOG OF TWO HEAD (PRT CDMP 8837)
IN THE ARMY NOW (Vertigo 830 049–2)

1987
THE COLLECTION (Castle Communications CCSCD 114)
PICTURESQUE MATCHSTICKABLE MESSAGES FROM THE STATUS QUO (PRT 8.26693 ZR)
SPARE PARTS (PRT 8.26694 ZR)
MA KELLY'S GREASY SPOON (PRT 8.26695 ZR)

1988
DOG OF TWO HEAD (PRT 8.26696 ZR)
QUOTATIONS – VOLUME 1 THE BEGINNING (PRT 8.26699 ZR)
QUOTATIONS VOLUME 2 – FLIPSIDES, ALTERNATIVES AND
ODDITIES (PRT 8.26700 ZR)
AIN'T COMPLAINING (Vertigo 834 604–2)

1989
PRT COLLECTOR (PRT GHCD3)
PERFECT REMEDY (Vertigo 842 098–2)
RECOLLECTIONS (Avanti RECCD 001)
PICTURESQUE MATCHSTICKABLE MESSAGES FROM THE
STATUS QUO (Castle Communications CLACD 168)
MA KELLY'S GREASY SPOON (Castle Communications CLACD 169)

1990
GOLDEN HOUR OF STATUS QUO (Knight KGH CD 110)
SPINNING WHEEL BLUES (Castle Communications 295 975)
B-SIDES AND RARITIES (Castle Communications CCSCD 271)
SPARE PARTS (Castle Communications CLACD 205)
DOG OF TWO HEAD (Castle Communications CLACD 206)
ROCKING ALL OVER THE YEARS (Vertigo 846 797–2)
INTROSPECTIVE (Baktabak CINT 5003)

1991
THE EARLY YEARS (Essential ESBCD 136) Three C.D. Box Set
NIGHTRIDING (Knight KNCD 10018)
WHATEVER YOU WANT AND JUST SUPPOSIN'
(Vertigo 848 087–2)
NEVER TOO LATE AND BACK TO BACK (Vertigo 848 088–2)
QUO AND BLUE FOR YOU (Vertigo 848 089–2)
IF YOU CAN'T STAND THE HEAT AND 1+9+8+2 (Vertigo 848
090–2)
PILEDRIVER (Vertigo 848 171–2)
HELLO! (Vertigo 848 172–2)
ROCKIN' ALL OVER THE WORLD (Vertigo 848 173–2)
ON THE LEVEL (Vertigo 848 174–2)
ICE IN THE SUN (Marble Arch CMA CD 108)
TO BE OR NOT TO BE (Pickwick PWKS 4051 P)
THE HITMACHINE (Woodford Music WMCD 5614)
LIVE AT THE N.E.C. (Vertigo 818 947–2)

ROCK 'TIL YOU DROP (Vertigo 510 341–2) {included six extra tracks}
BEST OF STATUS QUO 1968–1971 (Pickwick PWKS 4080)
BACK TO THE BEGINNING (Decal CD LIKD 81) Two C.D. Set
BEST OF STATUS QUO 1972–1986 (Pickwick PWKS 4087 P)

1992
STATUS QUO LIVE! (Vertigo 510 334–2) Two C.D. Set
THE EARLY YEARS (Dojo EARL D 8)
LIVE ALIVE QUO (Polydor 517 367–2) {included three extra tracks}
TUNE TO THE MUSIC (Ariola Express 291 008)

COMPACT DISC VIDEO ALBUMS

1983
LIVE IN CONCERT (Spectrum 790 688 1)

1988
ROCKIN' THROUGH THE YEARS (Polygram 070 170–1)

1991
ROCKING ALL OVER THE YEARS (Polygram 082 644–1)

PUT IN TRANSIT VAN
IN THIS ORDER
STATUS QUO

BOB YOUNG
EQUIPMENT LIST
1968

8 Sound City Cabinets (TWO WITHOUT WHEELS
FRONT LEFT.
(leave 1 out without wheels til last)
2 marshall amps
4 Marshall Columns
Organ
Organ legs case and feet (on left)
Snare drum and light legs (on right)
and lights switch box
1 Sound City. amp
1 small Tom-Tom
Still heads case

Bass Drum
Large Tom Tom
1 Sound City Cabinet
3 gnitars (TWO BLACK ONE GREY)
3 other Sound City Cabinets
3 mike stands
2 guitars (1 is behind drivers seat)
Any other odds

STAGE PLAN ON OTHER SIDE.

Quo on the Road, 1968

CASE CONTAINING:		£
Roger Griffen Custom Guitar S/N: 8617	1	400
Zemaitis Custom Guitar NSN	1	300
Ovation Viper Guitar S/N: E6548	1	300
Dobro Guitar S/N: 1896484	1	400
CASE CONTAINING:		
Schecter Guitar NSN	1	400
Fender Telecaster Guitar S/N: 156101	1	350
Fender Esquire Guitar S/N: 48937	1	400
Fender Telecaster Guitar S/N: L96877	1	350
CASE CONTAINING:		
Fender Telecaster Guitar S/N: 110850	1	400
Fender Telecaster Guitar S/N: L57781	1	350
Fender Telecaster Guitar S/N: 110959	1	350
GNL Telecaster Guitar S/N: 0025752	1	300
CASE CONTAINING:		
Fender Guitar S/N: 140454659	1	400
Steinberger Guitar S/N: N5253	1	375
GNL Telecaster Guitar S/N: G024284	1	300
Steinberger Guitar S/N: N7886	1	375
CASE CONTAINING:		
Marshall JCM 600 Amp Heads S/N: 13705, 20924, 13746	3	450
CASE CONTAINING:		
Marshall JCM 600 Amp Heads S/N: 30916, 13752, 13710	3	450
CASE CONTAINING:		
Marshall JCM 900 Amp Head NSN	1	150
Marshall JCM 900 Amp Heads S/N: 23497, 15931	2	300
CASE CONTAINING:		
Marshall JCM 900 Amp Head NSN	1	200
Marshall JCM 900 Amp Head S/N: 07980	1	200

Quo on the Road, twenty-four years later.

CASE CONTAINING:		£
Roland GP8 Guitar Processors NSN	2	650
Roland FC100 Foot Pedals NSN	2	160
Custom Overdrive Pedals	3	70
Marshall Overdrive Pedal	1	85
Custom Splitter Boxes NSN	2	70
Samson Radio Receivers S/N: 400778, 200909	2	550

CASE CONTAINING:		
Plugboards	8	30
Leads Set	15	45
Speaker Leads Set	15	20
Loomed Guitar FX Leads	2	35
Guitar Straps	6	25
Guitar P/Up Set	8	100
Manuals Set	1	15
Marshall Overdrive Pedal S/N: 00835	1	85
Samson Guitar Transmitters	4	120
Equipment Connector Cable	1	05
Machine Heads Set	1	45
Boss Tuner NSN	1	60
Spare Valves Set	1	120
Transmitter Leads Set	8	20
Drawer Unit	1	10
Korg Tuners NSN	2	50

CASE CONTAINING:		
Marshall 4×12 Speaker Cabinets S/N: 5122, 5114, 5116, 5118, 4956, 5117, 5115, 5125, 5123, 4958, 5121, 5121	12	1000

CASE CONTAINING:		
Speakers	8	60

CASE CONTAINING:		
Custom Fan NSN	1	80

CASE CONTAINING:		
Marshall JCM 800 Lead Series Amp S/N: 13732	1	150

		£
Marshall JCM 900 Lead Series Amp S/N: 34164	1	150

CASE CONTAINING:

Vox AC30 Amp S/N: 25837	1	140

CASE CONTAINING:

Yamaha Cab S/N: AS31357	1	600

CASE CONTAINING:

Yamaha Cab S/N: AS31350	1	600

CASE CONTAINING:

Akai S900 Tape Machine S/N: 11155–00312	1	800
Cheetah SX16 S/N: S21251	1	130
Hill Multi-Mix S/N: A7593	1	600
BSS Active D.I. Unit	2	200
Roland U220 S/N: CC79644	1	150
Roland U220 S/N: CC34465	1	150
Patch Bay	1	100

CASE CONTAINING:

Samson Transmitters S/N: 600586, 800613, 800577	3	300
Boss FU200 NSN	1	120
Yamaha Foot Pedal S/N: 8704	1	100
Foot Pedals	4	70
30 Piece Leads Set	1	30
Roland Piano Pedal S/N: 732145	1	400
Strings Set	1	150
Korg Volume Pedal	1	30
Korg S1 NSN	1	30
Korg S2 Foot Switch	1	20
Nady Transmitters NSN	2	150
Shure SM58 Microphones	3	120

CASE CONTAINING:

Tascam 34B R to R S/N: 250091, 330085	2	1000
Switch Box	1	40
Tandy Headphones	1	20

		£
Cables	2	20
Tapes	9	90

CASE CONTAINING:

Roland RD1000 S/N: 732145	1	800
Roland Key Stand	1	30
Mike Stands	2	40
Stool	1	20

CASE CONTAINING:

Marshall 2×12 Cabinet S/N: 05756	1	100

CASE CONTAINING:

Marshall 2×15 Cabinet S/N: 1715	1	300

CASE CONTAINING:

Marshall 4×10 Cabinets S/N: 1357, 1388	2	600

CASE CONTAINING:

Marshall 2×15 Cabinet S/N: 1719, 1718	2	300

CASE CONTAINING:

Marshall 4×10 Cabinets S/N: 1355	1	300

CASE CONTAINING:

Mirror	1	40
Dressing Gowns	5	40
Hanger	1	10
Rail	1	20
Tefal Iron	1	30
Carmen Hairdryer	1	20
Shirts	6	30

CASE CONTAINING:

Boss TU12 Tuner S/N: 957888	1	40
Boss TU12H Tuner S/N: 575900	1	40
Boss TU100 Tuner S/N: 592900	1	100
Korg WT12 S/N: 1002	1	60

		£
Yamaha MA10 Amp S/N: 81989	1	100
Equipment Connector Cable	1	0
Black & Decker Screwdriver	1	25
RS240–110 Transformer	1	40
Cable Tester	1	30
Switch Boxes	4	30
Sony Headphones	1	30
Multimeter S/N: 1004	1	30
BSS DI Box S/N: 1991	1	40
Tool Set	1	60
RS Rivet Gun	1	15
Drill Bit Set	1	20
R.S. Soldering Iron	1	10
Staple Gun	1	20
Cables Set	1	20
Torches	3	10
Marita Drill S/N: 3674E	1	40
B/D Jig Saw S/N: DN531	1	40
Panavise	1	30
Stool	1	20
Heat Gun	1	10
Brother P-Touch S/N: 09720744	1	120

CASE CONTAINING:

Premier 18" Floor Tom S/N: 9676	1	90
Premier 16" Floor Tom S/N: 19667	1	80
Yamaha S10X Speaker S/N: 7616	1	75
Yamaha S10X Speaker S/N: 7652	1	75
Tama Bass Drum Pedals Set	4	100
Drum Head Set	1	60
Electric Fan	1	15

CASE CONTAINING:

Tama Bell Brass Snare Drum S/N: 012116	1	300
Ludwig Black Beauty Snare Drum S/N: 2140528, 1839082, 2202685	3	2100

CASE CONTAINING: £

Drum Stick Set	1	100
Premier 10″ Rack Tom S/N: 20256	1	40
Premier Rack Tom S/N: 22889	1	50
Premier 13″ Rack Tom S/N: 20963	1	60
Premier 14″ Rack Tom S/N: 19682	1	70
Roland Drum Pads	4	200

CASE CONTAINING:

Tama 22″ Bass Drums S/N: 004129, 006846	2	300

CASE CONTAINING:

Tama Drum Frame	1	300
Tama High Hat Pedals	2	75
Drum Stools	2	50

CASE CONTAINING:

Paiste 14″ Cymbals S/N: 951213, 951262	2	100
Paiste 16″ Full Crash Cymbal S/N: 925633	1	70
Paiste 17″ Full Crash Cymbal S/N: 981344	1	80
Paiste 18″ Full Crash Cymbal S/N: 960859	1	90
Paiste 17″ Full Crash Cymbal S/N: 958390	1	80
Paiste 16″ Full Crash Cymbal S/N: 954531	1	60
Paiste 20″ Full Crash Cymbal S/N: 950485	1	100
Paiste 20″ Rough Ride Cymbal S/N: 954976	1	100
Paiste 21″ Power Ride Cymbal S/N: 954933	1	100
Paiste 10″ Splash Cymbal S/N: 925347	1	30
Paiste 8″ Bell Cymbal S/N: 919282	1	30
Paiste 13″ Heavy High Hat Cymbal S/N: 950109	1	50
Paiste 13″ Heavy High Hat Cymbal S/N: 950140	1	50
Paiste China Type Cymbal 14″ S/N: 950280	1	60
Paiste Rude 14″ C/Ride Cymbal S/N: 818169	1	60
Paiste 2002 20″ Nova Cymbal 720979	1	100
Paiste 2002 20″ Nova Cymbal NSN	1	100
Paiste 22″ China Type Cymbal S/N: 930949	1	100
Paiste 14″ S/Edge H/Hat Cymbal S/N: 95033	1	50
Paiste 14″ S/Edge H/Hat Cymbal S/N: 50287	1	50
Paiste S/Reflect 18″ C/Cymbal S/N: 843531	1	80

		£
Paiste S/Reflect 16" C/Cymbal S/N: 810956	1	60
Paiste S/Reflect 18" C/Cymbal S/N: 843534	1	80
Paiste 2002 15" C/Cymbal S/N: 634262	1	60
Paiste 2002 18" C/Cymbal S/N: 811686	1	80
Paiste 2002 20" China Type Cymbal S/N: 634282	1	100
Paiste 2002 18" C/Cymbal S/N: 811686	1	80
Paiste 2002 20" China Type Cymbal S/N: 634282	1	100
Paiste 2002 18" H/Crash Cymbal S/N: 628922	1	100
Paiste 3000 18" Crash Cymbal S/N: 848751	1	80
Paiste 3000 Rude 14" C/R Cymbal S/N: 818168	1	60
Paiste 3000 Splash Cymbals 10" S/N: 616429, 826517	2	80
China Type Cymbal NSN	1	50
Paiste Full Crash 20" Cymbal S/N: 005347	1	80
Paiste 18" Mellow Crash Cymbal S/N: 002686	1	50
Paiste 18" Full Crash Cymbals S/N: 009777, 009776, 00977	3	130
Paiste 16" Full Crash Cymbal S/N: 009976	1	40
Paiste 16" Power Crash Cymbal S/N: 010017	1	40
Paiste 17" Full Crash Cymbal S/N: 981341	1	40
Paiste 14" Full Crash Cymbal S/N: 958223	1	30
Paiste 17" Fast Crash Cymbal S/N: 950362	1	40
Metal Riser Frames	10	550
Carpeted Riser Boards	4	200
Tool Boxes	3	300

CASE CONTAINING:

Stage Costumes	15	1500
Clothes Accessory Set	1	300
Monitor Drapes	26	260

CASE CONTAINING:

Hammond Organ	1	500
Equipment Connector Cables	2	10
Cable Reel	1	200
Voltage Conditioner S/N: 8612378	1	200

CASE CONTAINING:

Leslie Cabinet NSN	1	300

		£
Shure SM77 Microphones	2	100
Sennheiser 421 Microphone	1	50

LOOSE:

Roll of Carpet	3	450
Pieces of Perspex	3	20
Vallen Pump Mic Stands	3	100

CASE CONTAINING:

Custom Made Variac	1	600
32A Mains Cable	1	25

CASE CONTAINING:

Boss TU12 Tuner	1	50
Korg DT1 Tuner	1	50
JHE Footswitch	1	30
Soldering Iron	1	35
KAT KDT–1 Drum Triggers	5	100
Hand Tool Set	1	300
Cable Set	1	100
Boss HAS Headphone Amp	1	50
Bss Dr. Beat	1	100
Vox Pedal	1	20
Bosch Cordless Drill	1	75
3 Cell Maglite	1	30
Mini-Mag	1	20
Stencil and Roller Set	1	75
Heavy Duty Staple Gun	1	30

CASE CONTAINING:

Drapes Set	1	200

CASE CONTAINING:

Stationery Kit	1	50
Plugboards	2	10
Laminator	1	150
Amstrad AT9600 Fax	1	400
Compaq 286 SLT Unit S/N: 8944HU4F0324	1	1000

		£
Cannon BJ10 Printer S/N: PAN24751	1	350
Pass Set	1	10

CASE CONTAINING:

Roland DDR-30 Digital Drums	1	200
Roland R-8M Percussion Module	1	150
BSS 4 Channel Active D.I.	1	125
Marshall 400W Bass Amp	1	200

CASE CONTAINING:

Marshall SE100 Speaker EMU S/N: 01933, 01329, 01903, 01857	4	600
Roland GP8 GTR Processor NSN	1	300
Ashley Split Boxes NSN	2	125

CASE CONTAINING:

Marshall JCM 900 Comboo S/N: 16763	1	275

CASE CONTAINING:

Marshall JCM 900 Combo S/N: 05323	1	275

CASE CONTAINING:

Marshall JCM 900 Combo S/N: 21220	1	275

CASE CONTAINING:

Aquaval S/N: 8503BO1218726	1	200

CASE CONTAINING:

Status Bass S/N: 007, 021, 018	3	900
Guitar Stands	3	45

CASE CONTAINING:

Nady VHF 700 RCVR. S/N: 211	1	450
Samson Radio RCVR. S/N: 800766	1	250
Ashby Split Box	3	125
Boss TU12 Tuner S/N: WO28672	1	125
Custom Split Box	1	50

CASE CONTAINING:		£
Cable Set/Plugboards	10	175
Martin CT2 Bass Cabinets	2	825
Martin CT2 Mid/High Cabinets	4	800
Martin PM3 Floor	2	500
Amcron 2400 Amplifiers	3	750
Martin MX4 Crossovers	2	35
EP3 Speaker Leads	2	1
Shure SM58B Microphones	3	10
Shure SM58 Microphones	3	80
Shure SM57B Microphone	1	35
Shure SM57 Microphone	3	75
AKG 451 Microphones	2	135
AKG 414 Microphones	2	243
Sennheiser 421 Microphones	4	165
AKG 460 Microphone	1	34
Sennheiser 509 Microphone	4	115
BSS Active Stage Box	1	1250
12 Way Microphone Sub Box	4	140
Martin MX4 Cross Over	6	1750
Martin CT2 Cross Over	1	175
Dennon CD Player	1	127
BSS 404 Com–Lim	1	335
BSS 504 Noise Gate	2	765
Midas XL3 40 Channel Mixing Console	1	7343
Midas XL3 Power Supply	2	145
Klark Teknik DN 360 Graphic	5	2040
Yamaha SPX 90 Processor	1	246
Talk Back System	1	69
Martin CT2 Speaker Cab	4	1425
Martin CT Sub Bass Cab	2	825
Martin LE 700 Monitor	10	3490
Martin PM3 Monitor	2	835
Amcron Macrotec 2400 Amplifier	12	7800
Microphone Stands	6	210
Shure SM57 Microphone	5	134
Shure SM58 Microphone	2	270
Sennheiser 509 Microphone	4	175

		£
Sennheiser 421 Microphone	3	156
Shure SM58 Beta Microphone	6	125
AKG 451 Microphone	3	97
AKG 414 Microphone	2	254
BSS DI Box	4	140
Martin F2 Bass Cabinets	2	750
Martin F2 Mid/High Cabinets	2	2367
125 Amp 3 Pohase Mains System	1	3547
Microphone Cable	95	154
EPS Speaker Leads	10	225
Midas XL3 40 Channel Mixing Console	1	15678
Midas 16 Channel Mixing Console	1	5000
Midas XL3 Power Supply	3	700
BSS DPR 901 Dynamic EQ	1	372
DBX 160X Compressor	5	760
BSS DPR 502 Noise Gate	5	1125
BSS DPR 402 Compressor	1	276
BSS DPR 404 Compressor	1	296
AMS DMX16 Reverb	1	1534
Roland SDE 3000 Delay	1	218
Dennon CD Player	1	75
Dennon Tape Deck	1	62
Lexicon PCM70 Processor	1	1324
Yamaha REV 7 Reverb	1	998
Yamaha REV 5 Reverb	1	825
Yamaha SPX 900 Processor	12	758
Sony DAT Player	1	397
Lexicon MRC	2	567

You are invited to:

STATUS QUO'S 25th ANNIVERSARY WALTZ

on Wednesday 10th October
at
Butlins Somerwest World, Minehead
with

and
special guest

with a
post gig party

**KARAOKE CONTEST: More accurate
than a Metropolitan Police breath test!**

The Quo Express departs Paddington 13.40 on 10th October
and departs Taunton 12.00 on 11th October

	YES	NO
(1) Do you wish to travel on the "Quo Express"?	☐	☐
(2) Do you wish to return to London by coach on the same night?	☐	☐
(3) Do you require accommodation at Butlins?	☐	☐
(4) Are you a vegetarian?	☐	☐
(5) Are you an alcoholic?	☐	☐

FROM _____

Butlin's Revisited.

BUTLIN'S – OUTLINE SCHEDULE
FOR QUO DAY

9.30 a.m.   Arrive at Butlin's.
                       Picture exclusive for The Sun.

10.00–12.00 a.m.   Soundcheck.
                       There will be assorted TV crews and reporters in
                       attendance.

12.00–12.40   Photocall.
                       To take place at Funfair and Go Kart track.

12.40–1.30   Press, Radio and TV interviews to take place in
                       Barnum's.

1.30–2.30   Personal appearance and autograph signing session
                       for punters in The Beachcomber.

5.00 p.m.   Media and guests arrive on site from train.

6.30–8.00   Media reception – Balmoral Rooms.

9.00   Band on stage – Prince's Ballroom.

Following show.   Party time.

12.30 a.m.   Coaches depart back to London.

ROCKIN' THE BUTLIN'S BALLROOM

Caroline
Roll Over Lay Down
Little Lady
Medley comprising: Mystery Song
                   Railroad
                   Most of the Time
                   Wild Side of Life
                   Rolling Home
                   Again and Again
                   Slow Train
Hold Ya Back
Down Down
Dirty Water
Whatever You Want
In the Army Now
Rocking All Over the World
Don't Waste My Time
Medley comprising: Roadhouse Blues
                   The Wanderer
                   Marguerita Time
                   Living on an Island
                   Break the Rules
                   Something 'bout you Baby I Like
                   The Price of Love
Burning Bridges

25 years!!
Isn't it amazing what you
can get away with

Tony Blackburn

TONY BLACKBURN

"I love all the music
can't wait to hear the 12" dance remix!"
congratulations
Gary Davies

GARY DAVIES

Status Quo. Didn't they support
the Flying Chimneys in 1962
Peter Powell

PETER POWELL

25 years of top-notch
entertainment!!
All the best
Jonathan Ross

JONATHAN ROSS

25 years of
Wine, Women and Song....
(well, wine and women!)
Congratulations,
Graham Dene

GRAHAM DENE

Happy 25!. Can I have My
Beethoven Guitar Book Back?
Adrian Juste   **ADRIAN JUSTE**

"Not only have they been busy lads since I
was a kid, but that bassist bloke is
still longer than mine as well"!!!
Rock on for 25 more years ....
Pat Sharp

PAT SHARP

The Midwives
of Boogie.
They deliver!
To
Vance.

TOMMY VANCE

Turn it down lads - it's all far too
loud !!
Congratulations
Simon Bates

SIMON BATES

Still the greatest little
rock 'n' roll band in the world !
David Hamilton

DAVID HAMILTON

"This is to confirm that I would
like to book 'Status Quo' for my
50th Birthday Party."
Bruno Brookes
B x

BRUNO BROOKS

"Hello" + Congratulations to the best
"Pilodrivin" no nonsense Boogie Band
in the business!
Glad there was some room in the world
for the Kosher Cowboys —
yours — David the Dustpipe -
Kid Jenson

KID JENSON

Before the Quo
Came in as guests
on my show I thought
they were dead — after
meeting them I became
Certain they were

CONGRATS BOYS! Steve Wright

STEVE WRIGHT

Status Quo?
my favourites!!

(Mind you, they were never
the same after Les McKeown left...
and as for those awful tartan
turn-ups..... UGH !!!)

Paul Burnett
(Capital Gold
1548 AM)

PAUL BURNETT

There's nothing I like more than to lock myself
in my little bedroom and bop about to my old
Status Quo records!

TERRY WOGAN

HERE'S TO THE BEST 25 YEAR RIFF
IN THE BUSINESS.
QUO, WE LOVE YOU !

Bob Harris

BOB HARRIS

Francis and Rick —
Well done on maintaining
the Status Quo !

Mike Read

MIKE READ

Years and years of musical
magic! Single, shy, unassuming,
modest, clean-cut, tone-deaf,
lads who have delighted us through
both world wars, and still are
the best band in the world.
I've personally been to all 73 of
their final farewell concerts and I
look forward to hundreds more ....

Congrats! Chris Tarrant.

CHRIS TARRANT

LISTEN !!!
'DO YOU WANNA'
KNOW A SECRET ???
.... IT'S 105 YEARS !!!
SO? DON'T ROLL OVER ....
DON'T LAY DOWN ....
AND HAPPY 25TH ANNIVERSARY
'MIGHTY QUO' !...
LONG LIVE ROCK 'N ROLL !'
Love + Stuff!

FLUFF!
x

ALAN 'FLUFF' FREEMAN

I can't believe that Status Quo have been
going strong for so many years. But
what is even more frightening is the fact
that I have been going longer than them!
Which all goes to prove the fact that
old farts have more than just wind.

Keep on Rockin'
Best Wishes

Dave Lee Travis

DAVE LEE TRAVIS

They know more 'bar
ropin' than they let on!!

MARK GOODIER

What a record! 25 years
on 3 chords !!!
Keep on Rockin'!

Tony Prince
The Royal Ruler
'94

TONY PRINCE

The Twenty-Fifth Anniversary – DJs get their own back.

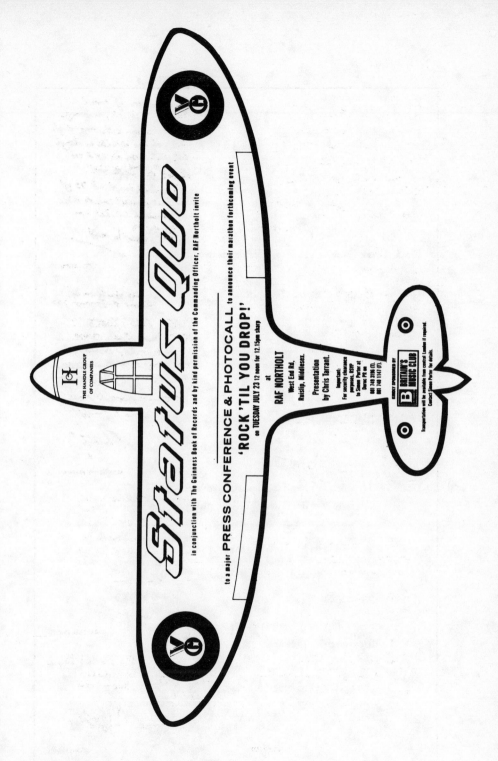

Rock 'Til You Drop – The Launch.

"ROCK 'TIL YOU DROP"
– SCHEDULE –
SATURDAY 21ST SEPTEMBER

9.45 **BBC Centre. Band arrive 'Going Live'.**

10.45 **BBC Centre, studio performance of 'Let's Work Together'.**

11.00 Media depart from Wembley Arena for Heathrow – coach.

11.00 (Doors open Sheffiend Int' Centre.)

11.15 **BBC Centre. Rehearse medley outside.**

11.45 Support team/Film crew depart Preston Manor School – Helicopter (×2) to Sheffield Int. Centre.

12.00 **BBC Centre, live performance 'Brits Medley'.**

12.00 Hallam FM Presenters – Jonathan Miles, Linda Joice and Dave Kilner on stage at Sheffield.

12.12 **'Going Live' ends. Depart for Northolt. RP/FR interview with Cheryl Baker plus camera, sound and director in one car for filming.**

12.20 Media depart Heathrow – Fixed wing.

12.30 Special guests Fahrenheit on stage at Sheffield.

12.35 **Band arrival at Northolt.**

12.45 **Band depart Northolt – Helicopter to Sheffield International Centre.**

13.00 Support team/Film crew arrive Sheffield Int. Centre. Support team transfer to coach for venue.

13.00 Media arrive Gamston – Transfer to helicopter (×2).

13.30 Media arrive Sheffield International Centre.

13.30	(Doors open Glasgow. Radio Clyde programming.)
13.45	**Band arrive Sheffield International Centre.**
	Photocall at landing site.
	Transfer to coach for venue.
13.55	**Photocall and interviews by stage ramp.**
14.00	**QUO ON STAGE**
14.30	Support team/Film crew depart Sheffield Int. Centre – Helicopter (×2) to Gamston.
14.40	Media assemble for departure from Sheffield Int. Centre.
14.50	Media depart Sheffied Int. Centre – Helicopter (×2) Gamston
14.50	**QUO OFF STAGE**
14.55	**Photos with guitar winners.**
15.00	Support team/Film crew depart Gamston – Fixed wing to Glasgow airport.
15.00	Media arrive Gamston.
15.10	Media depart Gamston – Fixed wing to Glasgow.
15.15	**Band depart Sheffield Int. Centre – Helicopter to Leeds/ Bradford airport.**
15.15	Special guests Nazareth on stage Glasgow.
15.45	**Band depart Leeds/Bradford – Fixed wing.**
16.00	Support team/Film crew arrive Glasgow airport – transfer to helicopter (×2).
16.00	Radio Clyde/Glasgow programming.
16.00	(Doors open Birmingham NEC. BRMB programming.)
16.00	Support team/Fim crew depart Glasgow airport
16.10	Media arrive Glasgow airport – Transfer to coach for SE and CC.
16.20	**Band arrive Glasgow airport.**
16.30	**Band depart Glasgow airport for SE and CC – Helicopter.**

16.35	Media arrive Glasgow SE and CC.
16.35	**Band arrive SE and CC.**
	Photocall at landing site – To include overseas media.
	Band transfer to coach for venue.
16.55	**Photocall and interviews by stage ramp.**
17.00	**QUO ON STAGE.**
17.25	Media assemble for departure from SE and CC
17.30	Support team/Film crew depart SE and CC – Helicopter (×2) to Glasgow airport.
17.30	Media depart SE and CC – Coach to Glasgow airport.
17.35	Support team/Film crew arrive Glasgow airport.
17.45	Support team/Film crew depart Glasgow airport – Fixed wing to Birmingham.
17.45	Special guests Rattle Snake Kiss on stage Birmingham.
17.50	**QUO OFF STAGE – GLASGOW.**
17.50	Media depart Glasgow airport – Fixed wing to Birmingham.
17.55	**Photos with guitar winners.**
18.05	**Band depart SE and CC – Helicopter.**
18.10	**Band arrive Glasgow airport.**
18.20	**Band depart Glasgow airport – Fixed wing to Birmingham.**
18.30	(Doors open Wembley. Capital Radio Programming.)
18.30	BRMB Programming – NEC Birmingham.
18.50	Support team/Film crew arrive Birmingham airport.
	Support team transfer to coach for NEC.
19.00	Media arrive Birmingham airport – transfer to coach for NEC.
19.10	**Band arrive Birmingham airport.**
	Transfer to coach for NEC.
19.20	**Photocall and interviews by stage ramp.**

19.30	**QUO ON STAGE – NEC BIRMINGHAM**
19.50	Media assemble for departure from NEC.
19.55	Media depart NEC – Coach to Birmingham airport.
20.00	Support team/Film crew depart NEC – Coach to Birmingham airport.
20.05	Media depart Birmingham Airport – Fixed wing to Heathrow.
20.10	Support team/Film crew depart Birmingham Airport – Helicopter
20.15	Special Guest Ethan Johns on stage Wembley.
20.20	**QUO OFF STAGE – NEC BIRMINGHAM.**
20.25	**Photocall with guitar winners.**
20.35	Media arrive Heathrow – Transfer to coach for Preston Manor School.
20.35	**Band depart NEC – Coach to airport.**
20.45	**Band depart Birmingham – Helicopter to Wembley.**
21.00	Capital Radio Programming.
21.15	Media arrive Preston Manor School.
21.25	**Band arrive Wembley – Preston Manor School.** **Photocall and filming at landing site.**
21.35	**Band/Media depart Preston Manor School for venue.** **RP/FR interview with Cheryl Baker plus camera, sound, director in car.**
21.50	**Photocall and interviews by stage ramp.** **Note: To include two fan presentations – Cheque and shields. Overseas media also to attend.**
22.00	**QUO ON STAGE – WEMBLEY**
23.00	**QUO SET ENDS – Presentation on stage by Norris McWhirter.**
23.05	**Photos with guitar winners.**

STATUS QUO
'ROCK 'TIL YOU DROP'

Media Information Sheet – Sheffield Leg

Saturday, September 21st 1991

Sheffield International Centre
Broughton Lane
Sheffield
S9 2DF

11.00	Doors open
12.00–12.30	HallamFM presenters Jonathan Miles, Linda Joyce and Dave Kilner live on stage.
12.30–13.15	Special guests Fahrenheit on stage.
13.40	**QUO arrive by helicopter. Photo and filming opportunity at landing site:** Sheffield Development Corporation Land Broughton Lane. Situated directly opposite venue.
13.55	**Photocall and interviews by Stage ramp.** Media to assemble at backstage area by 13.50
14.00	**QUO ON STAGE**
14.50	**QUO OFF STAGE.**
PLEASE NOTE:	**The above times are a guideline only. Please allow additional time either way.**

STATUS QUO

Rock 'til you drop!

Set List

SHEFFIELD

1. Whatever you want

2. Paper plane

3. Roll over

4. Medley

5. Rain

6. The price of love

7. R.A.O.T.W.

8. The Waltz

STATUS QUO
'ROCK 'TIL YOU DROP'

Media Information Sheet – Glasgow Leg

Saturday, September 21st 1991

SE & CC
Hall 4
Finnieston
Glasgow

13.30	Doors open. Radio Clyde programming.
15.15	Special guests Nazareth on stage
16.00	Radio Clyde programming.
16.30	**QUO arrive at SE & CC by helicopter. Photo and filming opportunity at landing site:** Car Park 7 SE & CC – Stobcross Rd. Landing site is situated to west of SE and CC. Drive past SE and CC and turn left. Do not confuse with SE and CC Helipad.
16.55	**Photocall and interviews by Stage ramp.** Media to assemble at backstage area by 16.50
17.00	**QUO ON STAGE**
17.50	**QUO OFF STAGE.**
PLEASE NOTE:	**The above times are for guideline purposes only. Please allow 15 minutes either way.**

STATUS QUO

Rock 'til you drop!

Set List

GLASGOW

1. Down down

2. Roll over

3. Little lady

4. Let's work together

5. Burnin' bridges

6. Medley

7. Whatever you want

8. Army

9. R.A.O.T.W.

STATUS QUO
'ROCK 'TIL YOU DROP'

Media Information Sheet – Birmingham Leg

Saturday, September 21st 1991

Birmingham NEC

16.00	Doors open. BRMB programming.
17.45	Special guests Rattlesnake Kiss on stage
18.30	BRMB programming.
19.10	**QUO arrive at Birmingham Airport.**
19.20	**Photocall and interviews by stage ramp.** Media to assemble at backstage area by 19.10
19.30	**QUO ON STAGE**
20.20	**QUO OFF STAGE.**
PLEASE NOTE:	**The above times are for guideline purposes only. Please allow 15 minutes either way.**

STATUS QUO

Rock 'til you drop!

Set List

BIRMINGHAM

1. Down down

2. Roll over

3. Little lady

4. Let's work together

5. Burnin' bridges

6. Medley

7. Whatever you want

8. Army

9. R.A.O.T.W.

STATUS QUO
'ROCK 'TIL YOU DROP

Media Information Sheet – London Leg

Saturday, September 21st 1991

Wembley Arena

18.30	Doors open. Capital Radio programming.
20.15	Special guest Ethan Johns on stage.
21.00	Capital Radio programming.
21.25	**STATUS QUO arrive by helicopter. Photo and filming opportunity at landing site, which will be lit for filming purposes:**
	Preston Manor School (Playing Fields). From Forty Avenue, turn left into Carlton Avenue East. 400–500 yards on left is a small side street with a gate at the end leading into playing fields.
21.35	Quo depart Preston Manor School for Wembley Arena.
21.50	**Photocall and interviews by stage ramp.** Media to assemble at backstage area by 21.45
22.00	**QUO ON STAGE**
23.00	**QUO SET ENDS – ON STAGE PRESENTATION BY NORRIS McWHIRTER from the GUINNESS BOOK OF RECORDS.**
PLEASE NOTE:	**The above times are a guideline only. Please allow 15 minutes either way.**

Media and VIP Hospitality available in Silver Mint Bar – Backstage from 20.45–22.00 and 23.00–23.45.

STATUS QUO

Rock 'til you drop!

Set List

WEMBLEY

1. Whatever you want

2. Paper plane

3. Roll over

4. Medley

5. Rain

6. Army

7. Burnin' bridges

8. R.A.O.T.W.

9. The Waltz

I, **STATUS QUO** of 27 Goudhurst Road Gillingham in the County of Kent **DO SOLEMNLY AND SINCERELY DECLARE** that I do hereby assume as from the date hereof the christian name of **STATUS** in place of my present christian name of **JAMES** and the surname of **QUO** in place of my present surname of **HALL** and in pursuance of such change of christian name and surname I **HEREBY DECLARE** that I shall at all times hereafter in all records deeds instruments and writing and in all actions and proceedings and in all dealings and transactions upon all occasions whatsoever use and sign the said name of **QUO** as my surname in lieu of the said surname of **HALL** as aforesaid and the said name of **STATUS** as my christian name in lieu of the said christian name of **JAMES** as aforesaid and I **HEREBY** authorise and request all persons to address my by the christian name of **STATUS** and the surname of **QUO**

I N   W I T N E S S whereof I have hereunto signed my christian name of **STATUS** and my surname of **QUO** and my former christian name of **JAMES** and my former surname of **HALL**

Dated this   21ST day of March 1991

....

....

AND I make this solemn declaration conscientiously believing the same to be true by virtue of the provisions of the Statutory Declaration Act 1935

SWORN before me this 21ST
day of MARCH 1991)
at Gillingham)
in the County of Kent.)

A solicitor/~~Commissioner for Oaths~~

MARTIN P. SMITH
A SOLICITOR EMPOWERED
TO ADMINISTER OATHS

The Ultimate Fan.